W. C. Cartwright

The Jesuits

Their Constitution and Teaching a Historical Sketch

W. C. Cartwright

The Jesuits
Their Constitution and Teaching a Historical Sketch

ISBN/EAN: 9783337002534

Printed in Europe, USA, Canada, Australia, Japan

Cover: Foto ©Lupo / pixelio.de

More available books at **www.hansebooks.com**

THE JESUITS:

THEIR CONSTITUTION AND TEACHING.

An Historical Sketch.

By W. C. CARTWRIGHT, M.P.

LONDON:
JOHN MURRAY, ALBEMARLE STREET.
1876.

The right of Translation is reserved.

LONDON:
PRINTED BY WILLIAM CLOWES AND SONS,
STAMFORD STREET AND CHARING CROSS.

TO

RAWDON BROWN,

This Volume is Inscribed,

IN GRATEFUL RECOLLECTION

OF

MUCH KINDNESS RECEIVED, AND OF MANY PLEASANT

HOURS ENJOYED

IN CASA DELLA VIDA,

BY

THE AUTHOR.

PREFACE.

THIS Volume is in substance a republication of two articles, that appeared in No. 274 and No. 275 of the 'Quarterly Review,' with some additions and corrections. The additions are in the first section, which treats of the Constitution of the Society of Jesus. They consist of historical matter calculated to illustrate more amply this branch of the subject. The corrections are in both sections—the most important one, however, being in the second, which relates to points of Doctrine. In reference to these corrections the Author would say a few words of general explanation. On appearance in the 'Quarterly Review,' the articles were fortunate enough to attract the attention of a well-known Roman Catholic periodical, the 'Month.' They were subjected to incisive criticisms in a series of papers in its pages, which have been ascribed to a competent master of the matter. These have been issued in a reprint, prefaced by observations, complaining that no notice had been taken by the present writer of the strictures passed on his statements, and charging him, on ground of this silence, with want of candour. It is desired here to assure the Critic in the 'Month' that never has there been any wish to evade the acknowledgment due to his valuable criticisms, and that the reason why no earlier response has been made to them is simply that soon after publication it was contemplated to re-issue the articles with emendations. To this re-issue the acknowledgment due to the Critic was postponed, and now here it is freely tendered. Several modifications have been made in the text, which have been in part suggested by what was stated in the 'Month;' and the Author is anxious to express his admission of the charge that he allowed himself to fall into a grave blunder in his remarks regarding two kinds of Mental Reservation, all the more blameable as arising from carelessness in the interpretation of a text that is perfectly plain. The Author is specially desirous to make this admission, as on many points he has been unable to concur in the views of the Critic, and has combated these in the additions to his original narrative. The points in question are closely connected with what is most characteristic of the Society as an active Institution. The Author is not sanguine enough to fancy that this new matter will induce the Critic in the 'Month' to abandon his opinions; but as he has been accused in print of having shown want of fairness, by wilfully abstaining "to avail himself of the many opportunities open to him of setting himself right with the public," he has deemed it proper to make these preliminary explanations.

There is but one word more which it is desired to add. In the account given of the circumstances connected with the doings of the Jesuit Fathers in China, allusion is made to doubts expressed by the writer in the 'Month,' as to the correctness of the allegation that certain *Mémoires de la Congrégation,* after having been put in type, have been wholly suppressed in deference to stringent commands from Rome. It should be mentioned that the doubts have been withdrawn in the reprint; not, indeed, in the text, but in a note affixed as an Appendix. The excuse for not having taken notice of this in the body of this Volume is that the reprint never came under the Author's eye until after this portion of the book was already in type.

In conclusion, the Author desires to record, as he has already done elsewhere, his lively thanks to Mr. Rawdon Brown, for the liberality with which he has allowed him to make use of his manuscript collection, some transcripts from which will be found in the Appendix.

September, 1876.

CONTENTS.

CHAPTER I.

Introductory observations—Present interest in the character of the Society of Jesus—Problem which bespeaks general attention—Scope of this publication .. .., .. Page 1

CHAPTER II.

Foundation of the Society—Names of Founders—Their original engagement—Proceed to Venice, and then to Rome—Paul III. by Bull confirms the Society—Formidable opposition amongst Roman Ecclesiastics to the Society—Paul III.'s Second Bull in favour of the Society—Its importance in respect to the Constitution of the Society—Great success which immediately attended the Society—Its special character symbolised in its title—Loyola's intention in this title of his own invention—Representations against its adoption—Observations from Father Michel Torres—Loyola's reply—Jesuit Fathers not Members of a Monastic Order—Technical meaning of term *Compañía*—Loyola's design that the Society should become the embodiment of the Church Militant—Protest by Sorbonne against assumption of the name of Jesus—French clergy at Assembly in Poissy demand change in title as conditional for admission of the Society into France—Sixtus V. determined on exacting such change—Congregation of Ecclesiastics appointed in Rome to consider modifications required by the Pope in the Society—Decree submitted by Acquaviva to Sixtus V.—His death—Accession of Gregory XIV.   5

CHAPTER III.

General character of Organisation elaborated by Loyola—Unparalleled Faculties vested in General—System of self-acting checks and counterchecks—*Ad Majorem Dei Gloriam*—Supreme importance of obedience in Loyola's estimation—Respective Symbolisms represented by Jesus and the Pope—Singular Faculties with view of making the General independent of the Pope—Curious combination of elements in the system: Despotism, Monarchy, Oligarchy, Democracy—Various Grades in Order—Their general character—Novices—Their Probation—Their position in the Order one of absolute dependence—Moral worth declared by Loyola no sufficient qualification—Rebuke given by him to Rodriguez—Unhesitating obedience to Superior the paramount object of Probationship—All direct intercourse with the world outside the Society forbidden to Novices—Condition of Fathers who have professed three vows—Apparent improvement—Real value thereof—Bull of Gregory XIV. empowering General to dismiss without trial—Conditions for attainment of Grade of Fathers who have professed four vows laid down in Constitutions—Incalculable Faculties of Dispensation in General which may lighten them—Nature of fourth vow—Estimate of proportion amongst Fathers admitted to this supreme grade—Stringent injunctions to ensure constant communication to the General of reports on all matters—These expressly ordered to extend also to dealings with those not of the Society—Precise instructions for periodical reports to be sent in, for employment of ciphers, and the incessant exercise of spying inspection .. Page 13

CHAPTER IV.

Mechanism regulating action of the System—General Congregations—How constituted—They appoint particular officers independently of General—Functions of these officers—Limitation of residence imposed on General—He cannot abdicate—In specified cases Order can depose him—Practical unimportance of checks on his authority—General virtually autocratic—The real spirit of the Society embodied in the General's Faculties of Dispensation, and not in the Regulations—Characteristic formula for engagement taken by every member of Order—General alone decides on admission and rejection—Quite irrespective of provisoes in the Statutes—System framed with view of facilitating enlistment of every force that might seem useful—At discretion General can promote rapidly or keep in life-long drudgery, expel with ignominy or dismiss in secrecy—Early perception of possible results from this system—Observations by St. Francis Borgia—Perversion of his words—Noteworthy persons refused admission to the Order 26

CHAPTER V.

Originally all professions to be made in Rome alone—Paul III. rejects this condition—General enabled to delegate power for receiving professions to persons not professed members of the Order—Extraordinary immunities secured by Pontifical Charters—Jesuits exempted from ritual observances—Obligation of poverty—Trading faculties granted by Gregory XIII.—Lavalette's failure—That of Coadjutor in Seville—Other instances of trading operations—Papal Brief empowering Order to modify according to expediency its Statutes independently of Papal sanction—Pius V. by Bull declares Privileges of the Society in perpetuity irrevocable by Holy See—*Oracula vivæ vocis*—Their force as stated by Order—Instances of their action .. .. Page 33

CHAPTER VI.

Allegations as to clandestine affiliation—The practice is stoutly denied by Jesuits—Definition of what is comprised within the pale of the Society, given in a Declaratory Gloss to the Constitutions—Important passage in Statutes—Evidence indicating that clandestine affiliation may have been sometimes practised—Francis Borgia—His secret admission into the Order—Synchronism between this and the Bull *Licet debitum*—Correspondence between a Venetian Nobleman and Oliva, General of the Order—Case of a Cardinal, believed to be Donghi—Admission made by a writer in the 'Month'—Sir Toby Matthews—Monclar's statement before Aix Parliament—Decree by First General Congregation—Lay members of Order of Christ—Suarez's proposition that Wedlock is compatible with Obligations involved by Religious Vows 39

CHAPTER VII.

Jesuits often accused of deliberate slyness in their dealings—Unfairness of the charge in connection with their having employed disguises in England during Penal Laws—More foundation in reference to proceedings in Sweden and elsewhere—King John III.'s inclination towards Catholicism—Arrival of Jesuits in Stockholm—Adopt the disguise of Protestant ministers—Reference to Rome—Father Possevino's mission to Sweden—Failure of attempt to restore the Roman Catholic religion 52

CHAPTER VIII.

Common practice by Glosses to modify tenor of Statutes—This the case in reference to vow of poverty—And to prohibition against accepting ecclesiastical dignities—Jesuits have preferred the influential position of Confessors, but have declined preferments only out of expediency—Names of Jesuit Fathers promoted to the Cardinalate—Official connection of the Order with Inquisition—Particularly in Portugal—Loyola's own words in regard to this Tribunal on application from King John III. that it should be under direction of the Order .. .. Page 57

CHAPTER IX.

Plea that the Order never countenanced Inquisition as operating in Spain—Cannot stand the test of facts—Father Nithard Inquisitor-General in Spain—Has to leave the country, and is then rewarded with the Purple—Case of Father Vieira in Portugal—Discrepancy between countenance accorded to these two and the action towards Father Fernandez by the same General, Oliva—Order associates itself with the intolerance practised in Spain against Jews and Moriscoes—Under Acquaviva's Generalship taint of Jewish or Saracen blood declared absolute bar against admission into Society—Nuevos Cristianos put under ban by formal Decree—Synchronism between the Decree and a peril of Spanish origin threatening Acquaviva's authority—Renewal of prohibition against Moriscoes by name in a subsequent Decree immediately before publication of Royal Edict proscribing the same 61

CHAPTER X.

Inordinate inflation of General's authority—This concentration of power not consummated without opposition—Acquaviva silently takes measures to counteract the same—His action stimulates Spanish jealousy—Oligarchical sentiment amongst primitive Jesuits expressed by Mariana—Action of Spanish Government—Acquaviva's tactics—Assembly of General Congregation—Acquaviva invites investigation—Triumphant result for him—Futile Reforms enjoined by Clement VIII.—Memorial of Grievances presented to him by some Fathers—Its six points—General Congregation of 1608—Francesco Contarini's report on its proceedings—Papal Brief prohibitory of discussions about Reforms—Acquaviva's authority rendered yet more absolute—Paul V.'s Brief fulminating Censures on those who had dared to memorialise the Pope in favour of Reforms—Constitution of Innocent X. in opposite sense—Revoked, however, by Alexander VII. and subsequent Popes 71

CHAPTER XI.

Generalship of Gonzalez—Illustration how, notwithstanding his great privileges, no General can infuse a Reform into the Order—Innocent XI.'s sentiments—Jesuit authorities forbid publication of a Treatise by Gon-

zalez—Mellini, Nuncio at Madrid, draws to it attention of Innocent XI.
—Approbation of its tenor expressed by Pope—Gonzalez attends
Congregation for election of a General—Nomination of Gonzalez with
marked concurrence of Innocent—Opposition to the General's action by
Members of the Society—Father Assistants protest against publication
of a book on which he is engaged—Gonzalez offers to submit it to
previous inspection by the same—Entire destruction of every copy is
demanded—Fear of Jesuits lest Pope should refer the book to a special
Congregation of Divines—Meeting of Provincial Procurators—Design
through it to effect sentence of removal from office against Gonzalez
—Motion for convocation of special General Congregation to that end
—Inadequate majority in favour—Matter referred to five Cardinals—
Vote of Procurators declared void—Opinion of Cardinal Noris on the
result .. .. Page 81

CHAPTER XII.

Episode of the Chinese Rites: demonstrative of even a Pope's inability to
make the Society acquiesce in orders if not agreeable to it—Authorities
for the facts of the case—The suppressed *Mémoires de la Congrégation*—
Exceptional favour which Jesuits from an early period secured in China—
Pretensions of Portuguese Crown—How the Jesuits accommodated them-
selves thereto—Their practices denounced by the Dominican Moralez—
Protracted investigation in Rome—Clement XI. refers the matter to the
Holy Office, which condemns Jesuit practices—Mission of Tournon as
Legate *a Latere*—His Faculties as such—His arrival at Pekin—Report
on the extent and nature of Jesuit establishments there by Tournon's
Secretary—Tournon's official statement to the Cardinal Secretary of
State as to the reception he encountered from the Jesuits—Intercepted
despatches—Money transactions carried on by the Jesuits—Legate's
sentence declaring void and usurious certain loans made in the name
of the Vice-Provincial—Change in the attitude of Chinese Emperor
towards Legate—He receives orders to leave Pekin, and await at
Canton return from Rome of two Jesuit envoys—Contumacious re-
sistance by Jesuits to the Visitation of the Catholics by the Bishop of
Pekin—Imperial Edict imposing conditions on all priests resident in
China—The Jesuits acquiesce, and accept to be the organs for communicating the same to the Missionaries—Legatine sentence against this
proceeding with promulgation of Papal Decree condemnatory of Chinese
Rites—Appeal of Jesuits to Rome—Legate obliged to betake himself to
Macao—Hostile reception from Portuguese authorities and the Bishop—
The latter pleads right of the Crown against recognition of Legatine
authority—Mandate from Governor-General transmitted by the Jesuit

Ammiani—Legate put in confinement, inveighed against in sermons, and subjected to sentence of Major Excommunication by the Bishop in a Decree formally promulgated—Legate's promotion to the Purple—Imprisonment of ecclesiastics from Rome who had been sent to bring the Cardinal's hat—The Legate's confinement made yet more stringent—Further fulminations by Bishop—Legate sickens and dies—Reflections on conduct of Jesuits—Bull *Ex illâ die* at last puts a stop to the controversy .. .. Page 90

CHAPTER XIII.

The foregoing not an unique instance of insubordination on part of the Society to the recognised authority in the Church—A memorable case in point, that of Bishop Palafox—Appointed to See of Puebla, in Mexico, by Philipp IV.—His character—Tithes of real properties in America—How Jesuits acted in reference to these—Statement of Palafox as to the financial condition of the Society in Mexico—Suit in a matter of tithes against Jesuits raised by Chapter of Puebla—They are called upon by Palafox to exhibit their licences in accordance with canonical regulations—Jesuits prove recalcitrant—They take the initiative in impugning Palafox's authority—Procure an invalid sentence of Excommunication against Palafox, who flies and lies hid for four months—Further improper proceedings—The See is declared deserted—Criminal prosecution before a sham tribunal—Indecent procession through streets of Puebla—Tidings from Spain check the confidence of Jesuits—Compromise whereby Palafox returns to Puebla—In Rome the decision of a Congregation specially instituted by Innocent X. in Palafox's favour—Deceitful conduct of Jesuits on receipt thereof in America—A second reference to Rome—Simultaneous machinations in Spain—Dismissal as frivolous of the Jesuit pleadings that the sentence published by Palafox had been falsified—How far the Society can be considered responsible for the proceedings against Palafox 114

CHAPTER XIV.

The plea of special privileges advanced by the Jesuits—Pius V.'s Brief barring revocation of privileges by the Holy See—*Oracula vivæ vocis*—Exemplified by action after suppression of the Order—Jesuits betake themselves to Prussia and Russia—Articles in the 'Cologne Gazette' hostile to Holy See—Their authorship by Father Feller—Vainly denied in the 'Month'—The evidence brought forward has demonstrably no bearing on the articles in question—Erastian propositions publicly sub-

mitted to discussion at Heidelberg—Statement by Nuncio Garampi—
Two spurious Briefs circulated—Their authenticity affirmed by Father
Curci—Allegation in like sense by writer in the 'Month'—Examination
of his statement—Despatch from Cardinal Corsini to Nuncio Garampi—
Clement XIV.'s Briefs to Archbishop of Gnesen and others—Reference
in 'Month' to Pastoral by Bishop of Mohilew—Explanations as to this
Prelate's position—Acquisition of White Russia by Catherine—Jesuit
establishment in that region—Attitude of the Fathers—Vice-Principal
Czerniewicz sent to St. Petersburgh—Becomes *ex officio* representative
of Society—In reply to an obsequious Memorial from Jesuits, Catherine
forbids publication of Brief *Dominus ac Redemptor*—The Fathers
acquiesce—Constitution devised by the Empress for the Latin Church
in her dominions—See of Mohilew instituted, and Siestrenciewicz appointed thereto—His antecedents—Catherine's intentions as to his
sphere of duties—The writer in 'Month' does not pretend that the
Pope confirmed his Pastoral—Positive evidence to the contrary—Papal
Brief addressed on this subject to various Catholic sovereigns—Benislawski's unfounded statement—Distinct disapproval of Bishop of Mohilew's doings in Pius VI.'s Brief—This no proof that Pius VII. was not
differently disposed—It is disingenuous to mix up the proceedings of
the two Popes—Question of clandestine revival of Order through
Oraculum vivæ vocis—Stated to have been affirmed by Father Roothan,
when General, in an Encyclical—Importance of the allegation in such
document, and of the declaration by the writer in the 'Month' that the
Oraculum would be perfectly legitimate .. .. Page 123

CHAPTER XV.

No foundation for attributing death of Clement XIV. to poison—Evidence
relied on for the report—Theiner wholly exonerates the Jesuits—Story
about antidotes found in Pope's apartments—Important testimony by
Tanucci to Pope's natural death—Account given by Dr. Huber of
incident in conference on Grace in Clement VIII.'s presence—Rests
on no authority—Serry does not bear out the statement, nor is it
warranted by Lemos—Statement of what really occurred on the
occasion 139

CHAPTER XVI.

Mechanism of the Society its mere skeleton—Mystic letters A. M. D. G.—
Signification thereof—Guarantee involved in official *imprimatur*—
Faculties of Examiners—General alone sanctions publication—The same

casuistry inveighed against by Pascal still prevalent in Jesuit schools—Authorities for this allegation—Father Gury .. .. Page 145

CHAPTER XVII.

Three cardinal propositions in Jesuit system—Probabilism—Mental Reservation—Justification of Means by Ends—Definition of *opinio probabilis*—What is sufficient to render probable an opinion—Its justificatory range—*Extrinsic* probability—Confessor shall not impose his opinion—Pascal's *Adoucissements*—Principle of dispensations—Latitude vested in Pope—Rulings by Gury that meet Jesuit proceedings in China—As to wearing Pagan vestments—Explicit belief in Trinity and Incarnation not indispensable in a Christian—Invincible Ignorance—Its operation according to terms of Jesuit definition—Case of Jesuits in China as judged by foregoing sentences 149

CHAPTER XVIII.

Mental Reservations—The Jesuit in the 'Provinciales' on them—Two kinds of Reservation according to Gury—Broadly mental reservations on occasions lawful—Condition *sine quâ non* for said lawfulness—Gury's doctrine as to force of solemn promises—Oaths not necessarily binding—Conditions that sanction repudiation—Statements by penitents to be accepted even though doubts exist as to their truth—Scope for equivocation—An illustration given by Gury—Another afforded by proceedings in reference to Suarez's '*Defensio Fidei Catholicæ*'—Acquaviva's alleged general prohibition of its objectionable maxims: only special to France as results from *Juvencus*—Reprints of Suarez's volume without censure—Modern propositions about Pope's Supremacy—Possible bearing of Mental Reservation on clandestine affiliations—'*Casus Conscientiæ*' stated by Gury—Single limitation apparently considered as of propriety—Note about Stark's affirmed secret conversion to Roman Catholicism 157

CHAPTER XIX.

Justification of Means by their End, third count in indictment against Jesuits—Has been affirmed by Jesuit divines of high authority at all times—Proofs of this—Busenbaum—Layman—Wagemann—Voit—Fathers Liberatore and Gury—Force of limitation contained in the term *media per se indifferentia* 167

CHAPTER XX.

Practical application of the foregoing cardinal principles—Two distinct groups of cases—Jesuit definition of Charity—On whom Acts of Charity are incumbent—In what cases, and to what extent, according to Gury—Evil **intention** does not **make a** deed wicked, though designed for compassing **death**—**Reparation** not obligatory on those by whose unjust **deed harm has been** wrought—Amazing exemplification—Extraordinary **character of Jesuit** maxims regarding Mine and Thine—The **red thread running** through all Jesuit doctrine—Absence of all test for **grounds** said to justify invasion of a neighbour's property—Communistic proposition—*Extreme* and *quasi* extreme necessity: what they are held **to** sanction—An imaginary case put—In extreme necessity all things **become** common .. .. Page 172

CHAPTER XXI.

Case of Jean d'Albe **in the** 'Provinciales': fully approved by Gury—Servants entitled to **recoup** themselves for over-work by clandestine compensation, which **means** robbing their employers—Gury's difficulty in fixing a figure **up to** which abstractions are merely venial offences—Provides a sliding-scale—Nice question in connection with this—Gury's thoughtfulness in devising exculpatory pleas—Case of woman robbing **her** second husband for benefit of son by first marriage—Every one justified in helping himself to his rights if recourse to legal means **involves** scandal or expense—The secreting of assets by insolvent—Informal death-bed gifts—Pope's right to alter their destination—Stories of pressure on dying persons to make bequests on Church—System **of** simulated donations sanctioned by Gury 181

CHAPTER XXII.

Gury's maxims approve transactions **ordinarily** deemed immoral—Hushmoney—Its extortion under false pretences—Bribery—Conditions under which it is practically sanctioned—Jesuit views on Courts of Justice—Judges can accept money if taken after delivery of sentence contrary to justice—Obligations to make restitution declared void by Physical or Moral inability—Latter defined as synonymous with grave inconvenience **to** the party in question—Illustrated by instance of a nobleman forced to reduce his establishment—The integrity required from witnesses—Cases **in** which the reproduction of documentary evidence would be excusable—Illustration how this **maxim** might have operated in a notorious suit—Bearing maxims of this kind may seem to have on the charge that Jesuits have not been foreign to forgeries—Relations between the sexes—Plighted troth may be broken for a fat inheritance—Seduction under promise of marriage involves no necessary obligation to wed—Exposure of offspring—Should wealthy parents, dropping their children at Foundling Institutions, make any payment?—Witchcraft—Black Art—Love philters—Sortilege .. .. Page 187

CHAPTER XXIII.

A second group of cases relating to demarcation between civil and ecclesiastical jurisdictions—The *Civiltà Cattolica*—Terms of Apostolical Charter conferred on it—Three noticeable points in this document—Maxims on obedience due by subjects—Father Liberatore—Question whether the wording is not artfully framed to warrant constructions not apparent at first sight—The only test for the bearings of Jesuit maxims to be found in application to them of the canons of Probabilism—" *Is it lawful to slay a tyrant?*"—Distinction drawn between rights of Sovereigns *de facto* and *de jure*—Emphasized in that between those of Sovereign Pontiff and all Princes—Distinct claim for Church of direct supremacy in civil matters—According to Liberatore, the State is strictly subordinate—Specially in all touching on Charity, Justice, or Morals—The Church has right to cancel all temporal arrangements not to its mind—This a peremptory article no true Catholic can presume to question 197

CHAPTER XXIV.

The advent of Christianity has narrowed bounds of State authority—The title-deeds for perennial maintenance of Pope's temporal sovereignty—Church can over-ride civil tribunals, and direct the employment of armed forces—Dogmatic character of Bull *Unam Sanctam*—Liberatore's demonstration of this character—Peculiar importance attaching to such utterance from Liberatore—Array of guarantees for the authoritative value of his opinions—Functions of State reduced to a police force at the command of Church—Application of coercion—" *The best form of government* "—Toleration to exist only under pressure of prudence—Right residing in a State that has apostatized—Force of any instrument concluded with a State that is Catholic—Affirmed existence of a legitimate power independent of public depositary of force—No Concordat binds Church—Vicomte de Bonald—Brief of approbation from Pius IX.—Concordats mere Indulgences—Revocable by Pope at will 204

CHAPTER XXV.

Apparent harmlessness of such extravagant views—But Jesuits dispose of more practical weapons—Capital importance for State of sound fiscal and military systems—Jesuit maxims capable of imperilling both—*Casus conscientiæ* relating to payment of taxes—Systematic smugglers guilty of no serious offence—Admirably distinct exemplification given by Gury—Another about defrauding the revenue in the matter of dues—Jesuit rulings as regards a soldier's duty to prove faithful to his flag—What constitutes a justification to desert—Plea to sanction a medical man taking money for a false certificate enabling a conscript to evade his obligations—Reference to political situations of recent times where such maxims were calculated to effect serious mischief—Illustration from instructions issued by the Holy Penitentiary .. .. .. Page 214

CHAPTER XXVI.

Increasing influence of the Society in Latin Church—Probabilism the essence of its teaching—Jesuit Divines recommend, indeed, strict observances—But through Probabilism their Rigorism is readily dissolved—Yet there is no deliberate purpose to corrupt—Desire to ensure influence alone has prompted the Society—Inevitable effect of such system—Instanced by the case of the priest Riembauer—State interested in the action on Constitution of the Church wrought by the spread of the Society—Substance of Absolutism precipitated by its agency—Independence of every kind hateful to it—Practical result of Jesuit Education—French clergy in seventeenth century—At present time no section of the Catholic community has ventured to do like it—Stealthy progress in destruction of ancient sanctuaries of Catholic sentiment—The culminating stroke dealt in the Vatican Council—Conversion of Latin Church into synonym with Jesuit Order—Proclamation of Pontifical Cæsarism, with the Society as a Prætorian Guard 222

APPENDIX I. 231
APPENDIX II. 233

THE JESUITS.

FIRST PART.

CHAPTER I.

Introductory observations—Present interest in the character of the Society of Jesus—Problem which bespeaks general attention—Scope of this publication.

THERE is hardly a phenomenon in History more deserving of investigation than that presented by the body of men termed Jesuits, who, though from the very day of their institution an object of suspicion in powerful quarters, and repeatedly of sharp proscription, have, nevertheless, asserted such enduring influence as to have become credited in popular fancy with the mysterious possession of a subtle faculty like that whereby some vegetable fibres contrive to defy extirpation. Barely a century has elapsed since promulgation of the Brief, through which it was confidently anticipated that Clement XIV. had at last laid the spirit of this occult force under the supreme spell of Pontifical exorcism; and public curiosity finds itself again drawn with unabated keenness to speculate, as it did then, on what can possibly be the vital principle that feeds the rank growth to which the Society has once more attained. Just as was the case a hundred years ago, the public is beset with publications about the Jesuits, varying in character from narratives worked up in the true Titus Oates colours to disquisitions bristling with learned quotations and counter-quotations. In the sharply-rolling fire of this controversy—due at the present moment mainly to the stringent measures which Germany has deemed it incumbent on herself to initiate against the Order of Jesus—both parties show themselves equally strenuous; and, if we are treated to some writings disfigured by a credulity that would still gravely adduce the 'Monita Secreta' as a genuine document, so also do we encounter rejoinders marked by a redundancy of declamation, in which the argument is made to converge upon the secondary and often very flimsy portions of the indictments advanced rather than upon their graver substance.

The point at issue in this hot dispute bespeaks attention on many grounds, and touches questions that practically affect serious interests. For upon the judgment arrived at in regard to the evidence brought forward will depend the question whether there can be a justification for the special sentence of outlawry which has been levelled in Germany against the Order of Jesus, on grounds which, if valid there, must likewise be deemed to hold good for a like sentence in other States. Are the Jesuit Fathers simply earnest, self-denying, devoted missionaries, who go forth only to pray, to preach, and to convert, with the fervour of souls rapt by transcendent devotion to a mystical call; servants of Christ, devoid of worldly guile and selfish interest, and whose preeminence over others engaged in like work is only what must be consequent on a higher degree of single-mindedness and the intenser zeal which they carry into the labours of spiritual conversion? Will it be pronounced, as the result of careful consideration, that only a visionary alarm, due to the sickly humours of morbid suspicion or the inventive spirit of calumny, can allege against the Society features distinct from those necessarily appertaining to every association destined to the exercise of spiritual duties, and composed of men absorbed in the enthusiasm of a religious vocation? Or will the conviction force itself on candid minds, that in the constitution and practice of the Order there is really something which warrants the charge, that the Society is an Institution curiously calculated to promote principles objectionable in their general tendency, and that it might even prove in certain contingencies a corporation dangerous to the State? It is with the view of helping to arrive at some opinion on these hotly-controverted matters, that the following pages have been written. We are fully alive to the impossibility of giving, in our limited space, an exhaustive survey of an Organisation so elaborate, and of a system so intricate, as appertain to the Jesuit Order. We must confine ourselves strictly to features at once typical and emphatically distinctive of the Society. In seeking to bring these out, we shall advance no statement that is not substantiated on authority which the Society itself would admit to be unimpeachable. At the same time our acknowledgments are due to various publications of recent date in Germany, of which that from Dr. Huber's pen deserves particular attention.* Dr. Huber's name is well known for several writings relating to Church history, and has been prominently connected with the movement against Ultramontane doctrine, which has resulted in the formation of an Old Catholic congregation. No book furnishes in so popular a form an equally comprehensive account of the Order. It is therefore to be regretted that Dr. Huber should not have expended the additional care which would have made his compilation, not merely a pleasant volume, but a trust-

* 'Der Jesuiten-Orden.' Berlin, 1873.

worthy handbook. The slovenly habit of either giving no authorities, or of giving them at second-hand, and often incorrectly, deserves censure; while in some instances Dr. Huber has made grave allegations for which the warranty is certainly not forthcoming in the authorities named in the references at the bottom of the page.

CHAPTER II.

Foundation of the Society—Names of Founders—Their original engagement—Proceed to Venice, and then to Rome—Paul III. by Bull confirms the Society—Formidable opposition amongst Roman Ecclesiastics to the Society—Paul III.'s Second Bull in favour of the Society—Its importance in respect to the Constitution of the Society—Great success which immediately attended the Society—Its special character symbolised in its title—Loyola's intention in this title of his own invention—Representations against its adoption—Observations from Father Michel Torres—Loyola's reply—Jesuit Fathers not Members of a Monastic Order—Technical meaning of term *Compañia*—Loyola's design that the Society should become the embodiment of the Church Militant—Protest by Sorbonne against assumption of the name of Jesus—French clergy at Assembly in Poissy demand change in title as conditional for admission of the Society into France—Sixtus V. determined on exacting such change—Congregation of Ecclesiastics appointed in Rome to consider modifications required by the Pope in the Society—Decree submitted by Acquaviva to Sixtus V.—His death—Accession of Gregory XIV.

It was a memorable moment in the history of the Latin Church when, on August 15th, 1534—the Feast of the Assumption—seven enthusiasts, prompted by the fervour of religious contemplation, met by concert in the little conspicuous church situate on the lonely heights of Montmartre, and there mutually engaged themselves by vow to exercises of pilgrimage, and a life of service in the interests of the Church, at the will and command of its Supreme Pontiff. The names of those constituting this knot of devotees, who then laid the foundations of an association which has acquired world-wide dimensions, and out of whose earnest prayer-meeting there has grown a Body which has materially influenced the character of the most powerfully-organised section of the Christian community, deserve to be remembered. At this humble beginning of a mighty structure there took part, besides Ignatius Loyola, four Spaniards—Francis Xavier, James Laynez, Alphonse Salmeron, Nicholas Bobadilla—one Portuguese, Simon Rodriguez, and one Savoyard, Peter Faber, who has left a written record of what passed on the solemn occasion. We learn that the engagements taken were to visit Jerusalem within a specified time, and after this pilgrimage to submit themselves absolutely to the Pope's disposal. But as a continued attendance in the Schools was felt to be needful for instruction, it was agreed that departure from Paris should be postponed until January, 1537. During the interval three additional recruits were admitted into this circle—Claude le Jay, from Geneva; John Codure, of Embrun; and Paschase Brouet, of Bretancourt, near Amiens; thus increasing the number of Father Founders to ten. At the appointed time these men set out by various routes to meet at Venice, the intended port of embarkation for the Holy Land. Circumstances, arising out of the hostilities then being waged between the Venetians and the Turks, however, prevented the realisation of the project, and accordingly the devotees proceeded to Rome, to present themselves before Pope Paul III. After not inconsiderable opposition Loyola succeeded in obtaining for the Society, whose drafted rules he had submitted, the sanction of Pontifical approbation.

On September 27th, 1540, the Pope promulgated the confirmatory Bull which is the Charter of the Society of Jesus. In it are recited by name the Founders, "the ten dear sons —Ignatius de Loyola and Peter Faber, and James Laynez, as well as Claude le Jay and Paschase Brouet and Francis Xavier, with Alphonse Salmeron and Simon Rodriguez, John Codure, and Nicholas de Bobadilla." It must be noticed that in this original deed of Constitution it is expressly enjoined that the Society shall be limited in numbers to sixty members—a restriction sufficiently explained by the serious opposition which had been raised in influential ecclesiastical circles against the sanction of a Corporation invested with such unprecedented faculties as were claimed by the constitution which Loyola framed. That Opposition comprised ecclesiastics of the highest rank and position in Rome, men of so pronounced zeal for the cause of the Church as the stern Cardinal Caraffa—afterwards Pope Paul IV.

Notwithstanding this active opposition, a marvellous success at once attended the infant Society. The extraordinary spread which it forthwith attained, the amazing rapidity with which recruits presented themselves for admission into its service, and the manifold calls which were received from many quarters for the ministrations of its members, conclusively testify to the singular qualities of those who were the Founders, and to the fact that this action must have happily responded to what at the period was felt to be a need. Within three years after institution Paul III., at the intercession of Loyola, issued a second Bull, which must be regarded as the instrument whereby what originally had been a carefully-limited Association, was converted into the nature of a World-Society, free to expand itself to the uttermost tether of elasticity. By this Decree the Pope, in expressed recognition of the circumstance how many fitting individuals were ready, as represented by Loyola and his comrades, to enter the Society, revoked the limitation as to numbers, and sanctioned indefinite enrolment at the will and discretion of the Superior. From this moment the Society was finally constituted as an Organisation of extraordinary force, and of incalculable dimensions. Such was the progress in numbers and in establishments made by the Society in the sixteen years during which Loyola lived to direct it, that at the time of his death, in 1556, it had penetrated into most European countries, and into several across the Ocean, and counted a hundred houses, which were grouped into twelve different provinces. These figures bear irresistible witness to the missionary merits that distinguished the early members of the Order. No candid student of History can possibly hesitate to recognise that to the efforts of the Jesuit Fathers mainly was due that work of Catholic reaction which successfully stemmed the in-rolling wave of Protestant reform. Wherever the seeds of heresy and schism manifested themselves, they were speedily confronted by the zeal and fervour of Jesuit ministration; and nowhere was the force of this element more strikingly exhibited than in those German regions which had been the cradle where the infant spirit of Reform had been first reared to strength and might. The practical efficacy of the service rendered at this conjuncture by the force which Loyola drilled, is a fact which invincible prejudice alone could affect to overlook.

The very special character which, from the outset, Loyola aimed to impart to his Institution, was clearly symbolised in the title he deliberately devised for it. To have introduced his creation under a designation of the type common to existing religious communities would not have answered the Founder's intention. Loyola contemplated calling into existence an Organisation novel in character and in scope, and that fact he sought to impress on the world by a title conspicuously expressive of superior pretension. That the choice of this peculiar designation was the deliberate and personal action of the Founder, is affirmed by Biographers, who, as members of the Order, write with the weight of plenary authority. It is likewise an established fact that Loyola, when met by criticism and opposition, insisted with pertinacity on the capital importance that the Society should bear a title plainly identified with the name of Jesus. On this head representations were addressed to Loyola not merely from quarters outside the community. From within the ranks of his immediate companions—for instance, from so intimate an associate as Father Michael Torres, to whom he himself entrusted, at a critical emergency, the interests of the infant Society in Portugal—Loyola had to hear entreaties that he would reflect on the propriety of obviating "scandal" and "dispute" by a change of name. To this disciple the Saint simply replied with unruffled imperturbability, "that the name had a deeper root than the world imagined, and that the substitution of any other for it was not to be thought of." *

The Jesuit Fathers have ever laid stress on the point that they are not members of a Monastic Body, and in this they are justified by their exemption from all those observances as to dress and ritual, which are stringently enforced in every Monastic Profession, as well as by being expressly not comprehended in the generic designation applied by the Council of Trent to Monastic Communities. "Est quorumdam militum societas" is the definition which the great Jesuit doctor, Suarez, gives of the Order to which he belonged; and its official historian, Orlandini, distinctly says that the term, *Societas*, was adopted as most closely rendering the Spanish *Compañia*, the technical term for a body of fighting-men under the direct control of a captain. Loyola's purpose was to effect an Organisation which should

* Father Genelli's 'Life of St. Ignatius,' p. 169, English Translation. Burns and Oates, 1871.

result in a thoroughly disciplined and mobilised body of men, moving like a highly-trained military unit at the word of command, and standing ever ready, under the proclaimed chieftainship of Jesus, to war against and smite by superior dexterity in arms the forces adverse to the absolute ascendency of the Papal system. In his design an Institution on such a model should be more than merely one amongst various organs of the Church. It should grow into the actual embodiment of the Church militant upon earth; and it was with the view of emphatically symbolising this superior scope, that he conspicuously affixed to his Foundation, as a declaratory inscription, the name of the common Saviour of Mankind. The pretensions involved in this attempt to monopolise so Catholic a name were instinctively perceived and strenuously resented, notably by the French clergy, then still animated with the spirit of the Gallican liberties. The Sorbonne protested against the presumptuousness implied in the claim of any particular corporation to style itself the special cohort of Jesus. At the Ecclesiastical Assembly held in Poissy, Archbishop Du Bellay, with the concurrence of his clergy, demanded that the admission of the new order into France should be conditional on a change of its objectionable title. But Paul III. had expressed the abiding instinct of the Holy See when, on perusal of Loyola's draft scheme, he exclaimed: "Hic est digitus Dei;" and, notwithstanding the opposition of minds that were veteran and venerable in the Church, the Order grew quickly into commanding influence under the fostering countenance of successive Popes.

At a later period, nearly forty years after the death of Loyola, there was a moment when it seemed, indeed, that the Society was irrevocably doomed to purchase continued existence at the expense of not a few privileges, and especially of its characteristic name. Under the impulse of his impetuously despotic nature, Pope Sixtus V. viewed with undisguised jealousy the exceptional character and constitution of the Society. He expressed an avowed resolution that modifications must be introduced into its Organisation. A Congregation of Ecclesiastics, presided over by the Cardinals Santa-Severina and Castagna, was specially instituted to consider the reforms sketched by the Pope himself as requisite to make the Society conformable to what, in the eyes of Sixtus, constituted a sound system. These reforms comprised curtailment of the Faculties vested in the General, admission of Capitular Bodies to a share in the making of appointments, modifications in the discipline of the Novitiate, and in the obligations of implicit obedience, but above all a complete change in Title. Sixtus V. would absolutely not tolerate that the Order should any longer go by a style derived from the name of Jesus. He pronounced that in this fact was implied a preposterous assumption. Vainly did its members strain every nerve to ward off so hateful a resolution. Notwithstanding the efforts and the arts of the General Acquaviva, Sixtus V. proved stubborn on this head. Upon other points he agreed to make some partial concessions in his demands; but on the matter of the name, the Pontiff remained inexorable.

Early in August, 1590, it was officially intimated to Acquaviva that, if his Society was to exist, it must be under a new style, and that he, as General, must issue a decree promulgating this resolution. No outlet for escape being apparently open, in presence of the Pope's grim determination, Acquaviva grudgingly acquiesced in the bitter necessity. He drafted a decree enforcing on the members of the Order a new Title. Before, however, promulgating it Acquaviva submitted the document to the Pope for inspection.

But on the 27th of the same month of August the days of Sixtus V. were suddenly cut short, before he had been able to affix to the decree that formal approval which would have given it the force of law. On his demise the uncompleted draft was found in the drawer of the Pope's writing-table. His successor was that Cardinal Castagna who, as one of the Presidents of the Congregation, took an active part in drawing up the schedule of demanded reforms, and had been the individual specially deputed to communicate to Acquaviva what he must perforce acquiesce in. A Pope of this stamp did not present much token of a kindlier sentiment. Once more, however, accident, and this time of a marvellous character, intervened to the rescue of the anxious members of the Society. Before he had time to perform a single act of Pontifical authority, before even the ceremonies of installation were completed by coronation, Urban VII. was gathered to his predecessors exactly eleven days after election. When the Cardinals next came out of Conclave, they had promoted to the Holy See in Gregory XIV. a Pontiff whose nature was cast in a different mould, and whose sentiments, so far from being favourable to a restriction, were, on the contrary, prone to an extension of the Faculties already conceded to the Society of Jesus. Thus, by the intervention of incidents, which might well seem to have a providential origin to those who profited thereby, the Order was rescued, at the eleventh hour, from a blow that would have been crushing, and relieved of the one Pope who seemed endowed with a fibre likely to have brought under control the supple elements of its subtle organisation.*

* See Hübner's 'Vie de Sixte Quint,' vol. ii. pp. 48, 54.

CHAPTER III.

General character of Organisation elaborated by Loyola—Unparalleled Faculties vested in General—System of self-acting checks and counter-checks—*Ad Majorem Dei Gloriam*—Supreme importance of obedience in Loyola's estimation—Respective Symbolisms represented by Jesus and the Pope—Singular Faculties with view of making the General independent of the Pope—Curious combination of elements in the system: Despotism, Monarchy, Oligarchy, Democracy—Various Grades in Order—Their general character—Novices—Their Probation—Their position in the Order one of absolute dependence—Moral worth declared by Loyola no sufficient qualification—Rebuke given by him to Rodriguez—Unhesitating obedience to Superior the paramount object of Probationship—All direct intercourse with the world outside the Society forbidden to Novices—Condition of Fathers who have professed three vows —Apparent improvement—Real value thereof—Bull of Gregory XIV. empowering General to dismiss without trial—Conditions for attainment of Grade of Fathers who have professed four vows laid down in Constitutions—Incalculable Faculties of Dispensation in General which may lighten them—Nature of fourth vow—Estimate of proportion amongst Fathers admitted to this supreme grade—Stringent injunctions to ensure constant communication to the General of reports on all matters —These expressly ordered to extend also to dealings with those not of the Society—Precise instructions for periodical reports to be sent in, for employment of ciphers, and the incessant exercise of spying inspection.

THE method elaborated by Loyola and his immediate fellow-workers, for securing the Organisation of a rigidly disciplined and yet admirably pliant body of ecclesiastical warriors, is a theme on which many writers have dilated. It is indeed impossible to consider the series of "Regulations" and "Constitutions,"— of minute injunctions and astute exemptions,— which make up the code of the Society, without becoming greatly impressed with the forethought and sagacity which could devise provisions so intricate and so nicely dovetailed. The law-makers of the Society have framed a set of ordinances and of privileges with skill that is perfectly marvellous. On the one hand, every conceivable guarantee is provided for crushing out any germ of independent impulse that could possibly allow momentary play in an individual member to some movement of dissent, however suppressed and strictly mental, from an order emanating from his Superior. On the other hand, everything is studiously calculated to instil into those entrusted with the supreme direction of the Society a sense of discretion so vast, so ample, and so wholly freed from all ordinary limitations, that they may become absolutely imbued with the consciousness of duty being centred in the keen observance of whatever at any particular moment might recommend itself as specially expedient for making particular minds acquiesce more readily in the ascendency of the Order. To this end Faculties are lodged with the supreme authority of the Order, which have no parallel in their range; while the whole plan of the extraordinarily protracted training, to which every member is subjected, has been carefully thought out with a view to the particular end of making him a thoroughly supple instrument ready at an instant to the hand of his superior for any purpose.

That powers of so vast a range might be diverted by some Superior to other purposes, under dictates of personal ambition, was a danger which did not escape Loyola. No part of his organisation is more noteworthy than the chain of checks and counter-checks for keeping each organ of the system, including the highest, to the precise mark of its intended functions, so as to let it neither lag behind nor yet exceed the measure thereof. A mechanism has thus been contrived, which, while exceptionally complicated, has yet worked with noiseless smoothness—setting in action a body of forces elaborately disciplined for the attainment of distinctly specified results, under the guidance of motive powers at once steeled into inflexible rigidity as regards ultimate aims, and yet capable of Protean suppleness in the adoption of forms of procedure at the dictate of policy. The circumstantial provisions of this machinery—the dry bones of the system—have been repeatedly dissected, but nowhere better than in the chapter devoted by Dr. Huber to this interesting section of his subject. We shall here merely draw attention to certain capital points, which it is essential to grasp as fundamentally characteristic of the Society of Jesus and as distinctive of its constitution from that of any confraternity of a simply devotional nature.

In the statutes and records of the Order, it is over and over again declared with emphatic solemnity, that the cardinal purpose of its labours is the promotion of God's Greater Glory; that all its powers and resources are to be devoted "*Ad Majorem Dei Gloriam.*" In a remarkable epistle to the Fathers in Portugal, to be found in every edition of the 'Institutes,'* St. Ignatius gave these instructions: "Other religious associations may exceed us in fastings, in vigils, and the like rigorous observances; it behoves our brethren to be pre-eminent in true and absolute obedience, in abnegation of all individual will and judgment." In the 'Constitutions' it stands again written: "Let all be convinced, that those who live under obedience

---

* Our references are all to the Prague edition of the 'Institutes,' in two volumes, 1757, published by the 18th General Congregation, which contains also the Decrees of the General Congregations and the Declarations by successive Generals, which rule the constructions to be put on the text of the statutes. It is this edition that was used in the pleadings against the Jesuit Order before the French Parliaments.

are bound to let themselves be set in motion and directed by Divine Providence through the medium of their Superiors, exactly as if they were dead bodies." In these sentences is comprised the quintessence of the principle whereon the Society was formed. It was meant to be the force that should break down by the sheer weight of solid pressure all elements adverse to the exaltation of God's Greater Glory; such exaltation demanding the reduction of the world to the implicit acceptance of a system culminating in the acknowledgment of an Absolute Pontiff. As the emblazonment of the name of Jesus symbolised in a speculative sense this Glory of God, so was it symbolised in the concrete by the Pope, to whose service every full member of the Order was sworn by a special vow. At the same time this bodyguard for the absolute authority of the Pope was curiously provided with Faculties calculated to justify its acting of its own accord for the assertion of its principles, in the event of some Pope proving unfaithful to the same. It will be found that, while the General professedly figured as a mere Lieutenant holding a commission from the Pope, he was yet invested with certain Faculties in virtue whereof, in particular contingencies, he might consider himself the depositary of powers that rendered the Order exempt from the authority of an innovating Pope. The same spirit of jealous precaution is manifested in the provisions for securing the maintenance of the principles of the Society against a General who might perchance be infected with ideas not conformable to its spirit. Though invested with absolute power in everything relating to the administration of the Society, the General is yet under perpetual supervision, and, by the rules, he would forfeit his powers in certain specified contingencies.

It is this chain of self-acting provisions which makes

the 'Constitutions' so wonderful. The system combines in most subtle proportions the elements of Despotism, of Monarchy, of Oligarchy, and of Democracy. The fully-professed Father — who is so closely bound to obedience that he must perforce bow without murmur to every command which he may receive from the General—is yet quite justified in reckoning on attainment, in due course, to a position that will give him influence in the administration of the Order, provided only his capacities are adapted to the character of its labours. Indeed, if only he were to appear possessed of superior qualifications, his promotion can be as rapid as if it were due to the most signal favouritism. The General, again, who is enabled to issue at discretion instructions that must be acquiesced in implicitly by every individual member, finds himself yet perforce surrounded by persons imposed upon him by the Society, of whose presence it is not in his power to divest himself, and who are for ever by his side like shadows—incessant spectres of admonition—that never forsake him for even the shortest interval. Finally, the Pope, who at first sight would appear to be exalted on the pinnacle of the absolute Commander of the Faithful—Lord over a host of myrmidons sworn to unmurmuring obedience to his whispered word—will be discovered, in the case of certain critical emergencies, to be hampered by limitations not indeed very ostensible but very singular, which, whenever they should come into play, must invest the General of the Jesuits, towards him, with the character rather of a great feudal magnate, strong in chartered rights, than of a mere captain in command of a body-guard in the pay of an absolute prince. By what elaborate provisions it has been possible for Loyola and his immediate partners to effect the blending of elements seemingly so incongruous into the production of an Institution which, while outwardly fashioned into the monotonous aspect of a cast-iron phalanx, possesses the most curious aptitudes for instantly falling into the loosest skirmishing order—this it what we now shall seek to illustrate from the Institutes of the Society, the Privileges recorded in Papal Bulls, the Decrees of General Congregations, and the authoritative Declarations given by its Generals.

It is matter of notoriety that there are various grades in the Order, and that the conditions surrounding the primary admission and gradual advancement of members constitute cardinal features in its Organisation. It would only bewilder the reader were we to give a catalogue (and within limited space it could be but a catalogue) of the intricate series of subdivisions and removes which make up the gradations through which a Jesuit may be made to pass. To grasp the peculiar significance of these intermediate steps, for the purposes of test or reward, would need a wearisome amount of detailed explanation. It is enough for the general reader to hold fast the fact, that the vast Organisation known as the Society of Jesus is composed of a body of men falling practically into three great divisions: —first, the division of Probationers, comprising a variety of sub-grades, to some of which are attached important trusts, but having this characteristic in common, that they are not connected as grades with any *solemn* profession of vows:— secondly, the division of Fathers who have made profession of the *three* vows:—and thirdly, the veterans of the Order, the select Fathers who have been proved worthy of admission to the innermost circle of the initiated, the Fathers who have made profession of the *four* vows. By the original statutes, no one under fourteen years of age should become a Novice, though, by a Brief of Benedict XIV., the General is empowered, if he sees fit, in special cases to admit at an earlier age.* Once admitted as such, which depends on the absolute discretion of the Superiors, the Novice is systematically subjected to a most rigid probation, extending ordinarily over a number of years, and in which advancement or non-advancement through the various stages is again wholly dependent on the opinion formed by the Superiors as to his qualifications. Assuming that he bears himself to their satisfaction, the aspirant will ultimately be permitted to make profession of the three vows, namely, of obedience, chastity, and poverty. It is perplexing to meet with special mention of these vows at this point, as they have been apparently exacted at earlier stages. The explanation is that all previous vows constitute mere moral engagements taken towards God, which strictly bind the individual *in foro conscientiæ*, without however involving any contract possessed of a bilateral force. Thus, by his vows, the Probationer binds himself indeed to absolute obedience towards the General for as long as the latter may see fit to command him (for the General can dismiss at pleasure), without, however, acquiring in return a particle of rights in the Society.

To all intents and purposes the Probationer is no more than the bondsman of the Order from the day he crosses its threshold; having renounced, on his part, every shred of individual liberty, while on the other part, nothing whatsoever is guaranteed him beyond admission to a course of trial. That course has been carefully framed with the view of instilling into the Probationer the peculiar sentiment of obedience which, in the opinion of Loyola, constituted the essential qualification for membership. In his selection

---

* "Præpositus Generalis admittere potest ad habitum Societatis et Novitiarum scholasticos ante 14 annum completum."—Ben. XIV., 1753; Inst. vol. i. p. 256.

of candidates, the Founder avowedly declined to be swayed by regard for the moral worth of an individual. There is preserved a manuscript collection of sayings by Loyola, the authenticity of which is vouched for by the Bollandists, and by Father Genelli, who both quote therefrom. In it we find Loyola reported to have said to his confidential secretary, Polanco, that, "in those who offered themselves, he looked less to purely natural goodness than to firmness of character and ability for business;" * inasmuch as without these the peculiar duties of the Society could not be fulfilled. But Loyola furthermore remarked, with emphasis, that, however remarkable might be the qualities of a Candidate, for him the value of these would be wholly conditional on their being strictly and exclusively brought into play only at the word of command. So sternly indeed did the Founder proscribe independent impulse, that he would not even tolerate self-prompted exercises of grief and devotion. When Rodriguez once exhibited a disposition to indulge in some devotional exercises in excess of those prescribed in the ritual of the Society, he was sternly rebuked in a letter by Loyola, who stigmatised his proceeding as an act of presumption that must rejoice the enemy of human nature, because not performed under that direction of obedience, which imparts to zeal its holiness.† To make the Probationer not merely acquiesce practically in the execution of commands, but so to renounce every shred of independence, that he will bring himself, on principle, to assent instantly with his whole mind and nature in any command from his Superior, simply because it is a command emanating from this source, constitutes the scope

* See Genelli, p. 341.
† Father Genelli (p. 334) informs us that this remarkable letter was preserved in the Archives of the Mother House in Rome at the time he composed his biography.

and aim of the training to which, by Loyola's directions, the Candidate for membership in his Society has to be stringently subjected. Accordingly, from the moment of admission, the Novice is absolutely forbidden every intercourse with the world outside the Society, except under the close supervision of his Superior. He may not see even his nearest relative, otherwise than in the presence of an appointed watcher, and then only, as is expressly enjoined, for brief moments. No letter may be written by the Novice but with previous permission, and then again subject to inspection. A letter from outside is first opened by the appointed authorities, with whom rests the discretion whether it shall be delivered or suppressed.* In a word, the condition of the Probationer is that of a prisoner, who is dependent on the humours of a jailer armed with absolute power.

Once the Novice has been admitted to make solemn profession of the three vows, his position would seem at first sight to be in so far improved that a sentence of expulsion apparently demands the concurrence of the great officers of the Order. Practically, however, this proviso involves no effective limitation of the General's power. In the first place, the officers of the Order are his nominees and humble creatures —the mere instruments of his pleasure. To credit them with a force which could control the General in the exercise of his disciplinary faculties would be to misapprehend the very essence of the Jesuit Organisation. But should, per-

* "Si aliquando permittendum videretur, ut consanguineos vel amicos, quos cum erat in sæculo, habebat, alloqueretur, coram aliquo a Superiore designato id fiat, et breviter, nisi particulares ob causas is, qui supremam curam habet, aliud statueret. Sic etiam, si aliquis ex iis. qui domi sunt, cuiquam scriberet, non nisi obtentâ facultate, litteris ei ostensis, quem Superior destinaverit, id faciat. Si ad eumdem litteræ mitterentur, ei primò reddentur, qui a Superiore fuerit constitutus, qui eas lectas reddet aut non reddet illi, ad quem sunt destinatæ, prout in Domino expedire ad melius ipsius bonum, et Dei gloriam existimabit."—Decl. A. in Cap. I. Const. Inst. vol. i. p. 374.

chance, in some instance, a disposition really manifest itself amongst these dignitaries to question an act of arbitrary persecution on the part of the General, the opportunity for staying his unjust hand would not be offered them. By a Brief of Gregory XIV.—issued in 1591—it is expressly approved that no investigation or inquiry whatever be requisite before sentence of expulsion is pronounced against a member of the Society by the General—it being sufficient that the ultimate authority which pronounces sentence should be inwardly satisfied as to its justification. In virtue of this Pontifical privilege, the powers of the General over a professed Jesuit Father are practically as absolute as they are over the Novice;* for he is expressly enabled to pronounce summary and ultimate judgment on the single ground that in his consciousness he is persuaded of its soundness.

If advancement up to profession of the three vows has been surrounded with conditions at once arduous and uncertain, it is yet more difficult to secure promotion into that choice class which constitutes the core of the Order. According to the letter of the statutes, no Jesuit should attain this supreme degree under the age of forty-five; consequently, if he became a Novice at the earliest legal period, he should perforce have passed thirty-one years in subordinate grades. Here, however, again may come into operation incalculable faculties of dispensation if an individual should happen to seem of special aptitude. There is

* "Quod vero attinet ad demissionem, declaramus, formam judiciariam adhibendam non esse, sed modum in Constitutionibus præscriptum, et hactenus in ipsâ societate servatum de cetero servari volumus; nempe ut etiam sine aliquo processu, telâ, aut ordine judiciario, ac nullis terminis etiam substantialibus servatis sola facti veritate inspectâ, culpæ, vel rationabilis causæ tantum ratione habitâ, ac personarum, aliarumque circumstantiarum (quarum consideratio est cum caritate et prudentiâ conjuncta) procedi possit, auctoritate prædictâ declaramus et decernimus."—Inst. vol. i. p. 103.

on record at least one very memorable departure from this apparently absolute regulation. Claudius Acquaviva entered the Society at the age of twenty-five. After only fifteen years of service he was promoted to the Generalship, which office he continued to hold for thirty-four years. A Father at this stage is required to renew the solemn profession of his former vows, to which is now added a vow imposed on no other Order—the vow of special obedience to the Pope, at whose word the Jesuit binds himself instantly to go forth on whatever errand it may please the Holy Father to command. Those who have sworn this oath compose what may be called the Old Guard of the Order. It has been calculated that not more than two per cent. amongst the received members of the Order come to be deemed worthy of admission to this supreme grade.*

Elaborately stringent injunctions are laid down with the view of insuring a continuous flow of correspondence and communication from every organ of the Society, that must reach the General in person and make him the recipient and centre of all things. The provisions to secure this object are devised with minute precision. Like a spider's web, the tissue of the Society is spun to sweep up everything to the General's individual benefit; for in him all is concentrated, to him all is rendered subordinate. The Superiors and Rectors of houses, if in Europe, have to report in writing every week to the Provincial—those in the distant regions of the Indies alone being authorised to regulate their correspondence according to intervals which the Provincial may fix. The reports, it is expressly commanded, shall treat at full not only of persons and matters relating to members

* Exception has been taken to this estimate by an authoritative critic in the 'Month,' who, without, however, adducing any evidence in support of his allegation, says: "This calculation is certainly very much below the mark; from twenty to thirty per cent. would be nearer the truth."

of the Society, but likewise of the dealings of the same with persons outside the Society, "so that the Provincial might contemplate all things as though he had them before him." The Provincial is then to make, once a month, his report to the General on what has been thus brought under his notice. To guard, however, against the possibility of suppression or misrepresentation on his part, all Superiors, Rectors, and Masters of Novitiates are bound, irrespective of their reports to the Provincial, once in three months to make another to the General himself. In addition, these officials are instructed that they must report to the General directly every time matter of any moment may occur, irrespective of the circumstance that the Provincial may have already expressed an opinion thereon. All letters of business, moreover, have to be directed to the General, "and not to others who are acting with him." Knowledge is meant to be carefully concentrated in one grand depositary, and to that end the most careful precautions are inculcated and enjoined. " In treating matters which demand secrecy, such terms are to be used as can be understood only by the Superiors; the method shall be prescribed by the General." Again, it is an instruction that whenever matters have to be written about "which relate to one outside the Society,"* care must be

* "Superiores domorum et Rectores scribant singulis hebdomadibus ad suum Provincialem in Europâ; in Indiis verò, ut suis Provincialibus visum fuerit commodum et opportunum . . . scribant autem ad suum Provincialem de statu personarum et rerum omnium, non solum quæ inter nostros, sed etiam quæ per ministeria Societatis erga externos in domibus suis vel collegiis fiant. . . . Provinciales omnium provinciarum Europæ scribant ad Generalem semel quolibet mense. Rectores autem et Superiores domorum et Magistri Novitiorum, tertio quoque mense. . . . Superiores domorum et collegiorum et Magistri Novitiorum scribant ad Generalem, quæ alicujus momenti fuerint etiamsi approbante Provinciali fiant. . . . Litteræ nostrorum, quæ negotia continent, solum ad Præpositum Generalem, et non ad alios qui cum ipso agent, destinentur. . . . In rebus, quæ secretum requirunt, explicandis, his vocabulis utendum erit, ut ea intelligi nisi a Superiore non possint; modum autem præscribet Generalis."—Inst. vol. ii. pp. 125, 126.

taken so to word the report that in the event of its falling into the hands of the person in question, it should not startle him. Three things are therefore **indisputably** implied in these injunctions. First, **a system of the closest inspection, and of the most detailed reporting and denouncing is inculcated;** secondly, **that system is explicitly extended to matters appertaining to individuals** who are not themselves members of the Society; thirdly, in the intention of the framers of these regulations, the system is to be of that spying character which renders the employment of conventional terms and ciphers expedient. Moreover, this elaborately-devised machinery for information is meant solely to operate with the purpose of furnishing the General with knowledge, which it is left to his discretion to turn to account as he may see fit in promotion of the interests of the Society.*

* The following characteristic passages occur in the chapter in which Father Genelli expounds the spirit and the discipline of his Society: "The members of the Society ought always to have the supreme object alone before their minds, '*the greater glory of God*,' and to wish for nothing else besides. On the contrary, they should be utterly indifferent as to the means which conduct to this end, unless they be directed in the choice of them by obedience. . . . The principle of the greater glory of God is the rule, and as this requires something more or less, the time, the place, or the person with whom dealing is to be had may require some particular line of conduct, and consequently circumstances, of a necessity, must be the guide."—'Life of St. Ignatius,' p. 192.
" . . . While, on the one hand, all depends on the free and living action of the individual, who must run with generosity in the race if he would win the prize, so, on the other hand, the direction and supervision of Superiors is ever following the religious into every detail of life. . . . That the Superior may have the necessary light to guide each one in a manner suitable and commensurate with his condition, every subject is obliged at least once a year to make a manifestation of his conscience to whoever is placed over him, and to conceal nothing from him that may be either useful or injurious to his direction. *Nor must he be angry if others discover to his Superior, as to a spiritual Father, his defects and failings*, which must be done, not out of dislike or illwill, but in a spirit of fraternal charity, and for the interests of his eternal salvation."—P. 202.

CHAPTER IV.

Mechanism regulating action of the System—General Congregations—How constituted—They appoint particular officers independently of General—Functions of these officers—Limitation of residence imposed on General—He cannot abdicate—In specified cases Order can depose him—Practical unimportance of checks on his authority—General virtually autocratic—The real spirit of the Society embodied in the General's Faculties of Dispensation, and not in the Regulations—Characteristic formula for engagement taken by every member of Order—General alone decides on admission and rejection—Quite irrespective of provisoes in the Statutes—System framed with view of facilitating enlistment of every force that might seem useful—At discretion General can promote rapidly or keep in life-long drudgery, expel with ignominy or dismiss in secrecy—Early perception of possible results from this system—Observations by St. Francis Borgia—Perversion of his words—Noteworthy persons refused admission to the Order.

IF we now proceed to examine the Mechanism regulating the action of this complicated body, we shall find a no less curiously contrived system of provisions to ensure the closest check and supervision at every turn and point, in combination with the vastest possible faculties for elastic play in the mainspring of the machinery. Through the medium of the General Congregation — comprising Elect Fathers, and particularly the high dignitaries called Provincials—the Order appoints certain members to be constant attendants on the General, who, while possessed of the entire patronage as regards every other nomination — including the Provincials—is wholly debarred from a voice in regard to these. The individuals thus holding commissions directly from the Order are the Assistants, four in number, each being the representative of a nation; the

Admonisher, a dignitary whose duty it is ever to be by the side of the General, like the personification of a pursuing conscience; and the Confessor, at whose hands the General, when falling back occasionally into the conditions of ordinary humanity, seeks to be shriven. The General is besides stringently bound to take up his residence nowhere but in Rome, and never to stay from home, except in company with a Father Assistant. He is likewise not at liberty to abdicate his office, which once accepted he must hold on in deference to the Order, without the consent of which he is also debarred from accepting any preferment or dignity. It is even within the competency of the Order, in specified cases, through appointed organs, to suspend and depose a General, and a serious attempt was once made to put this power in force against a General who had given offence to influential sections in the Order. Notwithstanding the apparent definiteness of these limitations, they practically amount to nothing as checks, except in the hardly credible contingency of a General proving traitor to the spirit of the Society, and seeking to undermine the basis of his own greatness. The real safeguard for the maintenance of the Order in the old lines resides in the extraordinarily careful probation every Jesuit has to undergo before promotion, which makes it well-nigh impossible for a false brother to escape detection at some point or other of his protracted apprenticeship. In practice, and this is quite conformable to the intentions of the Founder, the General of the Jesuits is an autocrat, provided only he will exercise his vast prerogative in astute furtherance of the special aims of the Order, namely, the ascendency of a particular ecclesiastical system and the extended subjugation of mind to certain habits of thought. It is true that, taken by themselves, the "Regulations" we have mentioned need imply textually no more than studiously careful dispositions for ensuring stringent supervision and discipline in a body devoted to spiritual offices and sternly trained to rigorous observances. It is not, however, from the "Regulations" that the working of the Order can be gathered. There exists a series of Privileges and Faculties and Declaratory Decrees which must be closely scanned if we would grasp the character of the Order as an active institution. It is no exaggeration to affirm that, barring one or two quite minor items, not a single point is laid down in the "Regulations" with the semblance of obligatory condition, the ready means for dispensing with which are not forthcoming in the Schedule of Faculties lodged in the General.

The first circumstance that commands attention is the quite exceptional formula in which the engagements contracted by members of the Order are taken. The Jesuit Father makes his solemn professions "to the Almighty God in sight of the Virgin Mother ... and to the General of the Society *standing in the place of God.*" The omission of any mention by name of Christ or the Trinity, coupled with the special invocation of the Virgin, is eminently characteristic of the theology uniformly advocated by the Order; while the altogether unapproachable elevation ascribed to the General is emphatically typical of the spirit in which the Order is to be administered. That a Society avowedly intended for the special advocacy of particular Church interests should be rigorous as to the selection of its members, is only natural. In the "Constitutions" it is solemnly declared that the Order shall be absolutely closed against whatsoever person has at any time been guilty of some delinquency, or labours under a serious imputation. But on perusing the less obvious portions of the "Institutes," we discover that the General alone decides as to what may or may not constitute a serious imputation. Nor is this all. If a candidate presents himself, who not merely labours notoriously under serious imputations, but actually stands convicted of delinquency, he is yet admissible if the General considers him possessed of natural advantages likely to prove of value to the Society. There is no ambiguity in the terms of the Faculty. The provisoes in the statutes as to conditions of exclusion are a mere flourish of the pen; for no disabilities can attach to any candidate—no matter what his antecedents—of whom the General believes that he is in possession of something whereby the "Society would be greatly benefited."* It is well to grasp the import of this vast dispensing power, for in it is epitomized the essence of the Order as an organisation.

The system is wholly framed to the end of facilitating, at all moments and at every point, the employment of any force of practical fitness that may chance to offer itself, through the medium of a General invested with unlimited discretionary power. Accordingly it is within his competency to throw open the gates of the Order, or to keep them closed; to retain an individual for his whole life in mean drudgery, or to promote him to high trust; to expel him in a manner that brands with public ignominy, or again to ensure his noiseless egress.† The head of no other religious community

---

* "Si in eo dona aliqua Dei illustriora cernerentur, ille, qui examinandi munere fungitur, antequam eum dimittat, rem cum Superiore conferat. (§ D in Decl. p. 343, Inst. vol i.) Qualia vero sint, vel non sint hujusmodi enormia peccata, judicet Præpositus Generalis. (§ D, p. 362, Inst. vol. i.) Si cerneretur aliquod ex his impedimentis in homine, qui talibus Dei donis ornatus esset, ut pro certo haberetur, Societatem ad Dei et domini nostri obsequium ejus operâ admodum juvari posse . . . posset idem Præpositus consensum ad eum admittendum præstare, dum tamen ostium non multis, imo nulli qui raris (ut dictum) dotibus non sit præditus, aperiatur."—§ G in Decl. in Cap. iii. Const., Inst. vol. i. p. 362.

† "Nonnulli occulte dimitti possunt, quando causæ (quæ plurimæ et quidem ex illis aliquæ sine peccato esse possent) essent occultæ, et si non dicerentur,

has ever been invested with powers approaching those of the General of the Jesuits for the enlistment of every desirable recruit and the easy dismissal of any one not to his taste. On the other hand, should it be the General's opinion that a member seeking to quit the Order might yet prove of value to it ultimately, he is empowered, not merely to compel his remaining in it, but he is provided with Faculties for humouring his disposition by indulgences that would allow of his having liberty for a period, but without being relieved from his obligation of obedience to the General.* "In proportion as the Society should be beholden to one as having deserved well of it, or as he might be endowed with special gifts of God for helping it in promoting God's governance, so should he be let go with greater difficulty; as on the contrary he to whom the Society may be less beholden, and who may be less fit for helping it in God's governance, can be let go more easily."† These maxims are laid down in the declaratory gloss attached to the chapter of the "Constitutions" which treats of the rules that should guide the General in regard to his flock.

At a very early period it did not escape the observation of men who had the best means of judging, that the pre-

---

in aliis aliquid perturbationis timeretur. Tunc enim conducibilius est aliquo prætextu (ut probationum) extra domum mitti, quam si eorum dimissio publiceretur." (Decl. A in Cap. iii. Const. Sec. Pars, Inst. vol. i. p. 368.) It is difficult to understand how a recognised and professed member of the Order, who had been publicly wearing its dress, could be *occultly* sent out of it—that is, severed from community with the Order without such severance being made manifest, unless, for concealment's sake, he should be permitted still to assume before the world the guise of a Jesuit.

* "Si hujusmodi essent [qui demissionem petunt] ut Deo gratum fore videretur, eos non sic relinquere . . . . privilegiis ad negotium hujusmodi concessis a Sede Apostolica, quantum Superiori in Domino videbitur, uti licebit." —Inst. i. p. 369.

† See Inst. vol. i. p. 365; Decl. A in Cap. i. Const. Sec. Pars.

ference given in the Order to special aptitudes rather than to mere godliness was likely to undermine the purity of its religious profession. Thus already St. Francis Borgia, in an Encyclical written by him as General, expressed fear lest the time might come, when, through undue consideration for what was opportune and apt, the Society might prove a field wherein ambition and pride would run riot without check, and he wound up with the remarkable words, "Would to God that, before now, experience had not more than once taught us this." A rebuke so sharp from one in St. Francis' high position was galling to the Fathers, and they accordingly had recourse to the simple process of altering the objectionable passage. The fact deserves notice, as the first important falsification of a text that can be established against the Order. In the Ypres edition of the Epistles of the Generals of 1611, the original words of St. Francis are to be found; while in the three subsequent editions a version is given that seriously modifies the tenour of his remarks.*
There is yet another very venerable testimony on this head. St. Charles Borromeo gave expression in a letter to the following observations: "The distinction drawn between those admitted to Profession and those not admitted to it is one likely to bring about some day a misunderstanding which

---

* "Profecto si, nullâ habitâ ratione vocationis et spiritûs quo quisque accensus veniat, litteras modo adspectamus et opportunitates habilitatesque corporis curamus, veniet tempus quo se Societas *multis quidem occupatam litteris*, sed sine ullo virtutis studio intuebitur, in quâ tunc vigeret ambitio, et sese efferret solutis habenis superbia, nec a quo contineatur et supprimatur, habebit, quippe si animum converterint ad opes et cognationes quas habent, intelligent illi siquidem propinquis et opibus affluentes, sed *omnino virtutum copiis destitutos*. Itaque hoc primum esto consilium et in capite libri scriptum, ne tandem aliquando experientiâ doceat quod mens demonstratione concludit. *Atque utinam jam non ante hoc totum experientia ipsa sæpius testata docuisset.*" The words in italics run thus in the later editions, as for instance in the one printed at Antwerp, 1635: "*Multis quidem hominibus abundantem—solidarum virtutum ac spiritualium donorum copiis egenos et vacuos—atque utinam nunquam docuisset.*"

will have consequences. What most makes me think this is seeing how the Superiors often do not admit the best subjects, while admitting with open arms those who are apt for sciences, though often they may be destitute of piety or devotion." It would be a curious chapter which should give the catalogue of those who under various pleas have been rejected by the Order: not a few names eminent for Catholic doctrine would figure therein. It is enough to mention some who in this generation have knocked at the threshold of the Order, but either were informed that it would be better for them to apply elsewhere, or after having been taken on trial received an unmistakable hint that their services could not be turned to account. Amongst the aspirants thus weighed in the balance and declared to be found wanting may be numbered the celebrated preacher Ventura, the Oratorian Theiner, who subsequently became Keeper of the Vatican Archives, and Father Passaglia.

CHAPTER V.

Originally all professions to be made in Rome alone—Paul III. rejects this condition—General enabled to delegate power for receiving professions to persons not professed members of the Order—Extraordinary immunities secured by Pontifical Charters—Jesuits exempted from ritual observances —Obligation of poverty—Trading faculties granted by Gregory XIII. —Lavalette's failure—That of Coadjutor in Seville—Other instances of trading operations—Papal Brief empowering Order to modify according to expediency its Statutes independently of Papal sanction—Pius V. by Bull declares Privileges of the Society in perpetuity irrevocable by Holy See—*Oracula vivæ vocis*—Their force as stated by Order—Instances of their action.

By the original constitution of the Order, it was enjoined that solemn professions could be made only in Rome, the obligatory residence of the General, the object being evidently to ensure that admission into the inner circle of the Society should never happen without the direct control of him who is its soul. Paul III., as early as 1549, relaxed this prescription, and sanctioned the General's delegating to individuals of his own selection the faculty of admitting candidates into the Order—a provision that would not appear anomalous if limited to deputies taken from its ranks. It is, however, a startling fact that, on reading through the Privileges declared to be vested in the General by the Declaratory Glosses appended to the Constitution, we find him empowered to confide this most delicate trust to persons who are themselves not professed members of the Order. A proviso so extraordinary irresistibly calls to mind rumours about Crypto-Jesuits. We shall presently revert to the latter topic; here we merely desire to establish the existence of this anomalous Faculty, the text whereof we subjoin in a note.*

No less amazing are the unique immunities conferred on the Order by Pontifical charters. The Jesuit Father is expressly relieved from such ritual observances as are obligatory on all other Religious, while he is merely bound to observe decorum, local custom, and the simplicity congruous to a mental profession of poverty. The measure of the latter receives a striking illustration from the Faculty to carry on trade operations, which was conferred by Gregory XIII. in terms of singular amplitude; while the public scandal attendant on Father Lavalette's commercial insolvency in the last century affords memorable evidence that the Society did not refrain from freely dealing in such operations. It has been sought to exonerate the Order from any connection with Lavalette's proceedings, but the circumstances of the case are not favourable to this allegation. Lavalette was not a simple Father, but the Superior in Martinique. As such, his operations in connection with trade-ventures attracted public attention as early as 1753, to such a degree, that on the part of the Society it was deemed advisable to institute an inquiry. After two years'

---

* " Quibusdam tamen Præpositis Localibus vel Rectoribus et aliis Visitatoribus aut Personis Insignibus poterit Præpositus Generalis hanc auctoritatem communicare, *imo et alicui qui de Societate non esset aliquo in casu*, ut Episcopo alicui vel personæ in dignitate ecclesiasticâ constitutæ, cum nullus ex Professis ejusdem Societatis eo in loco, ubi aliquis ita est admittendus, inveniretur."
—Decl. B, Cap. i. Const., Inst. vol. i. p. 407. Originally, in the 'Quarterly Review,' the quotation, for brevity's sake, terminated at *in casu*. This was denounced in the 'Month' as an instance of garbling. For this reason the whole passage is here given, though it is not apparent how the addition modifies the construction given above in the text. It is immaterial that no outsider should be named, except when no professed Father was in the locality. The point lies in the circumstance that a Faculty should be vested in the General enabling him to delegate, in any case whatsoever, to one not himself a professed member of the Society, a power of such capital consequence, as that of admitting recruits within its body.

investigation Lavalette was declared free from blame by his Superiors, and sent back to Martinique, where he forthwith renewed his former operations on an increased scale, and with the result of speedy insolvency. It is true that the authorities of the Order disowned Lavalette and repudiated all liability in his bankruptcy, but still the fact remains, that he had been denounced to his Superiors as engaged in illicit operations; that they had professedly inquired into this allegation, and that they had been content to dismiss it as without foundation. Nor should it be lost sight of that this is not an unique instance of one holding high rank in the Society having become involved in ruin from mercantile speculations. In 1646 the Coadjutor of the Jesuit establishment at Seville stopped payment. The ruin caused by this failure was prodigious. "All the great and populous city of Seville is in tears," wrote Bishop Palafox to Innocent X. "Widows, wards, orphans, young girls, good priests and laymen, all complain with cries and tears at having been miserably deceived by the Jesuits, who, after having drawn from them upwards of four hundred thousand ducats, have paid them only with this disgraceful bankruptcy." As in the case of Lavalette, the Order attempted to disengage itself from responsibility for the doings of its officer. The Spanish law courts, however, ruled otherwise. "The matter having been carried before the Royal Council of Castile," says Palafox in the same letter, "it ordered, that as the Jesuits carry on trade as it is practised amongst laymen, they should be treated as such, and brought before the secular tribunal." The consequence of this decision was that the Society ultimately made good the losses incurred by this failure. The same Bishop Palafox, as will be seen later on, gives an account of the vast possessions which he found owned by the Society in Spanish America; while it is recorded by Monsignor Tournon, who went as Papal Legate to China, that the Jesuits in Manilla were actively engaged in large and profitable speculations. These are sufficient testimonies to the fact that the Faculties accorded by Gregory XIII. were not left to become a dead letter.

Still more curious are the privileges whereby the Society is virtually put in possession of sovereign authority for its own administration, without preliminary deference to Papal sanctions. In 1543 Paul III., by a Brief, conferred on the Order the Faculty to modify its rules and statutes of its own accord, as *time and place might render expedient*, even to the extent of making quite new ones; such modifications and new enactments being declared *ipso facto* valid and through this charter surrounded at once with all the sacredness of express Apostolic confirmation.* Pius V.'s enthusiasm for the excellence of these new soldiers of the Faith, was not satisfied even with this. In his exuberant zeal he went the incredible length of issuing a Bull confirming to the Society all previously granted privileges—extending to it every privilege that ever had been or at any future time might be conferred on any Order with obligations of poverty—and furthermore declaratory that "these present letters at no time whatever shall be capable of being revoked, limited, or derogated from by Ourselves or the aforesaid Holy See, nor shall they be com-

* "Nos igitur ad eorumdem Ignatii Præpositi ac sociorum piam vitam et bonorum operum exemplum attendentes . . . . quod quascumque inter eas Constitutiones particulares, quas ad Societatis hujusmodi finem, et Jesu Christi Domini nostri gloriam, ac proximi utilitatem conformes esse judicaverint, condere, et tam hactenus factas, quam in posterum faciendas Constitutiones ipsas, juxta locorum et temporum, ac rerum qualitatem et varietatem, mutare, alterare, seu in totum cassare, et alias de novo condere possint et valeant; quæ postquam mutatæ, alteratæ, seu de novo conditæ fuerint, eâ ipsâ Apostolicâ auctoritate præfatâ, confirmatæ censeantur, eâdem Apostolicâ auctoritate, de speciali gratiâ indulgemus."—Iust. vol. i. pp. 10, 11. As the first General Congregation declared "Regulas condere solus potest Generalis," the powers sanctioned by this Brief were practically vested in the General.

prehended within any revocation of similar or dissimilar graces . . . but for ever shall stand excepted therefrom."[*] In virtue of this unique charter the Society is virtually constituted as a body which it is beyond the pale of Papal authority to control, inasmuch as that authority by this deed solemnly renounced in perpetuity all power to abrogate any one of the Privileges already appertaining to the Society, or accruing to it in the future by this anticipatory document. In the eyes of Pius V., the strengthening of the Order was the strengthening of the forces at the service of the Holy See; but it is well to consider that such unique privileges also tend of necessity to establish titles which can be fairly invoked as a warrant for considering invalid any sentence, however solemn, of the Holy See, which might be unfavourable to the action or existence of the Society.

Even this does not make up the sum of the possible immunities and liberties vested in the Order. We have hitherto dealt only with the category of privileges which are distinctly ascertainable, because declared and promulgated. But there is another category, of which all that is declared is the fact of existence—the category comprised under the vague term of *Oracula vivæ vocis*—privileges conferred by a Pope through word of mouth, without deed or document to leave a public trace that can establish their validity, which must accordingly rest on knowledge testified to by the original depositaries of Pontifical confidence, and handed down by tradition; or, if inscribed anywhere, then it must be in some secret records reserved for the eyes of only the innermost adepts of the Society. Let it not be supposed that the existence

---

[*] " Decernentes, præsentes litteras nullo unquam tempore per Nos, aut Sedem prædictam revocari, aut limitari, vel illis derogari posse, neque sub ullis similium, vel dissimilium gratiarum revocationibus, alterationibus, limitationibus, derogationibus, aut aliis contrariis dispositionibus nunc et pro tempore emanatis comprehendi, sed semper ab illis excipi."—Inst. vol. i. p. 43.

of such *Oracula* is open to the shadow of a doubt. It rests on absolutely unimpeachable authority—the declaration of the Society in its own Statute-Book. In the printed Compendium of its Privileges, the Order solemnly affirms " non minoris sunt efficaciæ et valoris *vivæ vocis oracula* quam si per Bullam aut Breve ad perpetuam rei memoriam essent concessa."* There is no gainsaying the explicitness of these words, though the advocates of the Order seek to explain away their significance, and to reduce the range of what could possibly come within the scope of such inscrutable instruments. These pleas are, however, strikingly invalidated by the inadvertent testimony of the Society itself. In 1703 there was printed at Prague, in the presses of the Jesuit College, a Compendium† of the Privileges of the Society—a compilation authenticated with every possible voucher for its official character. In this volume occurs the remarkable declaration, that the obligations binding on conscience attach not merely to the Faculties "contained within this Compendium, but likewise to those which are secret or not promulgated—*occultis seu non manifestis.*" It is acknowledged that the title whereby the Society of Jesus, in derogation from the Decrees of the Council of Trent, retains special privileges, rests on a clandestine warrant of this character given by Pius V. We shall point later to the allegation of a like warrant in respect to another matter of grave consequence. The two cases together indicate conclusively that the *Oracula vivæ vocis* should not be dismissed as a mere figure of speech which can never be credited with important bearings.

* See Inst. S. J. vol. i. p. 323.
† 'Compendium Priv. S. J. Pragæ, 1703. Typis Universitatis in Collegio Soc. Jesu.' The passage in question will be found at p. 58.

CHAPTER VI.

Allegations as to clandestine affiliation—The practice is stoutly denied by Jesuits—Definition of what is comprised within the pale of the Society, given in a Declaratory Gloss to the Constitutions—Important passage in Statutes—Evidence indicating that clandestine affiliation may have been sometimes practised—Francis Borgia—His secret admission into the Order—Synchronism between this and the Bull *Licet debitum*—Correspondence between a Venetian Nobleman and Oliva, General of the Order—Case of a Cardinal, believed to be Donghi—Admission made by a writer in the *Month*—Sir Toby Matthews—Monclar's statement before Aix Parliament—Decree by First General Congregation—Lay members of Order of Christ—Suarez's proposition that Wedlock is compatible with Obligations involved by Religious Vows.

No point connected with the Society of Jesus has given rise to angrier controversy than the supposed existence of a grade of clandestine members, affiliated through bonds, not of mere sympathy, but of positive obedience and direct engagement, while exempted, in deference to motives of particular expediency, from any overt signs of Membership. The Crypto-Jesuit, stealing about the world under disguise, figures as the typical representative of the Order with one class of writers, while his existence has been pronounced the invention of a heated fancy by critics so little prone to priestly propensities as Bayle. Dr. Huber is disappointing in his treatment of the subject, for, while he leaves the impression of his belief in a provision for secret affiliation, he has not substantiated the allegation by any conclusive evidence. It must be admitted that there would be nothing in the fact of a clandestine grade necessarily incompatible *à priori* with the spirit of the Institution. If the General is avowedly empowered to admit any candidate, though "notoriously infamous for enormous crimes," whose acquisition should promise to be of particular value to the Order, there cannot be anything incongruous in his being enabled to secure the accession of some equally valuable recruit through a secret engagement, in the event of particular circumstances barring such a one's ability to render full service to the interests of the Order if he were to appear publicly as a member—the more so as it is the distinctive condition of the Society to be exempt from any obligations of dress and from all the ritual observances compulsory on such as belong to the emphatically sacerdotal congregations. The Jesuits have, indeed, on all occasions stoutly denied the existence of a clandestine grade of Membership; but we are not acquainted with any writer of the Order who has effectually grappled with the particular texts and incidents which can be pointed to as giving colour to the allegation that to affiliate by secret profession, and to allow those thus affiliated to live on in the guise of seculars, is neither contrary to the letter of the rules, nor has been absolutely foreign to the practice, of the Order.

In a Declaratory Gloss appended to the 'Constitutions,' as a definition of what lies within the area of the Society, it is affirmed to comprise not merely Professed Fathers and Novices, but all who at any time may be under some probation with an inward intention of "ultimately living or dying in the Society," and of being admitted some day to one or other of its grades. Over all these the General's authority is declared to extend implicitly;* so that he would seem hereby empowered to assert a right of absolute command over individuals whose connection with the Order was merely that of an inward intention "ultimately to live or die in it." No doubt there

* See Decl. A, in Cap. i. Const. v., Inst. i. p. 402. By the first General Congregation these Glosses, the power of making which was exclusively vested in the General, were declared to be of absolute and unimpeachable authority.

is something cloudy about the wording of this passage, and if it stood alone we should certainly not consider it a sufficient warrant for the affirmation of an absolutely anomalous provision. But there is another capital passage in the Statutes of the Order, to which we have already alluded in passing, that is so clear in its wording as to be free from all ambiguity. In this passage it is laid down that the admission of candidates * can be effected only by the General in person, or through those on whom he has conferred special powers; and then follows the designation of the persons who may be so deputed. Amongst the persons designated are enumerated "individuals of distinction," without limitation as to their being of the Society, or even in holy orders, and then come these most remarkable words: "*Yea, even in some instances one who himself may not be of the Society.*" How words so clear and distinct can be made to bear plausibly any but their plain construction, baffles conception. Until some commentator of superior skill shall have performed this feat, we shall venture to consider them conclusive on the point that by the statutes of the Society it is expressly declared not unlawful in particular exigencies to employ the agency of individuals who themselves have made no overt profession of the Order. And that the Faculty thus legitimatized has not been allowed to remain wholly in abeyance—for this there is also forthcoming evidence of a nature which cannot be easily impugned.

The share due to Francis Borgia in the early fortunes of the Order is matter of notoriety, as also how he was a Spanish Grandee of illustrious lineage, holding high appointments in the State. For a man of his position to cast aside the glitter of the world's distinctions for a religious profession, at the call of an enthusiast, was necessarily a step beset by obstacles

* See Decl. B, in Cap. i. Const. v., Inst. i. p. 402.

of no slight gravity. But Borgia's soul was bent on the furtherance of the work preached by Loyola, and finding himself perforce tied for a while to the world through various obligations, Borgia craved to be allowed, during the interval before he could conveniently loosen himself from those ties, to make a secret profession of the vows that are compulsory on a member of the Order. The indulgence so demanded was accorded. In February 1548, Borgia, in the private chapel of his feudal mansion, made secret profession of the vows, after which to the outer world he still continued to be Duke of Gandia and Viceroy of Catalonia until circumstances were sufficiently matured to let him withdraw into the retirement of a religious house. Our knowledge of this case is drawn from no doubtful source. The occurrence is vouched for by Ribadeneira and Orlandini, two official writers of the Order. The only point in the transaction which can be open to question is how far the Profession made was more than mental—how far the Viceroy, on occasion of the solemnity in his private chapel, bound himself in those absolute obligations which are exacted for actual Membership. In the absence of positive information as to the tenour of the vows sworn on that occasion, a very striking light is shed on the matter through a Pontifical deed, which, when the date is considered, it is hardly possible not to refer directly to this incident. At the period of which we now treat, Paul III. had already solemnly approved the 'Constitutions' of the Order, and in special Bulls he had given his Pontifical sanction to the vast powers vested by the original scheme in the General. Everything needful for the confirmation of the General's unprecedented authority might, consequently, have seemed to have been fully secured. Nevertheless, in 1549 —that is, immediately after Borgia's profession—Paul III. saw fit to issue another Bull, known as *Licet debitum*. In this remarkable document the Pope first reaffirmed the General's jurisdiction over "all members of the Society," and then extended it likewise over such "persons as might be living under obligations of obedience to him, wherever they may be residing, even though *exempt* and *notwithstanding whatever faculties they may be holding.*" * It suggests itself with irresistible force that so extraordinary an increase of the powers deliberately conferred but a short time before must have been due to some particular circumstance having arisen in the interval; and does it not press itself upon us, with almost the weight of demonstration, that this circumstance must have been the peculiar case so exactly covered by the new provision—the case of Borgia's clandestine admission into the Order? At all events, the fact is manifest of a highly suggestive synchronism between the admission of Borgia under anomalous conditions and the immediately subsequent promulgation of a Bull which exactly legalises what might have been open to challenge in that admission. Moreover, evidence of no trivial nature can be adduced that the case of Borgia does not stand by itself as an instance of clandestine affiliation.

In 1681 there was printed in Rome a collection of Letters by Oliva, General of the Order,† which is presented with even more than the usual vouchers of authenticity. Besides bearing the customary *imprimatur* of spiritual censorship, the edition must have been prepared by Oliva himself, who died only some weeks before its publication; while, in a pre-

---

* The Bull is couched in terms singularly explicit as to the distinction between the two classes. "Plenam in *universos* ejusdem Societatis *socios* et *personas* sub ejus obedientiâ degentes, ubilibet commorantes, etiam exemptos, etiam quascumque facultates habentes, suam (jurisdictionem) exerceat."—Inst. vol. i p. 14.

† 'Lettere di G. P. Oliva, 2 vol., Roma, presso al Varese, M.DC.LXXXI. Con licenza dei Superiori. Imprimatur: Fr. Raymundus Ord. Præd. Sac. Pal. Apost. Mag.'

fatory statement, it is declared that every letter ascribed to Oliva and not contained in this collection is to be considered "spurious, apocryphal, and injurious to his name." In the collection of the General's letters thus emphatically authenticated, several passages occur which might be taken to corroborate a practice of occult affiliation; but there is one in especial, the explicitness of which seems to defy the possibility of any but a literal construction being put on the words. The 723rd Letter in the second volume is addressed to a Venetian nobleman, who sought to be publicly admitted as a Professed Member of the Society. Oliva saw reason why it would not be desirable to accede to the request, and in this letter he set himself to dissuade the nobleman from any public profession, on the ground that this step must materially impair his peculiar usefulness in behalf of the very interests which both had at heart. "Most readily," writes Oliva, " would I receive you amongst the servants of God with the veneration due to your fervour, if after protracted examination of the circumstances of the offer I did not clearly perceive that the Eternal Father meant you for a Minister of his Sublime Republic rather than for a nursling of so lowly a community." After further remarks in this strain, Oliva continues: " Nevertheless, in course of time I will show your Lordship *how to combine with the sacrament of wedlock the palms and crowns of religious profession* (la religione). *It was in this manner that under my direction a Cardinal dedicated himself to God while retaining the purple to serve the Church, and crucified himself to the Society* (la Compagñia), *so as not to forego the acquisition of holiness, by a clandestine* (occulta) *and sworn submission to whoever shall be and is the successor of the Holy Father.* To you the opportunity will not fail for promoting the interests of Divine service in the magisterial offices which high lineage ensures, and thus you will be more thoroughly one of us while retaining your independent station and being on the watch in our defence." It will not escape observation that the expressions employed by Oliva in regard to the engagement contracted "under his direction" by the Cardinal are those which are applicable, with the closest precision, to the specific vows demanded on full Profession. The Society is designated by its technical term of *Compagñia*, and the obligation, by which the Cardinal is affirmed to have bound himself in secret, is that obligation of implicit obedience to the Pope, which the Professed Jesuit of four vows has to contract. There seems no loophole here for disputing the character of the engagement entered into, as there is none for denying its secrecy or questioning the ground on which the proceeding was recommended. It is conceivable to set up a plausible plea against the literal construction of the flowery phrase about combining "palms and crowns of religious profession with the sacrament of wedlock;" but apparently none can be advanced against the plain and matter-of-fact language in which the counsel is given not to follow the strong inward call for a public Profession of religious vocation, on the one ground that by doing so a considerable worldly advantage would have to be sacrificed, to the consequent loss of desirable political influence.

This case is not the only one apparently confirmatory of occasional clandestine affiliations to the Order. The Cardinal referred to by Oliva is generally understood to have been Cardinal Donghi, to whom two letters in this collection are addressed, which are couched in a curiously mysterious tone. In the first—the opening one in the first volume—the General expresses ecstatic joy at a communication received from the Prelate, his reply to which is to be conveyed to the latter through a Father intimately acquainted with the sentiments that had been evoked in the General in relation to what had come from the Cardinal: "Your Eminence can conceive the amazement wherewith I read your letter. . . . I kissed it repeatedly and laid it on my forehead, the inditing thereof seeming to me not human, but of an angel or Apostle. Never shall I presume to oppose the dictates of the Holy Spirit, who, without doubt, devises singular altitudes of Divine glory in the ideas He is rough-hewing in your Eminence's soul with his finger. In relation to this I must refer to that which, in my name, will be expressed to your Eminence by Father Lamberti, who is wholly cognisant of the astonishment and inexpressible veneration wherewith I have considered the depths and fulness (*generosità*) of Divine Counsels." What were the sentiments conveyed through the medium of Father Lamberti, we have no means of knowing. They induced the Cardinal, however, to make a second communication, which elicited from the General a further reply—the 17th Letter in the Collection—in which occur some very remarkable expressions. "This last letter of your Eminence," writes Oliva, "is revered by me, as an Ark far holier than the ancient one, in which every sentence breathes eternity, and every word is the accent of an Apostle. I have been unable to peruse it without amazement, especially for the so serious offer made by your Eminence to Christ of all you love *and of all you are*, as ready as Abraham to sacrifice on Calvary that which you love more than children or life, *namely, that rank which puts you on a level with Kings and makes you venerable for Monarchs.* . . . *You will learn from our Interpreter what I am now engaged in arranging*, so as not to leave idle to your Eminence's soul the lights which God sheds through it."

It would be preposterous to make these mysterious utterances by themselves, the foundation for an allegation that clandestine affiliation was an established practice in the Society. The circumstance which alone can warrant our attaching particular significance to these expressions is, that they have been understood by Roman Catholic writers of standing as referring to the case of that Cardinal of whom mention is made in the letter to the Venetian nobleman. A critic in the 'Month,'* who is entitled to great authority in matters connected with the Society, himself identifies the Prelate in question with Cardinal Donghi. Indeed, this writer, while strenuously denying any general practice of clandestine affiliation, very candidly admits that evidence does exist of its having been had recourse to in some instances. He fully concedes that St. Francis Borgia was "secretly admitted to the solemn vows of the Society," and he grants that "a few other similar examples may perhaps be found—two or three, at the most." One would be that of Sir Toby Matthews, if Dodd can be relied on, who says that he had been during the last years of his life a member of the Order. That he died in a Jesuit house at Ghent in 1655 is beyond doubt. It is also not undeserving of note that Dr. Oliver alleges Sir Toby to have been a priest, though the fact was kept secret for prudential reasons.† The

---

* See the issue of the 'Month' for November, 1874.

† Sir Toby was converted by the celebrated Father R. Parsons. Dr. Oliver has the following:—"When and where he associated himself with the Institute of St. Ignatius I cannot discover; but it is an indisputable fact that he took holy orders from the hands of Cardinal Bellarmine; viz., minor orders, 4th May 1614; sub-deaconship, on the 11th; deaconship, on the 19th; and priesthood, on the 20th of the same month and year. 'Omnes simul cum D. Georgio Gage, uti constat ex litteris patentibus subscriptis ab illo Emo. Card. Bellarmino quas veneror ob memoriam S. Viri, et hic (in Romano Collegio) asservantur.' This I find in a MS. note, written at Rome about the year 1690." 'Collection towards illustrating the Biography of the Scotch, English, and Irish Members of the Society of Jesus. By the Rev. Dr. Oliver, St. Nicholas Priory, Exeter. London, 1845.' Only 250 copies were printed.

writer in the 'Month' refers also to the case—a well-known case, he adds—of a Cardinal Orsini; as to which, however, we have been unable to learn any details. What is, however, of far more weight in regard to the matter under consideration than any story of more or less doubtful authenticity, is the circumstance, that one so perfectly at home in the lore of the Society, and so devoted a champion of its Constitution, as the writer in the 'Month' acknowledges, the difficulty presented by Oliva's letter to the nobleman, and the "hopelessness" of "understanding what was the precise nature of his dealings with the Cardinal in question."

The marked nebulousness which surrounds the conditions attaching to the class of the Professed Fathers of three vows has induced the surmise that the affiliated members (assuming their existence) are to be found in this division. Such was the opinion expressed by Monclar in his masterly pleading before the Aix Parliament—one of the most critical disquisitions on the 'Constitutions' of the Order. " The creation of those Professed of three vows is one of the mysteries of the policy of the Society," are his words. " Wherefore add this intermediary class? No one has been able to understand the true ground. . . . The first mention of it occurs in Julius III.'s Bull of 1550. . . . Suarez informs us of the remarkable circumstance that they can be exempted from taking the priesthood, though simple Coadjutors, and even Scholars after a specified age, are bound to become priests. Through this dispensation it is possible for mere clerks and even laymen to hold positions superior to those of priests in the Society." Whoever has studied the intricate regulations of the Order will admit that Monclar is perfectly justified in asserting that there is nothing to bar recourse to such occult stratagems, though it must be of the essence of such devices to render conviction very difficult.

Before dismissing this obscure point of secret affiliation, it should be observed that the inference, which Oliva's words seem to warrant, may find further corroboration in a decree of the first General Congregation, and in an elaborate disquisition by one of the greatest luminaries of the Order, Suarez. In this Congregation the question was raised, whether Lay Members of the Order of Christ—a semi-religious, semi-military body of chivalry—could be admitted into the Society,* " though there might be ground

---

* " An sæculares qui emittunt vota in ordine militari vocato Christi possint ad Societatem nostram admitti, *licet credatur non emissuros Professionem apud nos*. Responsum est admitti fore."—Inst., vol. i. p. 480. The only ground which suggests itself why this particular Order should have been specially considered, is that it was a Portuguese Order, and that at this period the Jesuits were specially favoured at the Court of Portugal. Suarez, whose argument is to be found in the 'De Relig.' Tract. ix. lib. i. c. iv., is explicit in not confining his remarks to any one Order; and as to the status of such Knights, he concludes, " has personas esse Ecclesiasticas . . . quia censentur habere in Ecclesiâ proprium et specialem statum Ecclesiasticum et non sæcularem, nec clericalem, ergo religiosum." The terms of his thesis are singularly definite: " An etiam ordines militares qui castitatem tantum conjugalem vovent, sint proprie religiosi?"

The critic in the 'Month' has taken exception to the inferences drawn from this resolution of the First General Congregation. He does not dispute its terms as given here, but says that its import has been gravely misunderstood. According to him, it was simply meant to relieve the Knights of the Order of Christ from the impediment which by the Constitution of the Society prohibits admission of a candidate who has once assumed the dress of a religious order. In so far as regards these particular Knights, he therefore admits that they had a privilege to be affiliated, though they were of a " military order." The critic also makes the further admission that, although the above general impediment had already been solemnly affirmed in the Constitution, yet for some reason the *thirteenth* General Congregation saw fit expressly again to promulgate prohibition against admission of any chaplains of the Order of St. John of Jerusalem. He does not explain why it was found expedient to pass this special resolution of exclusion against one class by name, when already comprised in a general prohibition of many years standing, from which there should have been, according to him, but one particular exemption in force, namely, that of the Knights of Christ. These chaplains of St. John could by no possibility have been confounded with the

for believing that they had no intention to make profession amongst us," and the resolution was in the affirmative. Now, there was nothing distinctive of this Order from any other semi-religious Order of chivalry, so that what was explicitly ruled to hold good in the case of the laymen enrolled in the Order of Christ must hold good likewise in principle of those enrolled in kindred associations; and this Suarez unequivocally affirms in an argument singularly elaborate and explicit. This sublime doctor demonstrates at great length that the obligations consequent on religious vows can be deemed adequately fulfilled by any Member of such Orders, though living in wedlock, so that, according to this ruling, any individual doing service in behalf of the interests of this Society in some particular line might become affiliated to it while living with a wife, provided that he had contracted those engagements of obedience, &c., demanded from every one who enters into an Order. It is no part of our purpose to conjecture whether those who have administered the Society have often put in practice the Faculties sanctioned by these authorities. The point of importance is to establish

Order of Christ, for they must perforce have been publicly identified with a different Order. But while in this respect there could be no fear of mistaken identity, it seems positive that in essence there was nothing to distinguish the Knights of Christ from any other semi-religious Order of Knighthood in regard to their professions; a point conceded by the critic, who admits that he knows no special ground why this Order on its own merits should have been selected for special distinction. It must be borne in mind that the terms of the proposition, as stated by Suarez, are moreover quite general. As to whether affiliations have been frequent, we specially guard ourselves against being supposed to have insinuated, or have wished to insinuate, any opinion. Stories of crypto-affiliation are, in the main, far too vague to warrant reliance. The only cases which in our opinion appear to support its practice are those given in the text; while all we venture to infer from the decree of the First Congregation, and the disquisitions by Suarez, is that provision does exist in the Constitution of the Society which would legitimatize recourse to secret affiliation in the event of its appearing expedient to the authorities who administer the Society.

the existence of these Faculties, and to recognise how the **shrewd** minds ruling the Society have worked out and legalised a system of warrants, under which practices of stratagem and of hidden affiliation can be readily justified whenever these may be found expedient.

CHAPTER VII.

Jesuits often accused of deliberate slyness in their dealings—Unfairness of the charge in connection with their having employed disguises in England during Penal Laws—More foundation in reference to proceedings in Sweden and elsewhere—King John III.'s inclination towards Catholicism—Arrival of Jesuits in Stockholm—Adopt the disguise of Protestant ministers—Reference to Rome—Father Possevino's mission to Sweden—Failure of attempt to restore the Roman Catholic religion.

THAT on more occasions than one the Jesuits have been charged with a propensity to adopt courses of procedure more marked by a spirit of slyness than of openness is matter of notoriety. No fairminded person indeed would make it the ground for such accusation that, in the days of our harsh Penal Laws, Jesuit Fathers visited this country disguised as Protestants, in order to minister secretly to the spiritual wants of persecuted and forlorn co-religionaries. Here there was in existence a destitute flock of undoubted Catholic believers, who panted for the offices of their Church with that fervent yearning which is the outcome of a living faith. If men who had embraced the vocation of priesthood strove to furnish to longing devotees those ministrations which to their souls were as the breath of life, though to accomplish this purpose they stooped to evade the prohibitory action of a jealous police through acts of stratagem and even of subterfuge, there was that in the circumstances of the case which must render the proceeding excusable in the eyes of even strait-laced Rigorists. The duties of spiritual ministration are so supreme for a Catholic priest, and the services of the Church of such transcendent value to a believing Catholic, that for any priest to hang back from an actual appeal for his offices out of regard to an assumed impediment consequent on his having to wear a disguise, would be as if a person refrained from putting out a hand to save his neighbour who was calling for help, because to do so would oblige him to disturb the ordinary habits of his life. The persons whom the Jesuit Fathers came covertly into this country to administer were zealous, fervent, unfaltering Catholics, who abided by their faith with the tenacity of devotion under all the trials of persecution. Such persons felt urgent need for the spiritual consolations, which could be obtained only through the medium of consecrated individuals. It was the imperative duty of individuals in this condition to come to the aid of those who felt this need. But the conditions of England were then such as to make it impossible for any Catholic priest to pursue his vocation otherwise than under the cloak of disguise, and, therefore, to make it a ground for blame that disguise was adopted would be an act of monstrous unfairness. The question acquires, however, a different aspect when we have to deal with instances where it would appear as if disguise had been spontaneously assumed, not with the view of responding to the call of existing Catholics, but for the purpose of stealing into a country so as to proselytise surreptitiously under cover of a mask specially calculated to disarm suspicion. Plainly here there could be no justification arising from the irresistible force of an appeal made by destitute and yearning Catholics. The adoption of disguise under these circumstances would necessarily have been gratuitous, and such adoption would as necessarily have in it something startling and even shocking, if the disguise were one quite out of character with the profession of Catholic priesthood.

It certainly does seem that on this score the operations of the Jesuits in China and in Sweden were open to question. We shall refer more fully later on to the incidents that attended their proceedings in China. Here we will only indicate the capital facts which marked the attempt made by the Jesuits to win back Sweden to the Church of Rome. King John III., son of Gustavus Vasa, though the murderer of his brother, was a prince given to religious controversies, and who had studied himself into views leaning towards the Roman faith. What he really strove to evolve was a religious compromise which might have resulted in an union between the opposing currents of ecclesiastical doctrine. The Reformation had been introduced into Sweden, but was still of recent growth, and the character of the Protestant services retained much of the form and ceremonial proper to the Catholic ritual. It became known in Rome how King John showed sympathy for an order of theological ideas in many points favourable to the articles of the Catholic Church. His Queen, a Polish Princess, was in active correspondence with Cardinal Hosius, who readily encouraged these symptoms, and lured the King with hopes of concession on moot points, as, for instance, in regard to the Eucharist under both forms. In 1576 there arrived in Stockholm two individuals who professed to be Protestant preachers. In truth they were Jesuits from Louvain, by name Florence Feyt and Laurence Lasse, the latter being a native of Norway. The former has left an account of their proceedings on this mission.* Ac-

---

* See Geijer's 'Geschichte Schwedens,' vol. ii. p. 220, note. "Scriptum Magistri Florentii Feyt reversi ex Sueciâ anno 1577 de statu religionis in regno ex archivis Arcis S. Angeli." The Jesuit writes thus naively : "Insinuat se Pater Laurentius in amicitiam Germanorum, hi enim faciles sunt. Pergit Pater ad Ministros, sermonem miscet variis de rebus. Ministri, homines illiterati, promtitudinem latini sermonis et elegantium mirantur . . . miseri

cording to this statement these missionaries concealed their profession by command of their Superiors, and passed themselves off as sound Lutherans. A Protestant seminary had been recently founded in the capital as a nursery for efficient clergymen. The two Jesuits contrived to make such impression by their learning as to acquire the privilege to teach from the chairs of the institution. Their lectures became so highly considered, that it was enjoined on the Stockholm clergy to attend them. The method they pursued was to make a text of the writings of the Reformers, and then insidiously to impugn their authority without seeming to do so. After awhile these tactics appeared to produce their effect in a certain number of conversions. Nevertheless, King John could not be brought to take the final step of declared submission to Rome. There was then despatched to reinforce the apparently inadequate strength of those already in the field, a Jesuit Father of renown for his services to the Church—Anthony Possevino—who was speedily followed by others of his body under various disguises. Possevino was an adroit controversialist who admirably understood how to smooth down difficulties and dissolve into vapour the obstacles of conscience. He found the means for rendering it possible for King John to take the communion from him, to receive absolution, and to make a profession of faith, with which he then sped to Rome. There, however, Possevino failed in obtaining any of the con-

---

laqueum, quo suspendantur postea, sibi contexunt. Adeunt regem, commendant virum, Rex gratam sibi esse commendationem significat; gaudet in sinû rem dextre confectam. Hanc opportunitatem nactus Rex, Patrem Laurentium in Theologiæ Professorem cooptavit, statuens, ut quotquot Holmiæ ministri essent (erant autem, plus minus, 30) Patris lectionibus interessent. . . . Progreditur tamen Pater, quotquot auditores veniant, insinuat se in familiaritatem aliquorum, nunc hunc, nunc illum, dante Deo, a fidem occulte reducit."

cessions King John asked for, and which the Jesuit had plausibly held out to him a prospect of obtaining. When Possevino again landed in Sweden—this time no longer in the costume of a civilian, but clothed as a Roman ecclesiastic—he encountered a situation seriously modified. The disappointment of a Royal mind wounded in its susceptibilities, combined with the awakened strength of Protestant feeling, to thwart the further progress of Catholic reaction. Possevino and his fellow labourers soon saw reason to quit Sweden and to abandon their efforts as hopeless. It is not, however, the historical result attending their efforts, but the method in which their efforts were applied, which is deserving of attention. It is impossible to declare ingenuous and honest, a mode of procedure such as that which these Jesuit Fathers adopted with the view of paving a way into the entrenchments of Protestant Sweden. What they did, was done solely under calculation to steal a march, under protection of a treacherous mask, with the view of circumventing and ultimately getting the better of a hostile element, by means of a stratagem, that must be acknowledged to have been simply deceitful. For in this instance it cannot be alleged that entry into Sweden happened in dutiful response to a call which it must have been incumbent on priestly consciences to fulfil, but in sheer prosecution of a politic purpose, deliberately entertained, and spontaneously embraced.

CHAPTER VIII.

Common practice by Glosses to modify tenor of Statutes—This the case in reference to vow of poverty—And to prohibition against accepting ecclesiastical dignities—Jesuits have preferred the influential position of Confessors, but have declined preferments only out of expediency—Names of Jesuit Fathers promoted to the Cardinalate—Official connection of the Order with Inquisition—Particularly in Portugal—Loyola's own words in regard to this Tribunal on application from King John III. that it should be under direction of the Order.

THE practice of covertly modifying, through subsequent glosses of an unobtrusive form, the conditions clearly enjoined in the body of the Statutes, deserves particular notice in reference to the obligations of poverty, and the prohibition against acceptance of ecclesiastical dignities, which are both so stringently laid down in the Rules. It has been seen to how great a degree the Order has departed from the condition of impecuniosity. The proposition soon suggested itself to intellects trained in casuistry that, though the individual members could not themselves hold property, the words of the Founder need not forbid revenues, however large, being attached to the establishments in which these pauper members resided. In 1550, Julius III., by a Bull, expressly sanctioned the tenure of property by the General for the general benefit of the community, and the permission thus granted has been used with a freedom that needs no illustration. In regard to the other point, however, the conduct of the Jesuits has been sufficiently cautious to credit them, in the eyes of some grave writers, with a meritorious refusal of dignities, and particularly with the honourable distinction of not having connected themselves with the action of the Inquisition. The truth is that, though, as a practice, the Jesuits have been content to hold in Europe the less ostentatious but extremely influential position of Confessors to Sovereigns and persons of high degree, they have never declined ecclesiastical preferment when the acceptance did not seem impolitic. It is enough to recall the names of Lugo, Toletus, Bellarmine, Tolomei, Nithard; of Pallavicini, historian of the Council of Trent; of Salerno, who converted the Electoral Prince of Saxony; of Cienfuegos, who in the Spanish War of Succession distinguished himself as an Austrian partisan; and in quite recent times of Tarquini and Fränzelin; as of Jesuits who have been raised to the purple. So again in regard to the Inquisition, it is easy to give a list of Jesuits ranking high by their doctrine in the Order, as Castro-Palao, Tamburini, Marin, Pereyra, who were members of the Holy Office; while Father Nithard was for a time Grand Inquisitor in Spain. We have it besides, under the hand of Loyola himself, that the principles of this tribunal are quite in conformity with those of his foundation. The circumstances attending this utterance are too curious not to be specially noticed.

John III. of Portugal, the first royal devotee to Loyola's doctrine, being desirous to have a confessor who was of the Order, applied first to Father Gonzalez de Camara and then to the Provincial Miron. Both were simple-minded enough to consider the proposal incompatible with the profession not to accept proffered distinction, and reported to Loyola their having declined the request. Loyola replied in a letter eminently characteristic, and decidedly not expressive of concurrence in their view.[*] St. Ignatius in-

[*] The correspondence relating to this transaction is to be found in Genelli's 'Life of Loyola.'

structed Gonzalez that although preferments should never be courted, it was yet a duty to accede to a request of this nature, notwithstanding it entailed so heavy a cross as compulsory residence within the precincts of a Court—an opinion repeated in a letter to the Provincial, which the latter was directed to communicate to the King. John III., delighted at this sympathy on the part of the holy man with his longings, now proffered further privileges. When first this monarch contemplated introducing into his dominions the Tribunal of the Inquisition, it was through Loyola he had submitted to the Holy See an application for, and had obtained a grant of, the necessary Bulls and Faculties. He was subsequently desirous that the jurisdiction of the Tribunal to which was entrusted the duty of vigilantly repressing heresy in his dominions, should be vested in members of that new Order which the King looked upon as the soundest buttress of the Church. With that view John III. again made application to the Provincial Miron, who referred the matter to Loyola, and again Loyola showed himself most ready to meet the wishes of the King. Some difficulties, however, stood in the way. The Holy Office had long been the special appurtenance of the old-established Brotherhoods, and their influence in Rome might not improbably prevent the substitution of a new and encroaching Order. In a letter stamped with consummate astuteness, Loyola expressed his readiness to assume the proposed duties, and suggested means for circumventing opposition. "As in fact this charge is not directly contrary to the spirit of our Institute, there is no reason why the Society should seek to withdraw itself from the trouble of it, for it is decidedly a matter which nearly concerns the interests of religion in that kingdom. But to avoid many inconveniences, we think it would be good for his Majesty to write to the Pope requesting him to give us an order under obedience to accept of this charge, for then it would be on the express command of his Holiness, as Dean of the Cardinals, the Inquisitors, that the Society would undertake the office, and so all would be done with the Pope's full approbation. It would also be good for the King to write a letter to our protector, Cardinal Carpi, the acting Dean of the Inquisition, and another to his ambassador, to push on the affair." After some further counsel Loyola concludes with this suggestion: "If his Majesty shall not think fit to write, we shall nevertheless be ready to comply with his commands to the Greater Glory of God. . . . If his Majesty thinks that we should not wait for the Pope's reply to begin, one or two of ours can undertake the office provisionally, until such time as an official appointment from the Pope shall be made. Whatever may be the case, we will do in all things (as I have already written) what is most agreeable to his Majesty." To attempt to construe out of these courtly words an expression confirmatory of indisposition to participate in the practices essential to the principle of the Inquisition, is a task which must perplex the most consummate master in casuistry.*

* The above extracts are transcribed from the English version given in the English translation of the 'Life of Loyola,' by Father Genelli, who says that he had before him "a copy of the original, preserved in the chapel of Loyola."

CHAPTER IX.

Plea that the Order never countenanced Inquisition as operating in Spain —Cannot stand the test of facts—Father Nithard Inquisitor-General in Spain—Has to leave the country, and is then rewarded with the Purple —Case of Father Vieira in Portugal—Discrepancy between countenance accorded to these two and the action towards Father Fernandez by the same General, Oliva—Order associates itself with the intolerance practised in Spain against Jews and Moriscoes—Under Acquaviva's Generalship taint of Jewish or Saracen blood declared absolute bar against admission into Society—Nuevos Cristianos put under ban by formal Decree—Synchronism between the Decree and a peril of Spanish origin threatening Acquaviva's authority—Renewal of prohibition against Moriscoes by name in a subsequent Decree immediately before publication of Royal Edict proscribing the same.

ADVOCATES of the Society have, nevertheless, sought to make believe that it has uniformly abstained from identifying itself with the Inquisition as practised in Spain, and with the principles of persecution which, on various occasions, have imparted to the policy of that State a character of sanguinary and exterminating cruelty. Both pleas break down when subjected to the test of historical facts. That the Society did not associate itself with the Tribunal of the Inquisition in Spain in the same degree as the Dominican Order is, of course, beyond dispute. It did not care to conduct itself so that publicly and popularly the idea of the Inquisition, with its not pleasant associations, must become necessarily associated with the name of the Society. But whenever expediency suggested that the balance of advantage lay in connection with the dread Tribunal and in declared endorsement of cruel intolerance, then most positively the Society did lend itself in Spain, without perceptible indisposition, to the public adoption of such connection, and to the explicit affirmation of such principles. It has already been mentioned that more than one Jesuit Father can be shown to have been a member of that Tribunal. But it was not merely to subordinate grades that the connection of the Society remained confined. One Inquisitor-General of celebrity—we may even venture to say of notoriety—was a Jesuit Father.

Philip IV. being succeeded in 1665 by an infant son, the Queen-Mother, Maria Anna of Austria, became Regent with an appointed Council, of which the Inquisitor-General was to be an *ex-officio* member. This Princess placed implicit confidence in the counsels of her Confessor, the Jesuit Father Nithard, who had accompanied her from her native country. With the passion of a woman and a devotee, the Queen-Mother was bent on introducing this confidential adviser into the Council of Regency, and this end she attained by conferring on Father Nithard the office of Inquisitor-General. By the Constitutions of the Society it is, however, absolutely forbidden for a member to accept any dignity otherwise than with the special sanction of the General. It has never been alleged that in this case such sanction was not accorded. No insinuation has ever been thrown out that Nithard acted without adequate authority in accepting this post, and the ecclesiastical honours afterwards conferred on him by the Holy See afford conclusive evidence of the favour he continued to enjoy in that quarter. Father Nithard accordingly took his seat at the Board as Inquisitor-General. In that capacity he presided over the Holy Office, and during his four years' tenure of his high dignity, directed the actions of that Tribunal in a spirit, which certainly did not contrast by tolerance, or leniency, with the grimly stern temper that had distinguished the administration of his predecessors. Father Nithard, however, did not confine himself, as member of the Regency, to such duties as devolved upon him directly in virtue of his judicial dignity. He became the ruling Minister of Spain, and, through his influence over the Queen, he governed the State with supreme authority. The position publicly taken up by the foreign Jesuit Father was one of absolute ascendency,—he became the declared dispenser of all things and the guide of the State. But the Father's administration caused intense dissatisfaction, of which Don John of Austria made himself the conspicuous organ. Angry discontent spread throughout the land, until a popular rising ensued. Aragon and Catalonia declared openly against the obnoxious Minister. The remonstrants advanced successfully on Madrid in commanding force. Encouraged thereby the other members of the Regency Council summoned resolution to declare against the favourite, and to represent to the Queen-Mother the necessity for his immediate dismissal and his departure from Spain. After four years' tenure of power Father Nithard saw himself driven to leave the scene of his grandeur. Still he was destined to receive some compensation, in the guise of a distinction, expressive of the high esteem entertained for him by those, who were his immediate spiritual Superiors. He was promoted to the Cardinalitian rank; and in this circumstance lies the demonstration that the Society, as embodied in its General and as acting through the Pope, who was in intimate understanding with that dignitary, cordially approved of the action of a member who not only had identified himself with the Spanish Inquisition, but besides had assumed the character of a Minister of State.*

* The critic in the 'Month' does not dispute that Father Nithard did act as Inquisitor-General, but maintains that this circumstance proves nothing

In reference to this latter circumstance, the open assumption of a political part by Jesuit Fathers with the concurrence of their Superior, it is not irrelevant to note some cases which happened much about the same time in Portugal. It has already been mentioned how very favourably the Order was received in that country by the sovereign authorities from its commencement. The position acquired by the Fathers in Portugal was early one of singular influence. On the accession of John IV. this influence gained in force, so that we find Father Antonio Vieira—who was actually Provincial Councillor of the Order—despatched on a diplomatic mission to Holland and to France as the accredited Ambassador of the King, without any disapprobation being expressed by his Superior at having assumed such duties. King John was succeeded by Alphonso VI., a prince of worthless character. He married a French Princess, Isabella of Savoie-Nemours. The union was not happy, and the young Queen speedily allied herself with the elements of discontent in the country at the King's administration. She, too, like Maria Anna of Austria, had brought with her a Jesuit Confessor, the Père de Ville, and this ecclesiastic took an active part in promoting the Queen's ends, though these were connected with matter calculated to cause grave scandal. On the night of November 17, 1667, the Queen absconded to a nunnery, declaring she would no longer live with her husband, from whom she claimed herself entitled to a divorce. On King Alphonso's arrival at the nunnery, in pursuit of his run-away wife, with the view to carry her home by force, he found himself confronted by an armed body, at the head of which was his own brother Don Pedro. The result of

---

as regards the spirit of the Society, inasmuch as he had accepted the office only by the desire of Alexander VII. The force of the observation is not quite clear.

the commotion was a revolution, and the appointment of Don Pedro as Regent. The Queen then lodged her demand for divorce, and the Père de Ville, who had earnestly exerted himself during the critical moment when the success of the revolution was in the balance, now did the same for ensuring the attainment of her wishes. Through his efforts mainly the prayer was granted, and, by dispensation from the Cardinal Legate, the Queen was married in April, 1668, to her own brother-in-law Don Pedro the Regent. For the part taken in these transactions the Père de Ville does not appear to have encountered the slightest rebuke from his spiritual Superior—a circumstance the more noticeable that on another occasion, apparently much less open to moral censure, such was administered very decidedly to a fellow-member of the Order.* Don Pedro, like the others of his house, was singularly partial to the Society. He also chose his Confessor out of its body. The Father picked out for this trust was one Emmanuel Fernandez, and such was the confidence with which he inspired Don Pedro, that the latter came to consider it of essential importance for the security of his government to have this Jesuit Father in the Cortes. This was accordingly brought about, when the General of the Order interfered, and insisted on Father Fernandez forthwith resigning a position which he declared to be incompatible with his professions as a member of the Society. It must be matter of regret not to have the benefit of studying the text of the communication in which this opinion was conveyed, for the General who intimated this command to Father Fernandez was the very same Oliva who had been

* Crétineau Joly, the stanch champion of the Society, narrates, of course with a favourable colouring, these incidents in the fourth volume of his 'Histoire de la Compagnie de Jésus.' From so partisan a writer the following observation is noteworthy: "Le Père de Ville a, selon nous, excédé les bornes de l'affection paternelle envers cette jeune femme abandonnée."

in office when Fathers Nithard and De Ville acted in the manner described, without their having incurred a word of censure from him. It is consequently an established fact that Oliva dealt out different measures on different occasions in analogous cases; that while he made no protest against one Father fulfilling the functions of Ambassador, nor against another becoming Inquisitor-General and Minister of State, under altered conditions of time and general circumstances, the regard for what was incumbent on the character of the Order was made a plea by the General for peremptorily inhibiting a member of the Society from sitting in the Cortes on the ground that to do so was incompatible with his profession. These facts seem to furnish the demonstration that what is conformable and what is not conformable to the calling of a Jesuit Father depends on no fixed principle and no fixed regulation, but has to be determined by the untrammelled judgment of the General, in accordance to what appears to him, as each particular case presents itself, to be most in harmony with policy, or, as it is technically termed, the advancement of God's Greater Glory.

If we are thus driven to the conclusion, the plea cannot be sustained, that the Society of Jesus has kept aloof from the Inquisition as practised in Spain; further inquiry will also demolish the allegation, that the Society steadily avoided identifying itself with the principles of cruel persecution, which have given a repulsive aspect to certain leading events in the history of Spain. It will be admitted that the intolerance to which the Jews were subjected and the proscriptions the Moriscoes underwent, constitute the blackest chapters in the annals of that country. Can it be affirmed that on either point the Society of Jesus did anything in the direction of a charitable sentiment, or that it disconnected itself from association with the prevailing spirit of persecution? Upon this head testimony of the most authentic character is forthcoming. It is no evidence arrived at circumstantially and the result of inference. The evidence is written down in the clearest language in the official statute-book of the Society, and is embodied in the Decrees of General Congregations. Under the Generalship of Acquaviva there was convened in 1593 the fifth General Congregation, the fifty-second decree passed by which declares, that the taint of Jewish or Saracen blood shall be an absolute bar against admission to the Society. "The descendants of Nuevos Cristianos' ancestors (a progenitoribus modernis Christianis) having ordinarily introduced into the Society a vast amount of offence and injury, (as has been found by long experience,) many persons have strenuously demanded, it should be decreed by this Congregation, that none be henceforth admitted into the Society, who may descend from Hebrew or Saracen race, and that, should such a one have been admitted by error, he should be dismissed from the Society as soon as ever the existence of this impediment be established. It has been the pleasure of this Congregation unanimously to resolve, as by this decree it does resolve, that no one whatsoever out of the class of men descending from the Hebrew or Saracen race may henceforth be admitted into the Society." In respect of any thus labouring under the said taint who might already be admitted, the Congregation declared they should be dismissed if the defect were detected before actual profession, "for although the Society desires that all things be done by all for common salvation, so as to win to Christ as many as possible, yet it is not needful that it should derive its ministers from all manner of men."* There are several

* "Ii autem qui a progenitoribus modernis Christianis descendunt, plurimum et offendiculi et detrimenti (quemadmodum diuturnâ experientiâ compertum est) ordinarie in Societatem invehere consueverunt; ob eam

points to be noted in connection with this decree. First, it will be observed that it did not profess to give more explicit expression to a bar already involved in some original article of the Society's regulations, but that it avowedly purported to be a new declaration of incapacity made in response to the suggestions of experience and the demands of certain petitioners. By this decree a class of men previously admissible to the Society was branded as unworthy of this privilege.* Secondly, it must be noted that the wording of the decree is indisputably framed with the direct purpose of sympathetically responding to a specially Spanish sentiment, for in Spain alone there existed the so-called Nuevos Cristianos, mentioned by name in this decree. Thirdly, it should not be left out of sight that the enactment of this decree, which responded to a sentiment prevalent in Spain alone, happened at the very time when the peculiar powers of the General were seriously challenged from Spanish quarters, and when consequently to propitiate, if possible, in the Peninsula elements menacing to his authority,

causam multi efflagitârunt, ut præsentis Congregationis auctoritate statueretur, ne ullus post hac in Societatem admittetur, qui ex Hebræorum, aut Saracenorum genere descendat, et si quispiam eorum per errorem admissus fuerit, cum primum de hoc impedimento constiterit, a Societate dimittatur. Placuit autem Congregationi universæ statuere . . . ut nullus omnino ex hujusmodi hominibus, qui ex Hebræorum aut Saracenorum genere descendunt, deinceps in Societatem accipiatur. Quod si eorum quispiam errore aliquo admissus fuerit, cum primum de hoc impedimento constiterit, quocumque tempore ante Professionem id detegatur, . . . dimittatur. . . . Quamquam enim Societas pro communi salute omnibus omnia fieri optat, ut, quos poterit, Christo lucri faciat; non tamen necessum est, ut suos ministros ex quovis hominum genere desumat."—Inst., vol. i, p. 557.

* This fact that the prohibition here decreed was one not compromised within the intention of Loyola's legislation is illustrated by a very interesting circumstance. His own secretary, Polanco, was a Nuevo-Cristiano. Nevertheless the founder admitted him into the Society as many others who were of the same origin, and so high did Polanco stand in credit that in 1573 —after Borgia's death—he was within an ace of being elected General.

must have recommended itself as particularly desirable to the General.

That the prohibition here proclaimed had direct reference to Spain, of this additional testimony is afforded by a supplementary decree in explanation of the former, which was framed at the next General Congregation. This decree was professedly enacted to define the degree of genealogical investigation which should be applied in order to ensure safeguard against the admission of tainted blood. It was laid down that, in relation to those who by common report were of respectable or noble family, it would be enough to investigate back to the fifth degree inclusively; but at the same time there was incorporated in the decree a fresh enumeration of those wholly excluded, amongst whom are mentioned " *those who in Spain are called Moriscoes.*" *
There can be no possible dispute as to the specific bearing of this declaration. It was a distinct prohibition of an unfortunate class of human beings to be found only in Spain, and at that moment trembling under the impending descent of a relentless proscription. Moreover, the prohibition here pronounced with emphatic distinctness on the part of the Society of Jesus, through the medium of its authorities in Rome, was one publicly spoken at the precise conjunction when its utterance was calculated to give effective countenance to an act of ruthless cruelty then in preparation within the gloomy precincts of the Escurial. For the decree in question was promulgated in 1608 by the sixth Congregation under the presidency of that same Acquaviva who had

---

* " Exclusis iis, qui Morisci in Hispaniâ vocentur, vel aliis quibuscunque qui Cristiani specie tenus haberentur. . . itemque iis, qui hoc nomine generationis Hebræorum an Saracenorum infames habentur, qui enim juxta Constitutiones titulo infamiæ admitti non possunt; in ceteris, qui alioqui honestæ familiæ essent, aut vulgo nobiles, vel boni nominis haberentur, informationes fierent usque ad quintum gradum inclusive."—Inst., vol. i. p. 576.

so much cause to dread for his personal position the hostile action of Spanish influence, and that date preceded only by a few months the issue of the Royal Edict which converted the fairest regions of Spain into a scene of wailing and of desolation, and caused the most industrious of its inhabitants to be piteously driven into exile at the edge of a sword drawn in the name of God. In the presence of such clear and distinct utterances of proscription in the decrees of the Society, and of such remarkable coincidences in date between these utterances and events in their sense, can it be maintained that there is no serious ground for imputing to the Society of Jesus concurrence in abetting the cruel work of persecution that has disfigured Spanish history?*

* It can be shown that at the present day sentiments of the most intolerant character are being actively inculcated by those who rank as the choicest organs of the Society. Father Perrone's recognized eminence as a doctor can be open to no challenge. He composed for popular use in Italian a Catechism in which occur the following sentences: "Tra i ministri o propagatori del Protestantismo non bisogna cercare la probità," p. 59.—"Chi sono quelli che si chiamino Protestanti? *Sono la schiuma della ribalderia e della immoralità in ogni paese*," p. 60. "Non solamente dovete guardarvi dal Protestantismo e da coloro che cercano di propagarlo, ma li dovete avere in orrore ed in abbominazione. Intendo dire che al solo sentire a parlare di Protestantismo, voi dovete ricolmarvi di spavento, *più che se sentiste a parlarvi di un tentativo d'assassinio contro la vostra vita. Il Protestantismo e i fautori del Protestantismo sono nel ordine religioso e morale cio che la Peste e gli Appestati sono nel ordine fisico*," p. 93. It must be remembered that these sentences stand in a composition intended for popular instruction.

CHAPTER X.

Inordinate inflation of General's authority—This concentration of power not consummated without opposition—Acquaviva silently takes measures to counteract the same—His action stimulates Spanish jealousy— Oligarchical sentiment amongst primitive Jesuits expressed by Mariana —Action of Spanish Government—Acquaviva's tactics—Assembly of General Congregation—Acquaviva invites investigation—Triumphant result for him—Futile Reforms enjoined by Clement VIII.—Memorial of Grievances presented to him by some Fathers—Its six points—General Congregation of 1608—Francesco Contarini's report on its proceedings— Papal Brief prohibitory of discussions about Reforms—Acquaviva's authority rendered yet more absolute—Paul V.'s Brief fulminating Censures on those who had dared to memorialise the Pope in favour of Reforms— Constitution of Innocent X. in opposite sense—Revoked, however, by Alexander VII. and subsequent Popes.

It must be apparent to the reader who has followed us so far, that the Organisation of the Society of Jesus is a creation comprising an armoury of unique weapons, at the direct disposal of a General who is an Autocrat. So long as the General only puts in play his powers in furtherance of particular interests, technically designated those of God's Greater Glory, he is virtually free to strain them to any extent without check or trammel on his discretion. It is only if he should ever become tempted to deviate from the line of these interests, that the General instantly finds his strength incapable of making any impression on the grim stubbornness of a system stiffened into cast-iron rigidity through carefully methodical saturation by an essence as subtle as it is indelible. The irresistible effect of so much concentrated power must naturally be to efface the action of every organic force except the General's, whose authority becomes irresistibly inflated by the assumption of despotic pretensions, hardly in character with the profession of humility. On both heads—the inordinate extension of the General's powers, and yet his incompetency to effect with them any reform in the subtle essence of the system—the history of the Society furnishes striking illustration.

The concentration of so much authority in the General's hands did not take place without some notable manifestation of opposition within the body of the Society, especially from amongst its Spanish members. This was particularly the case after the elevation of Acquaviva to the Generalship in 1581. Until then the Spanish element had preponderated very markedly in the Society; and beyond doubt, national susceptibility, on transfer of the Generalship to Neapolitan hands, had somewhat to do with the umbrage which at this time was exhibited at the overgrown authority of the General. This motive, though it may have contributed considerably to inspire a declaration of opposition, does not, however, necessarily invalidate allegations which are supported by distinct references, so as to afford an opportunity of considering them on their merits. Acquaviva was endowed with the very qualities calculated to spread and assert with noiseless firmness the grip of absolute authority; he was a man of impassive and decorous exterior—given to no ebullition of temper, to no violence in action—with a strong power of will cloaked beneath an air of humility; a governor of inflexible purpose, shrouded under the smooth form of high-bred gentleness. Silently and stealthily Acquaviva made use of his prerogative, to promote to posts of importance those, whom he could depend upon as faithful creatures; silently and stealthily he took his measures to get rid of such elements of independent sentiment, as might reside in the survivors of the original generation of Fathers, and to introduce into the government of the Society the willing instruments of a central despotism. That procedure, however, gave umbrage in two quarters. It stimulated the jealousy of the Spanish Monarch—ever prone to look with suspicion at whatever might have the appearance of a strong organisation. It wounded the pride of the Spanish Fathers, who, though ready to obey a Commander in the service of the Church, never had contemplated enrolling themselves under the orders of a General, who should arrogate to himself the authority of a Caliph. These primitive Jesuits were permeated with an oligarchical sentiment, which found its forcible expression in Mariana, when he exclaimed that Monarchy without limitation must involve the downfall of the Society. That celebrated Jesuit composed a treatise on the defects from which the Society was suffering, wherein he enumerated the same with incisive vigour. To the movement so inaugurated, the Spanish Government lent practical help. Its influence was successfully exerted to make Clement VIII. command the convocation of a General Congregation. With the wary prudence of his nature, Acquaviva bowed before the storm as the best means to evade its brunt. Acquiescing with a semblance of readiness in the Pope's command, the General strove to neutralise what was menacing therein, through operation of the administrative machinery he had been steadily engaged in organising. The results were eminently satisfactory for him. Acquaviva had the gratification to experience, that the instruments at his disposal sufficed to ensure the Congregation consisting, in the preponderating majority, of individuals who were the obsequious creatures of the General. So decidedly in the ascendant was his influence, that even in Spain the nomination of marked opponents was prevented, including that of Mariana himself. Still, propositions of reform were formally brought forward at the meeting. They related particularly to the privileges which secured the permanent position of those in office. It was proposed that tenures should be for fixed terms, and that the Congregations should be held at stated intervals. The drift of these propositions was to impair seriously those privileges of absolute authority in the General which are sanctioned by the Constitution, and render the Organisation of the Society a thing which is without a parallel. With characteristic skill Acquaviva disconcerted his enemies by a bold stroke. At the opening sitting of the Congregation he declared himself conscious of having incurred the dissatisfaction of some sections of the Society, and, therefore, demanded an investigation into his conduct. This was instituted by the Congregation. It resulted, naturally, in a triumphant approval, and, consequently, in a confirmation of Acquaviva's authority. But though this Congregation thus put aside all propositions for practical reforms in the sense demanded from Spain, it was moved to enact the decree before alluded to, in bar of admission into the Society, of that Jewish and Saracen blood, which in Spain was being ostracised with so much cruel prejudice. It is true that subsequently Clement VIII. imposed some slight modifications— as, for instance, that the Superiors and Rectors were to retain office only for three years; but these alterations were of merely nominal consequence, for the General still preserved the same absolute powers of appointment, and so continued to pick his nominations from a select circle.

Though repressed and crushed, the sentiment for reform that existed within the Society had yet been undeniably real. An emphatic record thereof is preserved in a Memorial addressed to Clement VIII., the authenticity of which is not challenged. In this document—emanating from Jesuit

Fathers—certain evils complained of in the Society are enumerated with a telling precision of language. We perceive here an outspoken indictment of the system existing under Acquaviva, which is inspired by the clear light of experience. In this Memorial, which bears on it the inscription, "That it is intended solely for the Pope's own hand," six points of grievance are given, whereupon the intervention of his remedying action is invoked.*

I. It is prayed that it be made compulsory on all members of the Society holding offices in it not merely to vacate them at stated periods, but also thereupon to pass a fixed term without holding any other office in the Society. The prevailing system is stated to have had the result of setting Superiors above all restraint, inasmuch as they had nothing to fear from any quarter as long as they enjoyed the countenance of the General, while those of subordinate rank had no appeal, if desirous to guard themselves against the calumnies of their Superiors, or in self-vindication to bring a rebutting charge against those who, as mortals, must be fallible. II. The Pope is besought to provide against the favouritism consequent on the General's absolute discretion in the distribution of appointments. Acquaviva is directly charged with having shown himself unduly partial to his countrymen. "The General, being a man, has also his particular affections, and when so affected towards a person, he promotes him." Hence it is alleged to be a common spectacle, "to the serious detriment of the Society and to the scandal of the world, that the General appoints at his will Superiors, without respect to their seniority, their services, or their merits, and often men who are mere

* This remarkable document will be found in 'Tuba altera Majorem Clangens Sonum de Necessitate longe Maximâ Reformandi Societatem Jesu,' Argentinæ, 1715, p. 583. 'Sanct. Patri et Pont. Max. Clementi VIII. Soli et in Manu propriâ, Memoriale.'

youths and novices."* To obviate this state of things the Pope is petitioned to modify the existing system whereby the nomination of Superiors rests with the General alone; "for though he has his counsellors, he is not bound to abide by their advice, but is lord of lords, doing as he listeth, bound by no laws, so that he deadens and quickens, degrades and exalts, at pleasure, as if he were a God who should be free from disturbances of mind, and cannot err." III. It is represented that advancement to the grade of the Professed should no longer depend on the discretion of the General, who admits or rejects as he likes; "for in this matter there is a great regard for persons, to the great scandal of the whole world.... This is positive, that in the Society few are content, with the exception of some Superiors and Professed." IV. The Bull of Gregory XIV., investing the General with summary authority over every member, without being obliged to have recourse to any judicial inquiry, is protested against as "iniquitous and odious." Such powers are declared to set the General above even the Pope; "for your Holiness condemns no one, without having first heard the parties,"† and a remedy is earnestly implored against a state of things which utterly deprives the members of the

---

* "Provideat Sanctitas sua, ne sit in potestate solâ Generalis promovere ad praelaturam quem velit; nam videmus cum magno detrimento Religionis nostrae et scandalo mundi, quod Generalis, nullâ habitâ ratione, nec antiquitatis, nec laborum, nec meritorum, facit quos vult Superiores, et, ut plurimum, juvenes et novitios. Et donique Generalis, quia homo est, habet affectus particulares, et cum afficitur erga aliquem, promovet illum, etiamsi vere indignus; et quia est Neapolitanus, melioris sunt conditionis Neapolitani.... Licet Generalis habet suos Consiliarios, tamen non tenetur stare ipsorum consilio, sed est Dominus Dominantium, et facit quod vult; nullis legibus adstrictus, unde mortificat et vivificat, deprimit et exaltat quem vult, ac si esset Deus, qui liber esset ab omni animi perturbatione, et non posset errare."

† "Hoc est adeo iniquum et odiosum, ut plerique putent totam illam Bullam esse subreptitiam.... Certe hoc est facere Generalem majorem Papâ; nam Sanctitas sua neminem condemnat, nisi prius auditis partibus, et prolatâ sententiâ juridice."

Society of every shred of protection against arbitrary treatment. V. The like protest is made against the clause of the same Bull which, under pain of excommunication, forbids a word being spoken in difference from anything in the Institutes, inasmuch as it is affirmed "there are many things which, were he alive, Father Ignatius, under the lessons of experience, would alter." VI. The Pope is requested to enact that in Provincial Congregations votes be recorded secretly, "because, from dread of the General, many do not speak freely as they feel, being aware that everything is reported in writing to the General." In reference to this last point it is not amiss to mention, in corroboration, that Mariana, in his Treatise on 'The Evils affecting the Society,' dwells on the systematic denunciation which, he says, was practised to such an extent that, if the General's archives could be looked through, hardly a single member would be found to have escaped some denunciatory relation. This remarkable Memorial is no solitary record of the existence inside of the Society of a desire to curb the absolute power of the General through the operation of organic rights to be vested in constituted bodies.

In 1608, Acquaviva found himself again in a position that made it advisable to summon a General Congregation. This was the one which passed the before-mentioned decree directed against the Moriscoes. At that time Francesco Contarini was Venetian Ambassador in Rome, and this admirably-informed diplomatist, in confidential reports to his Government, has preserved to us some highly valuable notices in regard to the proceedings of this Assembly. We learn from a despatch, written at the time of convocation, that there was a section known to be animated with the desire of getting rid of Acquaviva, who then had held the reins of government for more than twenty-five years; that the Spaniards particularly wished to have more provinces allotted to their nation, which would increase their voting power; that it was not thought likely they would obtain this concession, although probably the favour withheld from them would be granted to the French; that there were rumours of some intended attempts at reform, particularly in restraint of the Society's interference in matters of State; and that, in provision of possible inconveniences arising out of the mooting of unpleasant points, "the General had contrived to secure, as much as possible, the nomination of individuals who were his creatures (*dipendenti da lui*), particularly in the Italian province." Contarini's anticipations were proved correct by events. Directly after the opening of the Assembly, notwithstanding the sacred obligation of secrecy, under pain of excommunication imposed upon its members, he was in a position to inform his Government how an attempt had been made to moot certain proposals "in restriction of the General's authority," and had instantly been met by an insuperable obstacle which Acquaviva had contrived to prepare in secret. This was nothing less than a Papal Brief "forbidding the discussion of anything relating to regulations in the original rules of Ignatius." The Ambassador adds that the Brief was artfully couched in terms making show of fair and legitimate grounds, but that it had been inspired "with the specific view of sustaining the General's reputation and command." This bold step broke the neck of the Opposition in the Congregation. The schemes entertained for decreeing periodical assemblies and limiting the tenures of office were quietly dropped, for, as Contarini reported, in presence of such august influences, the would-be reformers in the Society lost heart. "The Jesuits have closed their General Congregation," he wrote under date of April 5, 1608, "which, according to my information, was convoked under the semblance to reform certain abuses in the Society, but in reality with the intention to lessen the authority of the General. Those, however, who entertained this intention, perceiving the feeble ground (*fondamento*) they could rely on, and the vigorous preparations that were made against their efforts, in the conviction that they had no chance of success, fell away, and felt no courage to promote any provisions, but abstained wholly therefrom, not merely as regards the existing General, but likewise as regards the future one, as had been apparently contemplated, so that the General, who is an individual of great capacity, and has known how to withstand other storms, continues to guide himself well through this one, and has come out triumphant with even greater authority than ever." [*]

Such was the upshot, as related by Contarini, of the feeble effort towards reform of their Constitution, which some members of the Society had felt a disposition to make in the Congregation of 1608. Acquaviva emerged a yet more absolute General, and the administration of the Society was only rendered more confirmedly centralized through promulgation of a Papal Brief, which fulminated the direst censures expressly against those evil sons of Loyola, disturbers of the harmony of the Society, who had dared to address to the Pope himself written charges and incriminations, and even, most presumptuously, suggestions for shortening the General's tenure of authority, and introducing into the Society elements, in the shape of local Superiors and permanent Visitors, that would break its unity and established discipline. This Brief of Paul V. is a notable monument of the extraordinary influence which Acquaviva had secured,

[*] In the Appendix will be found the text of Contarini's despatches, which by the great kindness of Mr. Rawdon Brown have been copied out of Contarini's letter-books in his possession. See Appendix No. I.

and is even more illustrative than the original Pontifical privileges, of the peculiar character the Society of Jesus, through the agency of its great Generals, contrived to acquire in the Organisation of the Church. It is true that Innocent X., in 1646, issued a Constitution whereby General Congregations were to be held every nine years, the Assistants thereat to be always different from those at the previous Congregation, and all dignitaries of the Society, with the exception of the Superiors of Novices, should vacate their offices every third year, without being eligible to another till after an interval of eighteen months. This Constitution was, however, solemnly revoked by his immediate successor, Alexander VII., on the express ground that, according to the intentions of St. Ignatius, all matters relating to the administration and the nomination of officers must be left to the discretion of the General, so that he might do as would seem most expedient, *Ad Majorem Dei Gloriam.* This revocation was subsequently confirmed by Papal utterances of the same solemnity on two occasions, by Clement IX. and by Benedict XIV., so that, as regards the expression of Pontifical authority, the government of the Society of Jesus has been emphatically declared to be vested solely in the absolute hands of the General.

CHAPTER XI.

Generalship of Gonzalez—Illustration how, notwithstanding his great privileges, no General can infuse a Reform into the Order—Innocent XI.'s sentiments—Jesuit authorities forbid publication of a Treatise by Gonzalez—Mellini, Nuncio at Madrid, draws to it attention of Innocent XI.—Approbation of its tenour expressed by Pope—Gonzalez attends Congregation for election of a General—Nomination of Gonzalez with marked concurrence of Innocent—Opposition to the General's action by Members of the Society—Father Assistants protest against publication of a book on which he is engaged—Gonzalez offers to submit it to previous inspection by the same—Entire destruction of every copy is demanded—Fear of Jesuits lest Pope should refer the book to a special Congregation of Divines—Meeting of Provincial Procurators—Design through it to effect sentence of removal from office against Gonzalez—Motion for convocation of special General Congregation to that end—Inadequate majority in favour—Matter referred to five Cardinals—Vote of Procurators declared void—Opinion of Cardinal Noris on the result.

UNDOUBTEDLY the Popes who were parties to these transactions were, of themselves, much predisposed to favour the spirit and the temperament best represented by a despotic authority. It may, however, be fairly questioned whether at this period even Popes of a reforming disposition would not have proved powerless to counteract the peculiar essence which had systematically taken hold of the Society of Jesuits. The episode of Gonzalez' Generalship, and of Innocent XI.'s failure in combination with him to restrain the affirmation of Probabilist doctrines which had become habitual with the Fathers, indicates that, at all events, in this instance, the inveteracy of imbibed principles was able to defy even the action of a Pope and a General, when in concert they strove to fight against teachings that had become prevalent. The story of the interlude is emphatically illustrative of the incompetency that attaches even to a General of the Order, notwithstanding he is invested with so vast an armoury of power, if he should seek to apply them in a sense not exactly consonant to the maxims that have been identified with the traditional action of the Order.

Exception has been taken to the assertion that Innocent XI. had Jansenist leanings. It cannot, however, be gainsaid by any candid inquirer that this Pope, at least, was not disposed to look favourably on the manner in which the Jesuits bore themselves in the Jansenist controversies, and that he was decidedly more prone to Rigorist than to Probabilist views. It is equally positive that Innocent promoted the nomination of Gonzalez to the Generalship with a full cognisance of his entertaining Anti-Probabilist opinions, as will be seen to irresistible demonstration from a brief statement of the facts.

Father Tyrso Gonzalez occupied the Chair of Divinity in the University of Salamanca. He composed a theological Treatise to demonstrate that no merely probable opinion, but sincerely believed truth alone, could constitute a sufficient guide in morals. The manuscript was transmitted for inspection to Oliva, then General, to whom it was the author's desire to dedicate it, expressly as thereby the publication would acquire the weight of authoritative demonstration against the impression that the contrary view enjoyed the official countenance of the Order. The Treatise was handed for examination to five Revisors, and they unanimously reported against its publication being sanctioned, on the ground that the doctrine promulgated was characterised " by an undue rigidity, opposed to that spirit of gentleness with which it behoves to lead minds on to heaven." *

* " Unanimi consensu opus improbarunt, negatâ illud edendi facultate. Judicarunt æquo rigidiorem doctrinam, in hocce tractatu defensam, minusque

Finding it impossible to obtain permission for the issue of this Treatise, Gonzalez subsequently sought to be allowed to insert in another work then in the press some short and simple propositions, pointed against the most extreme formulas of lax Probabilism. In this application he was, however, equally unsuccessful, and Gonzalez had to acquiesce in the prohibition signified to him by his General Oliva.* Seven years later, in 1679, Innocent XI. issued his celebrated Bull, condemnatory of sixty-five propositions; amongst which was comprised the maxim that a barely probable opinion could be safely accepted as a warrant. On promulgation of the Bull in Spain, the Nuncio Mellini drew the Pope's attention to the fact that the views expressed in this document had been maintained in that country by a Jesuit divine of standing some time before in a treatise that had not seen the light of day. Hereupon Innocent instructed the Nuncio to get a copy of the manuscript sent to Rome; and this having been done, it then was, by the Pope's commands, submitted for examination to two specially-appointed Censors. The opinions of both were unequivocally favourable to the Treatise. According to the one the Treatise was specially useful and appropriate to the improvement of Christian morals, while by the second it was pronounced as the most solid production on the subject-matter that had come from the Jesuit

---

congruam suavitatis spiritui, quo dirigendæ in cælum animæ sunt."—Concina ad Theol. Christ. Apparatus, vol. ii, p. 184.

* The forbidden propositions were of such plain character as, for instance: "Nemini licet in praxi sequi opinionem faventem libertati adversus legem, quando ipse judicat esse falsam. . . . Nemo potest licite sequi opinionem faventem libertati adversus legem, quando absolute habet fundamentum majus ad judicandum illam esse falsam quam ad judicandum esse veram."—Concina, ad. Theol. Christ. App., vol. ii. p. 186, where are all the propositions.

presses. In accordance with these reports, Innocent XI. issued a Decree under date of June 26th, 1680, expressive of absolute approval of what Gonzalez had written, and of encouragement to him to preach, teach, and write, in the same sense with manful vigour.* Gonzalez, nevertheless, did not deem it proper, on the strength of this Pontifical encouragement, to print the Treatise, in face of the distinct prohibition which had been intimated to him by the General of the Society. Under the plausible plea that the Treatise needed ample revision, Father Gonzalez was content to keep by him the manuscript, and continued to attend unobtrusively to his local duties, until, in 1687, he found himself called upon to proceed to Rome as Elector for the Province of Castile, on occasion of the Congregation convoked for election of a General on the demise of Oliva's successor—Father Noyelle. The result was that Gonzalez himself was elevated to this dignity; and that this was due in the main to the influence which the Pope was able to exercise, is a circumstance distinctly affirmed by testimony of superior weight. Concina says that Innocent manifested in the clearest manner the desire he felt for Gonzalez' election, and the Jesuit Father Segneri, a strong Probabilist, never ventured expressly to deny the correctness of this allegation. There is, however, evidence of a yet more direct nature on the matter—the evidence of Gonzalez himself,

---

* The text of the decree is given by Concina, 'Theol. Christ. App.,' p. 195, vol. ii. "Die xxvi. Junii, 1680; Factâ relatione per P. Lauriam contentorum in litteris P. Tyrsi Gonzalez Soc. Jesu, Sanctissimo Nostro directis, Eminentissimi dixerunt scribendum per Secretarium Status Nuncio Apostolico Hispaniarum, ut significat dicto P. Tyrso, quod Sanctitas sua benigne acceptis, et non sine laude perlectis litteris mandavit ut ipse libere et intrepide prædicet, doceat, et calamo defendat opinionem magis probabilem, nec non viriliter impugnet sententiam asserentem licitum esse sequi minus probabilem in concursu probabilioris sic cognitæ et judicatæ, eumque P. Tyrsum certum faciat, quod quidquid favore opinionis magis probabilis egerit, et scripserit, gratum erit Sanctitati Suæ."

recorded in a Memorial which he presented to Clement XI. In that document he states, in the plainest terms, that on election he was told by the Pope himself that he had been made General with the view of rescuing the Society from the abyss into which it was in peril of falling, through the adoption as its own of the Probabilist principle in its larger sense. This statement was made on a grave occasion in a most solemn document by Gonzalez, and the accuracy of the allegation, as far as we know, was never challenged at the time. Quite irrespective thereof, however, the case seems perfectly clear. That Innocent XI. was well acquainted with the theological opinions held by Gonzalez, is a matter beyond dispute. That with this knowledge the Pope in no degree manifested any desire that his election might be frustrated, is also a point conceded on all sides. The unavoidable inference from these plain facts can only be that Innocent XI. willingly concurred in the promotion of Father Gonzalez, because he considered the elevation of one holding his opinions the likely provision for checking the continued assertion by the Society of certain theological views which it is notorious he himself did not contemplate with favour.

The success attending this design proved, however, eminently unsatisfactory, for it was found that the force acquired by the organisation of the Society was strong enough to render futile the action of a General who was not in everything conformable to its established spirit. Gonzalez encountered at every point solid and stubborn hostility. He had summoned from Spain the Jesuit Father Alfarez to teach Theology in the Roman College; but such was the opposition manifested to him, that he found it necessary not to broach distinctly Anti-Probabilist propositions. Thereupon the Pope saw reason to make remonstrances, in consequence of which the General Congregation issued a decree affirming that the Society never had forbidden the doctrine according to which a person had to guide himself by the light of the more probable opinion. This demonstration was soon seen to have been a mere feint. With the view of giving force to the resolution, Gonzalez composed a treatise vindicating the original divines of the Society from the imputation of that lax Probabilism which had permeated the writings of its subsequent members. Against the publication of this work the Father Assistants deemed it incumbent to combine in protestation. They drew up a formal memorial calling upon the General to suspend the impression of, and, if already in type, then to cancel and suppress, every copy of the Treatise he was understood to have composed. To grasp the import of such a demonstration it must be borne in mind that, according to the Constitutions, the sanction for what can be published by a member of the Society is vested in the General absolutely, and that, consequently, the proceedings of the Assistants was virtually tantamount to an insurrectionary demonstration. The reply made by the General was singularly conciliatory. To suspend the impression, he said, was not in his power, as it was completed; but in grateful recognition of representations which he could not but believe to have been inspired by a sincere zeal for the good of the Society, he offered to have copies of the Treatise, which was being printed at Dillingen, brought to Rome for examination before publication by the Father Assistants, whom he invited thereupon to favour him with their views as to its contents. Having these views before him, he would then carefully consider and weigh what course it would be most conformable to the interests of the Society that he should pursue. So far from being at all appeased by this conciliatory declaration, the Father Assistants proceeded to request that the General should forthwith destroy at the place of impression the whole edition of his Treatise so completely, that there could be no question of any copies being brought to Rome even for examination. To this demand Gonzalez naturally declined to assent. To affirm of a book that its nature was such as to require wholesale destruction, could be understood but in this sense—that it was not merely objectionable in regard to particular passages, but that it was thoroughly unsound in doctrine. An imputation of this serious character on a Treatise composed by a General, Gonzalez deemed no less injurious to the reputation of the Society than to that of his own person. He repeated his readiness to submit the work to an examination, from which it was technically exempt by the fact of its being composed by the General, but this proposal was distasteful to the Father Assistants, who were apprehensive lest the Pope should refer the inquiry to a specially-appointed Congregation of Divines, from which the Treatise might then go forth with the endorsement of a distinct approbation.

To obviate this danger they addressed to the Pope a suggestion that the whole matter might be fairly postponed until the next meeting of the Procurators of the Society. That body did come together in Rome in November, 1693. By that time the animosity of those hostile to the General had grown so much in intensity, that it was no longer satisfied with merely seeking to restrain the General from a specific action. What was now contemplated by the representatives of a powerful malcontent element was to bring about the deposition of the existing General—to effect the removal of Gonzalez from his office through a solemn decree from a specially-convened General Congregation. As early as April, 1693, Cardinal Aguirre wrote word to Charles III. that the General was in great affliction at the persecution he was suffering at the hands of those who ought to be under his orders, and that matters were being pushed to a point at which the Cardinal considered likely an attempt to deprive Gonzalez forcibly of his authority.* The event verified his anticipations. On the assembly of the Congregation of Provincial Procurators, a motion was made for the convocation of a General Congregation, with the view of, in virtue of its supreme authority, removing Gonzalez from the Generalship. By the rules of the Society the majority requisite to give validity to a decision must be one more than the half. The Congregation consisted in all of 33 members. On the division 17 voted in favour of convoking the General Congregation, and 16 against; whereupon a question arose as to the majority being valid, inasmuch as the half of 33 would be $16\frac{1}{2}$, and consequently it would need $17\frac{1}{2}$ to attain the figure indicated by the Regulations for an effective majority. The point continued to be hotly contested by the rival parties, until at last it was referred for decision to a Congregation consisting of these five Cardinals—Marescotti, Campagna, Spada, Albani, Panciatici. After mature deliberation these Prelates, on August 3rd, 1694, pronounced the vote of the Procurators null and void, a decision solemnly confirmed by the Pope, with the further instruction, *et non amplius audiantur*.† "Thus Father Tyrso has

---

* "El P. General de la Compañía, como sujeto tan exemplar, y docto, como V. Mag. sabe, y que tanto fructo ha hecho con sus missiones y predicaciones continuas in essos regnos, se halla muy perseguido de los suyos, y en grande afflicción .... la persecucion ha passado, y passa a querer formar una Congregacion Generale para deponerla de el gubierno." April 26, 1693, Cardinal Aguirre to King Charles.—Concina, 'Difesa dei Gesuiti,' p. 36.

† "Non constare de validitate Decreti Patrum Procuratorum Provincialium et ideo non esse cogendam Congregationem. Die 3 Augusti horâ noctis pro referente Card. Panciatico Sua Sanctitas confirmavit. E vi aggiunse S. Beatitudine *et non amplius audiantur*."—Concina, 'Dif. d. Gesuiti,' Sec. Parte, p. 20.

remained the victor," wrote Cardinal Noris to Magliabecchi, "and Father Segneri's opinion has been declared the *less probable*." Notwithstanding this check, it cannot be said that the Fathers of the Society acquiesced in the spirit of this august sentence. The Order continued to prove persistently mutinous to the General during the years he still lived to retain his dignity. There exists a memorial to Clement XI. from Gonzalez, written "at the very verge of life, and when awaiting death at every moment," * which records in sadly-touching language the insuperable hostility he had to encounter throughout, and constitutes a signal monument of how inadequate is even the combined influence of a General and a Pope to get the better of that stubborn spirit which, through systematic infiltration, has become so thoroughly instilled into the fibres of the Society, as apparently to defy the powers of extirpation.

* " Libellus supplex oblatus Sanctissimo Dom. Nost. Clementi XI. pro incolumitate Soc. Jesu, ab ejus Præposito Generali Tyrso Gonzalez, anno 1702." —Concina, ad Theol. Christ. Apparatus, vol. ii. p. 202.

CHAPTER XII.

Episode of the Chinese Rites : demonstrative of even a Pope's inability to make the Society acquiesce in orders if not agreeable to it—Authorities for the facts of the case—The suppressed *Mémoires de la Congrégation*—Exceptional favour which Jesuits from an early period secured in China—Pretensions of Portuguese Crown—How the Jesuits accommodated themselves thereto—Their practices denounced by the Dominican Moralez—Protracted investigation in Rome—Clement XI. refers the matter to the Holy Office, which condemns Jesuit practices—Mission of Tournon as Legate *a Latere*—His Faculties as such—His arrival at Pekin—Report on the extent and nature of Jesuit establishments there by Tournon's Secretary—Tournon's official statement to the Cardinal Secretary of State as to the reception he encountered from the Jesuits—Intercepted despatches—Money transactions carried on by the Jesuits—Legate's sentence declaring void and usurious certain loans made in the name of the Vice-Provincial—Change in the attitude of Chinese Emperor towards Legate—He receives orders to leave Pekin, and await at Canton return from Rome of two Jesuit envoys—Contumacious resistance by Jesuits to the Visitation of the Catholics by the Bishop of Pekin—Imperial Edict imposing conditions on all priests resident in China—The Jesuits acquiesce, and accept to be the organs for communicating the same to the Missionaries—Legatine sentence against this proceeding with promulgation of Papal Decree condemnatory of Chinese Rites—Appeal of Jesuits to Rome—Legate obliged to betake himself to Macao—Hostile reception from Portuguese authorities and the Bishop—The latter pleads right of the Crown against recognition of Legatine authority—Mandate from Governor-General transmitted by the Jesuit Ammiani—Legate put in confinement, inveighed against in sermons, and subjected to sentence of Major Excommunication by the Bishop in a Decree formally promulgated—Legate's promotion to the Purple—Imprisonment of ecclesiastics from Rome who had been sent to bring the Cardinal's hat—The Legate's confinement made yet more stringent—Further fulminations by Bishop—Legate sickens and dies—Reflections on conduct of Jesuits—Bull *Ex illâ die* at last puts a stop to the controversy.

How futile it is for a Pope to deem himself able, of his own authority, to make the Society concur in executing commands, however solemnly intimated, if they should not be according to the humour of its spirit, despite that oath of special obedience to the Supreme Pontiff, which every Professed Jesuit Father swears as his distinctive obligation—of this demonstration has been afforded by what happened in connection with that most curious Episode known as the controversy about the Chinese Rites. The facts relating to this remarkable passage in the Annals of the Society are not quite easy of access. They are stowed away in publications, some of which have become so scarce, that it would seem as if they had been systematically removed out of circulation. Of these two deserve special notice. In the 'Anecdotes sur l'État de la Religion en Chine,'* printed by the Lazarist Fathers, we have a detailed narrative of the principal events, running over a course of years. Subsequently the celebrated Cardinal Passionei compiled Memoirs of Cardinal Tournon, the Papal Legate despatched to China in settlement of the question.† This work is of great scarcity and of startling interest, on account of the documentary records embodied therein. The allegations contained in these volumes are of so strange a character that the genuineness of the evidence has been freely questioned, particularly by those who have written in defence of the Society of Jesus with the semblance of authority. It is, however, no longer possible to entertain a doubt as to the perfect authenticity of the documentary proof given in both publications. Some years ago, the Lazarists, whose head-quarters are in Paris, contemplated a new issue of reports illustrative of the missionary labours of their Congregation in various parts of the world.‡ Amongst the countries in which these had

* 'Anecdotes sur l'État,' etc. 7 vols. Paris, 1734. Aux dépens de la Société.
† 'Memorie Storiche dell' Em. Card. di Tournon,' 8 vols. Venezia, 1761.
‡ The collection was entitled, 'Mémoires de la Congrégation de la Mission.' 8 vols. Paris, 1865.

lain was China. Members of the Congregation had been actively engaged there, at the period of the events that led to the particular controversy in question, and on the occasion they had been brought into contact, and likewise into conflict, with the Jesuit Fathers. Sensible of the imputations to which they might plausibly be liable, of having advanced statements of grave import on the strength of data that could not bear the test of criticism, the Lazarist editors, before entering upon the narrative of the transactions in connection with the Chinese missions, sought to obtain authoritative verification of the evidence on which their story would rest. They applied to Father Theiner, then Keeper of the Vatican Archives, to collate for them the versions given in translations by Passionei and by the compilers of the 'Anecdotes,' with the original official reports preserved in the Archives. Father Theiner not merely testified to the correctness of what was given in these volumes, but he permitted this testimony to be inserted in the Lazarist collection.* Nothing can be more explicit than the deposition made by Father Theiner, and the crushing weight whereof was demonstrated by what ensued. The fact that the Lazarists were engaged in the compilation of this collection had been perfectly well known for years in Rome, without the shadow of an objection having been raised from that quarter. All of a sudden, however, there came from Rome a stringent injunction peremptorily forbidding the issue of the volumes already printed; and so rigidly has this suppression been carried

---

* " Une troisième raison (qui nous oblige d'entrer dans les détails, c'est que tous ces faits ont été imprimés et publiés en particulier par le Cardinal Passionei dans son ouvrage intitulé : Memorie Storiche dell' Eminentissimo Msgr. Cardinale di Tournon, qui renferme une partie des documents authentiques conservés dans les Archives du Vatican ou de la Propagande, et dont la parfaite conformité nous a été attestée par le Préfet des Archives du Vatican, le Père Theiner, Oratorien." —Vol. iv. p. 126.

out, that practically the work may be said not to exist. It has been impossible to obtain hitherto a copy for the British Museum. At present we know of but two complete copies, one in the Library of the Benedictines at Munich, which is not communicated to a student, another in the possession of an ecclesiastical dignitary in Austria. Dr. Huber, indeed, makes reference to the book as if it were an ordinary publication, within everybody's reach. One volume of the collection—the very one Dr. Huber refers to—does exist in Dr. Döllinger's library. It is a volume treating of the Chinese Missions. We owe it to the kindness of the venerable owner, that we have been permitted to make free use of this precious book,* and so to support the brief narrative we now shall proceed to give by references, which those who, in the interest of the Society, may possibly care to scan these pages, will doubtless have the means of satisfying themselves to be correct quotations. This practically complete suppression in the nineteenth century of a book to which no other possible objection could exist except that it contained well-established matter not creditable to

---

* A capital source whence the compilers of this volume drew is a manuscript of which they give this account : "Nous ne pouvons avoir de meilleurs renseignements sur cette matière que ceux qui nous sont fournis par un ouvrage de Msgr. le Secrétaire de la Sacrée Congrégation de la Propagande chargé en 1726, par le Pape Benoît XIII, de rédiger par écrit ses réflexions sur un certain mémoire que les Jésuites avaient présenté au Pape Innocent XIII., son prédécesseur. Ces réflexions du Secrétaire de la Propagande forment un ouvrage considérable, dont des extraits ont été publiés autrefois sous différents titres. Nous avons jugé ne pouvoir mieux faire que de recourir aux sources, et sans nous arrêter aux ouvrages publiés, nous avons consulté les manuscrits qui se trouvent à la Bibliothèque Corsini à Rome, et qui y ont été laissés par le Cardinal Corsini, neveu du Pape Clément XII. . . . Ce recueil de tout ce qui s'est fait à la Sacrée Congrégation de la Propagande au sujet des Jésuites de Chine n'a pas moins de douze volumes."—p. 131. The Secretary who compiled this elaborate report was Passionei. We give these details because the critic in the 'Month' says, "*Quod gratis asseritur, gratis negatur* ; and so, until further proof, we may be allowed to doubt the story of the Lazarist work on Chinese Missions, said to have been suppressed by an order from Rome."

the action of the Society in transactions nearly two hundred years old, is a fact worthy of notice. It is strikingly indicative of the extraordinary efforts made by the Jesuits to ensure obliteration of every particle of evidence that can be unfavourable to the reputation of the Society, no matter what may be the circumstances of the case, or how long a period may have elapsed since the event.* It is also signal evidence of the extent to which their special influence predominates in the official circles of the Church, so as to be able to bring into the field the full weight of the highest Church authority for the expunging of historical records, when these happen to prove inconvenient to the credit of the specific interests of the Society.

At an early period the Jesuits secured a footing of advantage in China, which they forthwith sought jealously to maintain against participation by missionaries of other religious communities. In support of the position they had acquired, they relied on the double action of the Portuguese Crown, and of the Chinese Emperor. Portugal held then extensive possessions in India, and had pushed its authority

* To what extent Jesuit writers, down to the present day, observe the principle, never to make a candid admission of error on the part of those who have represented the Society, however trivial the point may be, of this a curious instance is afforded by Genelli. Loyola despatched a mission into Abyssinia, and provided it with a long epistle addressed to the Sovereign of that country, whom, according to the geographical knowledge of the day, he took to be the legendary Prester John. It might well be thought that the existence in the flesh of an individual who had given rise to the idea of this personage was, at the present time, an utterly exploded notion, and that even the most sensitive disciple of St. Ignatius would not deem it incumbent to protect him from adverse criticism because he shared in this matter the prevalent error of his age. Such, however, cannot have been Father Genelli's view, for he so words his text that an ignorant reader—and the book is composed for popular circulation—would carry away the impression that Loyola had merely been guilty of a slip of the pen in the superscription of the epistle: "The Saint also sent a letter to the so called Prester John, the King of Abyssinia, *whose real name was Claudius.*"—'Life of St. Ignatius,' p. 270.

even to Macao, within Chinese limits. In connection with this colonial empire the Portuguese Crown put forth claims to commensurate ecclesiastical rights. The Archbishop of Goa styled himself Primate of the Indies, with the concurrence of the Holy See; and assumed to exercise metropolitan powers over all Christian bodies in these regions. The Jesuits, who on all occasions had been greatly favoured by Portugal, found it to their decided interest to recognise, and even to amplify, these pretensions. Their missionary detachments in these parts were advisedly composed, in large proportions, of Portuguese recruits, so as to cement the union with the leading Christian power in that region, and in return secure its cordial countenance to their operations as pioneers of Portuguese interests, and for the exclusion of missionaries not of Portuguese origin. This was carried to a point, that in the Jesuit community itself there was a declared hostility on the part of the Portuguese Fathers against those of other—particularly of French—nationality.* These dissensions were patent, and are repeatedly dwelt upon in the correspondence relating to these transactions. A point which the Fathers had particularly at heart was to ensure immunity from the jurisdiction claimed by Vicars-Apostolic despatched from Rome. To

* "D'après les lois faites par les Rois de Portugal à l'instigation de leurs Confesseurs Jésuites, l'entrée de la Chine était défendue à tous les missionnaires non-seulement séculiers ou réguliers de tout autre ordre, mais encore aux Jésuites eux-mêmes, à moins qu'ils ne fussent Portugais ou attachés à la Province de Portugal. Ceux-ci prétendirent avoir le monopole de cette Mission nonobstant les Brefs en sens contraire émanés des Souverains Pontifes Clément VIII, Paul V, Urbain VIII et Clément X, dans lesquels on donnait à tous les ordres mendiants, de quelque nation que fussent les Religieux, pleine liberté d'annoncer l'Evangile en Chine."—Cardinal Passionei, 'Memorie Storiche,' vol. vii. p. 241, as quoted in 'Mémoires de la Congrégation,' vol. iv. p. 214.

"Les Jésuites Portugais prétendaient qu'aucun Missionnaire ne devait venir en Chine qu'en passant par le Portugal et en se faisant sujet de ce Royaume."—Relation de l'Abbé Sala, 'Mém. de la Cong.' vol. iv. p. 320.

this end, it is stated in his Report by the Secretary of the Propaganda Congregation, the Fathers systematically applied for nominations, making them dependent on the Portuguese Bishops, particularly as Commissaries of the Tribunal of the Inquisition at Goa, which had a subordinate court at Macao.* The powers acquired by these means over missionaries of other bodies were furthermore strengthened by the influence which the Jesuit Fathers contrived to obtain quickly at the Court of Pekin. That this influence was due to the practice of acts which, in many respects, were characterised by a spirit of lax acquiescence little in accordance with a strong sense of principle, is of course the contention of those who disapprove of the Jesuit proceedings in China; and this view is undoubtedly borne out by the sentence of condemnation which Rome pronounced. It is, however, no part of our purpose to enter into the consideration of the speculative and dogmatic points raised in the controversy. The intrinsic merits of the views maintained on either side—of the doctrinal soundness of the opinions and propositions which were exchanged in ecclesiastical controversy—constitute no portion of what it is necessary to bring under review. That which bespeaks our attention are merely the historical facts connected with the action which the Society adopted toward the appointed representatives of the Holy See on an occasion when it found the latter not look with approval on a line of conduct which the Society itself deemed beneficial. Such facts are perfectly

---

* "Afin de tenir les Vicaires-Apostoliques occupés dans des disputes et dans des controverses étrangères à cette question (des Rites), ils entreprirent de soutenir à tout prix contre le Saint-Siége et ses délégués leur prétendue indépendance. Dans cette vue, ils se procurèrent des patentes de Vicaires de Vara ou Vicaires forains et de commissaires de l'Inquisition de Goa."—Report by the Secretary of the Propaganda Congregation in 'Mém. de la Congrégation,' vol. iv. p. 136.

capable of ascertainment, without troubling ourselves as to the moral value of the points that were raised.

The foundations for the influence acquired by the Society at the Chinese Court were laid by Father Ricci, who entered the country in 1581 with some companions and speedily won the Emperor's favour, which he is represented to have directed to the studied obstruction of other missionaries, whom he got either expelled or subjected to jealous supervision. About the middle of the seventeenth century complaints reached Rome from more quarters than one, but particularly through a Dominican friar, Father Moralez, who had himself experienced Jesuit hostility, that the Fathers owed their exceptional position in China to questionable connivances in pagan practices. An inquiry was instituted which resulted in a succession of decrees from various congregations, some of them being marked with a nebulousness, which practically tended to render the subject-matter under discussion only more perplexed. This was particularly the case on Alexander VII. issuing a decree which from its wording afforded the Jesuits a plausible ground for representing it as the reversal of an adverse sentence that had been given by his predecessor. They steadily continued to act in China as if their proceedings had been approved, and met representations which were periodically made against their doings in Rome, by specious subterfuges with promises of deference, while in reality they contumaciously disregarded alike the remonstrances of struggling fellow-missionaries and the summonses made by dignitaries armed with powers from the Pope. At last a Charge by Monseigneur Maigrot, one of the Vicars-Apostolic sent out, but, like the rest, baffled in the assertion of his authority, in which the Jesuit practices were reprobated with great detail, brought matters to a crisis. This Charge was referred to Rome; the Jesuits claimed to be heard against its allegations; the Congregation of the Holy Office was seized with the matter, and for upwards of four years the whole question was argued before this august tribunal with all the vehemence and all the subtleness that characterise theological pleadings.

Clement XI., the reigning Pope, was known to be himself favourably disposed towards the Society. Notwithstanding these leanings the ultimate decision was against the Fathers, and on November 20, 1704, the Pope confirmed the condemnation. He, however, reserved public promulgation of the sentence for the present on account of a very fair reason. A year before Clement had already come to the conclusion that the condition of affairs in China was such as to call imperatively for the prompt intervention of a dignitary invested with the highest powers of the Church. Accordingly he had named Monsignor Tournon Legate *a latere*, and had sent him out to China before the termination of the process. In the belief that his superior authority could not fail to ensure acknowledgment, and being desirous to treat the Society tenderly, Clement XI. postponed proclamation of the decree until after it had been intimated on the spot by the Legate, who was amply invested with discretionary faculties, to the Fathers immediately concerned, and as he fondly anticipated had been obediently acquiesced in to the happy avoidance of scandal. It must be borne in mind that there had not been previously sent out to China any ecclesiastic with a character equal to that with which Monsignor Tournon was clothed. Those who had preceded him were merely Vicars-Apostolic with a faculty to inspect the existing mission, but Monsignor Tournon as Legate *a latere* was canonically invested with *jurisdictio ordinaria* throughout the ecclesiastical province, and thus possessed an authority to which all Bishops in the same, according to the established system of church discipline, were bound to defer, and therefore still more all ecclesiastics of whatever degree they might be or whatever corporation they might belong to.

In the beginning of 1705 Monsignor Tournon reached Canton. After some months' interval he set out with the concurrence of the Chinese authorities for Pekin, where there existed flourishing Jesuit establishments. In the Legate's following there had come with him from Rome a private secretary, by name Marcello Angelita. This individual lived to return to Europe, when on request he drew up a statement of what befell his master, which was printed by Cardinal Passionei, and has been largely incorporated in the text of the 'Mémoires de la Congrégation.' The document therefore has the benefit of that corroboration which is due to Theiner's collation. The following is the curious account given by this witness of the condition in which the Jesuit establishments in Pekin were found. "At that time there were at Court no other missionaries than Jesuits, and these owned much property, a number of houses and of shops in various quarters of the city for which they got rent. The oldest of the houses owned, though neither the biggest nor the best, was named the Sitang College or the Western Temple. The second had been purchased in his own name by Father Adam Scholl, who in his day had instructed the Emperor, grandfather to the reigning one, in mathematics. This Father Scholl being desirous to enjoy at greater ease the liberalities and favours of this Prince, withdrew from the other Jesuits and the obedience to his Superiors, took a wife and lived in his private domicile. After enjoying the Imperial favour he ended his days sadly, leaving behind him two children by her whom he had made his wife. The Fathers contrived to take this house away from the children, and this was the one allotted for the residence of any Jesuits who happened to be neither French nor Portuguese. The third house, Pe-tung, was the largest and most imposing; it was more spacious than the others and had been constructed by the French Jesuits who had retired thither on expulsion from Siam some years before the coming of Monsignor Tournon. These good Jesuits, French and Portuguese, were divided amongst themselves, and their discussions excited the pity of the Chinese themselves, the division extending even to the neophytes of either section who had no intercommunion. The Jesuits themselves treated each other as declared enemies; till previous to the Legate's arrival they came to terms so as to make opposition to him, and put on an appearance of reconciliation." *

The most influential Jesuit at this time in Pekin was a Father Pereyra, a Portuguese, who had been many years in the country—was thoroughly conversant with the language, and had acquired the particular favour of the sovereign. Father Pereyra had himself taken an active part in the elaboration of that system of practices which constituted the subject-matter whereon the Legate was to pronounce sentence, and throughout the official correspondence he is designated as the most subtle and determined agent in the machinations to baffle the Legate's action, and to stir up against him the jealous and suspicious feelings of the Chinese Emperor by whom Monsignor Tournon was at the beginning received with decided friendliness. In a letter to the Secretary of State, Cardinal Paolucci, under date 27th December, 1707, written from Macao after expulsion from Pekin, the Legate says: "For reasons stated in a long despatch, it has not been possible for me to write to your Excellency all that befell me at Pekin. From the first moment to the last of my stay

* 'Mémoires de la Congrégation,' vol. iv. pp. 296, 297.

in that city, I encountered from these Fathers continual opposition in everything relating to obedience towards the Apostolic See. . . . The opposition was mainly directed against the establishment of direct relations between the Emperor and the Pope, against the establishment in China of the authority of the sacred Congregation of Propaganda, and lastly against the presence of missionaries of the Congregation."* It may be reasonably inferred that one of the reasons why the Legate had found it not possible to write fully was the circumstance, of which he acquired the conviction, that his correspondence was liable to interception through the agency of the Fathers. This point is repeatedly affirmed in the extended report to Propaganda;† allusion being made in particular to an intercepted despatch of the Legate's dated 23rd April, 1706, while in the same report special mention occurs of "a waiting man of the Portuguese Fathers by name Thaddeus, who had served as the chief instrument for intercepting the letters which the Legate wrote by the route ‡ through Muscovy."

In the letter to Cardinal Paolucci already referred to, the Legate emphatically ascribes the hostility which the Fathers showed as mainly due to the "question of the Chinese Rites which united against him the Portuguese and the French Fathers."§ There was, however, still a secondary cause which supervened to inflame the animosity of the Fathers resident in China. The reader has learnt, from the statements by the Legate's secretary Angelita, the outward financial condition in which the Jesuits stood at Pekin. It came, however, to the knowledge of the Legate that besides these considerable possessions the members of the Society, not in their individual capa-

* 'Mémoires de la Congrégation,' vol. iv. p. 215.   † Ib. p. 264.
‡ Ib. p. 188.   § Ib. p. 230.

cities but as representatives of the Society, were largely engaged in banking transactions on terms of an usurious character. This transpired in consequence of steps taken to ensure repayment from a Chinaman of a loan which the Fathers saw reason to call in. The bond in question was to Father Grimaldi, Visitor of the Jesuit College, and to Father Pereyra, Vice-provincial in China and Rector of the College in Pekin, consequently to the most conspicuous official representatives of the Society. The Legate, as soon as the matter was brought under his notice, issued a charge which emphatically condemned as " void and usurious the said contract," and censured Fathers Grimaldi and Pereyra as having by this act rendered themselves unfit to hold any office in the administration of the Society.* This sentence was promulgated on the 17th May, 1706.

Before August was over the Legate saw himself obliged to leave Pekin in consequence of a command from the Emperor. The command was certainly not in accordance with what the Legate had reason to expect from the favourable reception he had met with at Court on his arrival. In his official correspondence Monsignor Tournon distinctly attributes the change in the Emperor's action towards him to the machinations of Jesuit Fathers, and he substantiates his allegation by repeated and very precise relation of particular occurrences with which he couples the names of the Fathers whom he affirms to have been authors of the same. The aim of these devices as described by Tournon was to prevent the recognition of those plenary powers in the Legate which must have subjected the Jesuit establishments to his supervision. To this end the Fathers

---

* This edict is to be found, *in extenso*, in ' Anecdotes de l'Etat de la Religion,' vol. ii. p. 8. The Jesuits pleaded that their action was not usurious, as they took only 24 per cent., whereas 30 per cent. was no uncommon rate in China.

are represented to have craftily wrought upon the natural jealousy of the Chinese mind at all foreign authority, and at the same time to have plied the favour they enjoyed with the Emperor so as to induce him to declare that the Legate should not exercise within his dominions any direct supervision over the Jesuit foundations in the metropolis. This was a reassertion, under protection of a Chinese injunction, of that exemption from authority other than of their own General, which in practice the Jesuit Fathers had systematically striven to secure in China. When, by further suggestions on the part of the Fathers, the Emperor had been brought to intimate to the Legate that he must retire from the capital, and await at Canton the result of a reference to the Pope, to be made through the medium of Fathers Barros and Beauvilliers, two Jesuits whom the Chinese Sovereign had selected for this Mission, the spirit in which the Members of the Society intended to construe their assumed exemption from supervision in the Metropolis was exemplified in a striking manner.

The Legate had been prohibited by the Emperor from exercising, in virtue of his particular powers, any inspection over the foundations in Pekin, and he had abstained from any attempt to do so. But there existed, and had existed since long, a Bishop of Pekin, who as such was of course empowered in virtue of his authority as Ordinary to visit all the places of worship in his diocese. The chief sacred edifice in Pekin, which was the recognised Cathedral, was served by Jesuit Fathers. On April 22nd, 1706, the Bishop, in the exercise of his indisputable jurisdiction, proceeded to visit the Cathedral. He found the gates locked and admission stubbornly denied him; Father Barros, the same whom the Emperor selected to go to Rome, acting on this occasion as the representative of the Order, and the champion of its contumacious pretensions. Unable to effect an entrance except by force, the Bishop yielded and returned home. The Jesuits, not satisfied with this success, lodged a protest against the assumption by the Bishop of any faculty to visit the Cathedral. The latter in rejoinder referred the case to the Legate, who summoned the parties before him, and finally gave judgment in a decree enumerating in detail all the incidents of the case. That decree can be read *in extenso* in the 'Anecdotes sur l'Etat de la Religion,' and the authenticity of the document has never been challenged to our knowledge, although the severity of its tone has been reprobated as excessive by those whose bias in this controversy is towards the Fathers of the Society. The substance of the contention is, however, singularly simple. The Bishop, in pursuance of his undoubted episcopal functions, was prevented from exercising them by the Fathers. Whether he may have been inwardly animated by sentiments favourable or unfavourable to the Society, is a matter wholly irrelevant. In proceeding to visit the Cathedral the Bishop was simply seeking to do that which was part of the ordinary and prescribed discipline of the Church. To obstruct him in the exercise of this function was therefore to obstruct the prescribed discipline of the Church. To prove that the Fathers who rendered it not possible for the Bishop of Pekin to visit the Cathedral, were guiltless of the charge that they conspired to make null and void the organic faculties of Church discipline, it would be necessary to demonstrate that the whole story was a myth—that the Legatine degree, which was made public in China, was an audacious forgery—and that the entire narrative of the transaction was a deliberate invention. So much is at all events positive that up to the present time no serious attempt has been made to demolish the authenticity of the version printed in the 'Anecdotes' of the Legate's decree; and yet nothing could be easier than to establish its fabrication if the text there given of this document had been really spurious.*

Close upon this incident there supervened another and even graver scandal. In obedience to the Imperial command, the Legate started for Canton. The journey was greatly protracted by obstacles proceeding from the Chinese officials, so that he found himself detained for months at Nankin. While staying in this city, Monsignor Tournon acquired cognisance of an Imperial edict, issued after his departure from Pekin, that prescribed conditions on which

---

* The Legate's sentence will be found, 'Anecdotes de l'Etat,' &c. vol. ii. pp. 31-34 :—"Il est constant par les actes de la sainte Visite, que le Révérendissime Evêque de Pekin, après les avertissements juridiques, s'est transporté le 22 Avril 1706 à l'Eglise Cathédrale, appelée *Sytan*, pour la visiter. . . . Mais non-seulement il a trouvé la porte de la dite Eglise fermée, il a encore eu l'affront, qu'après qu'on lui eut refusé l'entrée de la dite Eglise, le Pasteur a été par force empêché d'entrer dans son Bercail. En sorte que ce que l'autorité Impériale ne nous a pas permis de faire . . . les Jésuites, de leur autorité privée, ont attenté de le faire, en fermant la Porte de l'Eglise au plus doux des Pasteurs. Le Père Barros était celui qui, à la place du Visiteur des Jésuites, s'opposait le plus fortement à la visite de la Cathédrale, et ce qui aggrave considérablement ce forfait, c'est que le Prélat . . . reçut de la part de ces Pères un nouvel affront par une protestation qu'on eut la hardiesse de lui présenter. Comme le dit Seigneur Evêque a porté ses plaintes par-devant nous, de l'attentat de ces Pères contre sa Juridiction, le P. Barros ayant été interrogé le 26 dudit mois et an, et étant interpellé de produire ses moyens de défense, allégua verbalement, pour sa justification, certains priviléges d'exécution, dont il ne produisit point les preuves. En sorte qu'après que nous l'eûmes renvoyé avec ordre à lui donné par écrit, de revenir dans huit jours, nous le fîmes de plus avertir par le Père Kilian-Stumpff de se rendre à son devoir, et de produire les preuves de ses prétendus priviléges ; mais après avoir méprisé les avertissements particuliers et juridiques, il ne parut plus devant nous, et ne fit aucune exhibition des prétendus priviléges, que nous déclarons être nuls . . . et par notre Sentence nous disons, nous jugeons, et nous prononçons, que la susdite protestation est nulle et de nul effet, et que le droit du Révérendissime Evêque doit passer pour incontestable, ayant le pouvoir de visiter la dite Eglise *Sytan* des Jésuites de Pekin, et d'y exercer les autres actes de juridiction, suivant les Règlements du Concile de Trente, et des Décrets Apostoliques pour les Missions."

alone Christian priests would be permitted to carry on their functions in the Empire. It was enjoined hereby that no priest would be in future allowed to ministrate without an Imperial licence, the issue of which was conditional on the priest expressing his acceptance of certain specified formularies of ritual and Chinese terms in the sense which the Emperor declared the same to bear. No missionary, according to this edict, would be tolerated until after he had submitted himself to an examination in regard to these points, which could be made only in the metropolis. Another command, issued at a later date, imposed the further obligation of an engagement on all missionary priests, once admitted to residence, never to go again out of China. It is undeniable that the conditions thus regulating the grant of licences involved the substance of the matter at issue in the controversy that had been pending so long in the Roman Courts. It is equally positive, therefore, that for ecclesiastics of the Roman Church to accept the injunctions of this decree, and to make declaration of this acceptance, without the authority of Rome, could not but be a proceeding of flagrant lawlessness. If there is anything in the world clear and distinct, it must be the fact that no Roman Catholic can recognise in any tribunal, but that of his Church, the slightest faculty to prescribe and enjoin aught that relates to ritual and to formularies. The Jesuit Fathers in Pekin, nevertheless, did not deem it incompatible with their duties to acquiesce in the edict,* and to make themselves the vehicle for communicating it to the missionaries in various parts of the Empire. It is but natural that, as soon as ever

---

* In subscribing to the engagement never to leave China, these Jesuits violated moreover the obligation every Father contracts to be ever ready to go on any mission at the command of his Superior. The practical importance of the engagement was, that it made the missionary in China the subject of the Emperor, and removed him from the jurisdiction of his ecclesiastical chief

knowledge of this transaction reached the Legate, he should at once have done what was in his power to record his solemn condemnation. From Nankin he launched a Legatine sentence, giving, for the first time, public proclamation to the decision at which the Holy See had arrived on November 20, 1704, against the Chinese Rites. He also was careful to specify in full his own powers, as extending "over all missionaries, secular and regular, of whatever Order, even of the Society of Jesus." After the issue of this document there could be no pretence about some unauthorised or mistaken utterance on the part of a misled dignitary. The voice of Rome had now spoken distinctly, and the words of its sentence had been transmitted with unmistakable precision through an organ of indisputable legitimacy.* Nevertheless, the Jesuits proved contumacious. They drew up a long and curious appeal to Rome against a Legatine sentence, which itself was but the promulgation of a decree made by Rome. The patent flimsiness of the plea did not come into consideration, for the practical object was merely to devise a pretext for litigation, which might give a colour for prolonged resistance. The appeal had affixed to it the signatures of four and twenty Jesuit Fathers.

Meanwhile, the Legate was slowly wending his way to Canton, where he expected to be made to await the return from Rome of the Jesuit envoys, Fathers Barros and Beauvilliers, despatched thither by the Emperor, when he was overtaken by a peremptory Imperial order that he was not to be allowed to stay in Canton, but should be forthwith transported to Macao, there to remain in forced residence. In this locality the jurisdiction was composite. The native

* This elaborate sentence of the Legate will be found in 'Anecdotes de l'Etat,' &c., vol. ii. pp. 182-7.

population was subject to Chinese authorities; but the Portuguese possessed a settlement with sovereign rights over all Europeans in the town. There was, accordingly, a Portuguese governor with a Portuguese establishment and force, as there was also a Bishop of Macao. The Legate might therefore have fairly hoped that transference to this town would ensure to him relief from the personal vexations to which he had been painfully liable when under the direct control of the Chinese, and that on taking up his residence within the jurisdiction of the Portuguese Crown his ecclesiastical character would meet with the deference due to its unquestioned rank from the officers of a Roman Catholic Government. If he did indulge in these natural anticipations, they were speedily dispelled.

The Legate landed at Macao on June 30, 1706, and the welcome that met him was the intimation of an appeal to Rome by the Bishop of the Diocese, in correspondence with the one lodged by the Jesuit Fathers, against the Decree in which he had proclaimed the decision of the Holy See. The Bishop of Macao was a certain Don John Cazale, who was entirely in the hands of the Society, at whose suggestion he had been named to the See. By the Jesuits this Prelate had been prompted to issue a formal protest against the execution of this Legatine sentence, partly on the ground of its resting on imperfect knowledge, but still more on the ground that in Macao it must be null and void as emanating from an illegitimate authority, because not of Portuguese sanction. The Bishop tells the Pope's Legate, that his action must involve a "violation of the incontestible rights of our Sovereign over all lands discovered and to be discovered in the East Indies," and that no decision of the Holy See shall be of force within his jurisdiction except with the previous sanction of the Portuguese Courts. In fact, the tenets expressed in this document are of the most decidedly Erastian character. The Bishop declares that no Papal sentence and no Papal faculty shall be of any validity in his Diocese unless previously endorsed by the secular authorities. This view, though frequently contended for by the State, is one certainly not in harmony with the established doctrine of the Roman Church. But even though it can be shown that some Prelates, whose religious faith in the dogmas of the Catholic Church cannot be impugned, have at various times recognised in the secular authority a power to control in a certain degree the exercise of faculties derived from Rome, it is beyond doubt that the assertion of such power in the secular authority must be wholly at variance with the principles of the Society of Jesus, and with the particular profession made by every Jesuit Father. Nevertheless, the Fathers at Macao were not content, merely to benefit practically for repudiation of a Pontifical sentence which they disliked, by the diversion the Bishop had already made through the fact of his protest, but they actively identified themselves with the affirmation of the Erastian principles he had publicly enunciated. A Jesuit Father, by name Ammiani, accepted from the Governor-General at Goa the mission, to carry to the Provincial Pinto at Macao a mandate issued on May 12, 1706, declaratory of the rights of the Portuguese Crown, and specially inhibiting the said Provincial from recognising any jurisdiction in the General Legate. With this mandate the Provincial waited on the Legate, and solemnly intimated that he wholly declined to acknowledge his authority.* Tournon naturally demurred

* See 'Memorie Storiche del Cardinal Tournon,' vol. i. pp. 251–2, for the Governor-General's mandate. After communicating it Pinto says: "E letta questa lettera, protesto, che non potea riconoscere la sua giurisdizione Apostolica e che *de facto* non la riconosceva."

to this intimation. He reminded the Provincial of the Jesuit vow about special obedience to the Pope, and having failed to make any impression, he proceeded to launch, as well as he could, his censures. This was the signal for instant adoption of measures of violence against the unfortunate Legate. He was put under close confinement by the Portuguese authorities; a guard of soldiers was set over him, and his claims to Legatine faculties were publicly proclaimed as invalid, and undeserving of any consideration. To such monstrous length was ridicule openly showered on Monsignor Tournon by those who, in Macao, represented the Church, that on the day of St. Francis Xavier, Father Fereira, preaching in the principal church of Macao, drew a parallel between the great Jesuit Apostle to the Indies, and the Legate, in which the latter was held up to derision under the nickname of Lucifer.

This was, however, a mere antic by the side of what the Bishop presumed to do. On July 24, 1707, the Bishop of Macao published an Episcopal sentence, solemnly declaring null and void all censures pronounced by the Pope's Legate,—enjoining on all Diocesans, under penalty of excommunication, to repudiate the authority of Monsignor Tournon,—calling on the latter, in deference to his obligations of sacred obedience, and under penalty of Major Excommunication, within three days to revoke all sentences that he might have uttered against Diocesans of the See of Macao, on the express ground of his authority being illegitimate;—and, finally, in the event of contumacy, pronouncing on him sentence of Major Excommunication '*ipso facto incurrenda*,' with all the provisos and technical formulas which are requisite to hedge round a judgment of this nature with binding force. The sentence was publicly proclaimed in strict observance of the formalities which, by canonical practice, are customary when a person is to be put under the ban of the Church. It was officially promulgated in the sacred edifice at times of worship, so that patently the appointed Legate of the Pope, with the concurrence of the Jesuit Provincial in the locality, was pilloried as an arrant impostor, and subjected to that treatment which should be the lot of a proclaimed outlaw.* The Legate, of course, protested in his prison against this stroke of Episcopal proscription, but without obtaining thereby any relief. On the contrary, Monsignor Tournon was subjected to yet more stringent treatment when the notice reached the authorities in Macao, that he had been promoted to the purple by the Pope. Six ecclesiastics who officially brought him from Rome the red hat, and who by the Pope had been appointed missionaries to China, were forthwith thrown into prison in the fort as

---

* A translation from the Portuguese of this episcopal sentence will be found in 'Memorie Storiche del Card. Tournon,' vol. i. pp. 272-5. "Noi il Dottor Giovanni Cazale Vescovo di questa città . . . facciamo sapere . . . perche, ci costa che l'illustrissimo Sig. Carlo Tommaso, intitolandosi Patriarcha d'Antiochia, Visitatore Apostolico, con facoltà di Legato *a latere* cercha d'introdursi in questo nostro Vescovado . . . dichiaramo nuovamente per nulle tutte le Censure imposte del detto . . . ordinando a tutti i nostri sudditi che sotto pena d'ubbidienza, e di Scommunica Maggiore *ipso facto incurrenda*, non obbediscano ne riconoscano per Giudice il detto Illustrissimo . . . Inoltre in virtù di Santa Ubbidienza, e sotto la medesima pena di Sommunica Maggiore *ipso facto incurrenda*, a noi riservata, commandiamo al medesimo, che in termine di tre giorni, che gli assigniamo per le tre Canoniche Ammonizioni, un giorno per ogn' una, a termine preciso, e perentorio desista, e revochi le scommuniche, che ha fulminate . . . e sotto le medesime pene, e termini ci faccia legale presentazione delle lettere della sua delegazione . . . e non facendolo . . . anzi non avendolo fatto, essendo stato da noi richiesto per molte volte, e ultimamente per una lettera requisitoria . . . poniamo, ed abbiamo per posta nella sua persona per questo presente scritto sentenza di Scommunica Maggiore *ipso facto incurrenda*, e come tale lo dichiaramo, perche cerca d'usurpare la nostra ordinaria giurisdizione, e per questo lo citiamo, e chiamiamo, e l'abbiamo per citato e chiamato per tutti gli atti, e procedure *in futurum*, e per tutti i gravami e rigravami di Censure, finche desista d'esercitare atto alcuno giurisdizionale."

interlopers. The Cardinal himself was curtailed even in the scanty liberties previously allowed him. On the plea that the authorities had reason to believe he was planning an escape to Spanish territory in the Philippine Islands, and so to break bounds in defiance of the Chinese Emperor's command not to move out of Macao until his envoys returned from Europe, the Cardinal was put under yet closer confinement, deprived of intercourse with attendants, and even exposed to such wanton hardships as the stoppage of fresh water supply. At the same time, the Bishop was induced to renew his fulminations, and to put under interdict a church served by some Austin Friars who sympathised with the suffering Legate. His health, never strong, at last broke entirely down under this continued bad treatment, and on Whitsunday, 1710, the Jesuit Fathers saw themselves happily freed from his hateful presence by sudden death.

This story may well appear one which makes a strong call on credulity, and yet it is thoroughly authenticated. It is not possible to conceive a more glaring example of persistent contumaciousness against the clear utterances of the Holy See than was exhibited throughout these transactions by Fathers of the Society, which professes to be its special body-guard. It is also beyond the possibility of question, that what prompted them to strive with such determination against the decisions of the Holy See on this occasion, was that they were sensible how these, if carried out with sincerity, must infallibly indispose the Chinese mind, and imperil the peculiar influence they themselves had obtained at Court. Without expressing any opinion, as to whether the practices, and customs, to which the Jesuits had conformed since the days of Ricci, did involve a recognition of heathen superstitions, it is positive that by adoption of the same the Jesuits had mainly succeeded in making themselves agreeable at Court. It is likewise undeniable that the maintenance of their influential position depended on their continuing to show themselves equally accommodating in the future. The motive which weighed with them in first making these concessions to Chinese sentiment, and then in defying Papal rescripts, was consequently one of sheer policy, namely, the consideration that their special influence in high quarters would be seriously menaced through a particular action demanded by the Holy See, and this is the really interesting and characteristic circumstance in these mutinous proceedings. Ultimately the Jesuits had to give in, but it was only after Clement XI., in 1715, issued the Bull *Ex illâ die*, which contained such precise and stringent provisions as to leave no longer a loophole for any shadow of plausible evasion.

CHAPTER XIII.

The foregoing not an unique instance of insubordination on part of the Society to the recognised authority in the Church—A memorable case in point, that of Bishop Palafox—Appointed to See of Puebla, in Mexico, by Philipp IV.—His character—Tithes of real properties in America—How Jesuits acted in reference to these—Statement of Palafox as to the financial condition of the Society in Mexico—Suit in a matter of tithes against Jesuits raised by Chapter of Puebla—They are called upon by Palafox to exhibit their licences in accordance with canonical regulations—Jesuits prove recalcitrant—They take the initiative in impugning Palafox's authority—Procure an invalid sentence of Excommunication against Palafox, who flies and lies hid for four months—Further improper proceedings—The See is declared deserted—Criminal prosecution before a sham tribunal—Indecent procession through streets of Puebla—Tidings from Spain check the confidence of Jesuits—Compromise whereby Palafox returns to Puebla—In Rome the decision of a Congregation specially instituted by Innocent X. in Palafox's favour—Deceitful conduct of Jesuits on receipt thereof in America—A second reference to Rome—Simultaneous machinations in Spain—Dismissal as frivolous of the Jesuit pleadings that the sentence published by Palafox had been falsified—How far the Society can be considered responsible for the proceedings against Palafox.

Though the most curious example of insubordination on the part of the Jesuit Fathers against the recognised authorities of the Church, these Chinese transactions by no means are a solitary instance of this insubordinate spirit. The powers of the Episcopate have been repeatedly set at nought on the plea of privileged exemption, when it happened that a Bishop was not disposed to look with favour on some proceeding, within the limits of his jurisdiction, which the Fathers considered conducive to the interest of their Society. A memorable case in point was that, of the treatment which Bishop Palafox encountered at their hands in South

America. Though the story has been often told, its leading facts may be here briefly stated with advantage, for they show with striking force what extraordinary things the Jesuits have ventured to perpetuate under particular circumstances. Palafox, according to universal testimony, was a man of quite saintly character, personally much disposed to countenance all religious zeal, but also one whose rigid nature absolutely rejected supple acquiescence in questionable transactions for purposes of worldly expediency. He was an earnest and fervent zealot. Philipp IV. named him in 1640 to the See of Puebla de los Angelos in Mexico, and so high did he stand in estimation, that the duties of the Vice-royalty were for a period confided to him. But Palafox's sphere was that of the pastor and not of the governor, and in it he soon found enough to occupy his attention owing to the peculiarly unsatisfactory condition into which, under his predecessors, a large section of the clergy, but especially the Jesuit Fathers, had slided. Before long he was engaged with the latter in conflict on two points, both the outcome of abuses that had been allowed to spring up. The first touched money interests. In America the tithes of all real properties had been allotted for endowment of the Cathedrals and Chapters. The Jesuits silently contrived to secure to a large degree exemption for their lands from payment of these dues, and as their possessions speedily attained vast proportions, the loss to the Church became proportionately serious. The amount of property, which the Society of Jesus had come to own in these regions, was indeed of an extent which had better be indicated in the words used by the Bishop himself in a memorial to Pope Innocent X. "Holy Father, I found in the hands of the Jesuits almost all the wealth, the stock, and the opulence of these American provinces, and they still are owners of the same. Two of their Colleges at present possess three hundred thousand sheep, besides large cattle. While all the Cathedrals and Religious Orders taken together own barely three sugar plantations, the Society itself owns six of the largest in the Mexican province, where they have only two Colleges. Now, Holy Father, a plantation of this kind is on the average valued at five hundred thousand dollars and upwards, some of them drawing near to a million dollars, and there is such as brings in a hundred thousand dollars a year. In addition they have farms of such prodigious size, that while the homesteads are four to six leagues apart, the boundaries of the land touch. Likewise they have very rich silver mines, and so immoderately are they increasing their might and wealth, that if they continue at the same rate, the priests will have to become dependent on the Society, laymen to become its tenants, and other Religious must beg at its gates."

The inevitable result of such progressive acquisition would be to make the Fathers almost the monopolists of real property, and consequently if, as this was bought up by them, it became freed from tithe, the revenues of the Church would be grievously reduced. A case having arisen where a lay property again passed into Jesuit hands, the Chapter of Puebla raised in the courts of law the contention that the plea of exemption set up by the Fathers was invalid, and though the ruling Viceroy favoured the Society, judgment went against the same—of itself an intelligible ground why the Fathers should be grievously irritated against Palafox, and should seek, as they did seek, to raise in various tribunals of America and Europe, vexatious issues against the Prelate. This unfriendly feeling came to be keenly fomented by the action of the Bishop in arresting an usage on the part of the Fathers which he considered as an invasion of his episcopal rights, and a breach of the safeguards incumbent in a diocesan jurisdiction for the insurance of a proper administration of spiritual offices. The attention of the Bishop was drawn to the extraordinary number of Fathers who, as Confessors and Preachers, were active in the diocese, and of whom it was to his knowledge that not a few were of quite recent arrival. This circumstance induced inquiry, which brought to light the fact that since several years the Jesuits had not applied for the Episcopal licence, which, according to the Decrees of Councils and Papal Bulls, is requisite to enable a person to ministrate. Accordingly Palafox caused an official intimation to be made to the Fathers that they should exhibit any licences, they might hold, to Episcopal inspection. To this order the Jesuits paid no attention; those who made any response simply pleaded specific privileges, which they affirmed that they could not exhibit except at the express desire of their Provincial, who lived at a distance in the city of Mexico. In Puebla itself, under the eyes of Palafox, a Jesuit Father had been announced to preach. The Bishop inhibited him from doing so until he had shown his licence. In defiance thereof, the Jesuit appeared in the pulpit and preached his sermon. In presence of such contumacious conduct, a more stringent intimation, accompanied with a menace of penalties, came from the Ordinary, but with no better result. The Jesuits stood on their assumed privileges, and abstained from deferring in any substantial degree to the Bishop's intimation. They did more than this. They took the initiative in getting the Bishop's authority impugned before the Viceroy, of whose friendship they stood assured; and having contrived to induce two ecclesiastics to assume the duties of Conservators, they went to the length of procuring from a spurious tribunal a sentence of Excommunication against Palafox, which the Viceroy had proclaimed in Mexico amidst the flourish of trumpets. In presence of these proceedings and what threatened to follow, it would appear that Palafox lost courage. He had already despatched to Rome two ecclesiastics to invoke the intervention of the Pope. He now saw himself impelled to fly for his life from those ready to go to extremities. Accompanied by only two companions the Bishop sought refuge in the depths of the wilderness, where he lay hid during four months, as he himself describes, amidst intense hardships and sufferings.

Meanwhile the Jesuits profited by his flight to venture on proceedings, which would seem absolutely impossible, were they not vouched for by the Bishop himself in his memorial to the Pope, and confirmed by the fact that the sentence pronounced by the Holy See on these transactions was in favour of Palafox. The Jesuits of Puebla got the so-called Conservators to come there from Mexico; when they were escorted into the town with an extraordinary pageant, as if they were dignitaries legitimately armed with superior faculties. A professed High Court of Ecclesiastical Jurisdiction was instituted, which, in the first place, declared the Bishop to have grievously exceeded his rights in demanding of the Jesuits that they should exhibit their licences before venturing on ministrations. This judgment having been published from the pulpits, secular pressure was brought to bear—and with success—on a portion of the Chapter, to make it declare the See deserted—although, before his retreat, Palafox had duly appointed a Vicar-General—and to usurp its administration. The proceedings to which this intrusive body is represented to have lent itself partake of a saturnalian type. Not merely was there instituted against Palafox —before the installed tribunal—the form of a criminal procedure, but his person and his dignity were publicly subjected to gross and ribald outrage, with the view of holding them up to derision. On the day of St. Ignatius, the pupils in the Jesuit College paraded the streets of Puebla in a mock procession, which was characterised by the features of a masquerade, worthy of some Pagan pantomime. Amongst other improprieties, a mounted figure was led about, with a paper mitre hanging from the stirrup, and a crosier dangling from the animal's tail; while, amidst jeers and derisive shouts, the accompanying scholars made the streets of Puebla ring with a parody on the Lord's Prayer, in which occurred the petition, 'deliver us from Palafox,' and with satirical rhymes in burlesque imitation of sacred hymns. All this is narrated with much detail by Palafox himself, both in a memorial to the Pope and in a letter to the Jesuit Provincial; and though many allegations in this letter were combated by the Society in counter-memorials to the King of Spain, there is no evidence of its having challenged the correctness of the statement in reference to this particular incident. The arrival from Spain of an order transferring the Viceroy to other functions, however, induced the Jesuits to moderate their action. Palafox was known to have referred his case to Rome, and it began, therefore, to be deemed prudent to seek some compromise in time; and to this he himself was willing. The Bishop returned to his See, having agreed to refrain from attempts to interfere in the status of the members of the Society until the expected decision of the Holy See on the case already before it. The object of the Fathers was to secure, anyhow, tacit acquiescence in their continued enjoyment of faculties which relieved them from Episcopal supervision, so as to gain time for influencing Rome in a sense favourable to them. Palafox, on the other hand, was prompted by a desire to repress the disorders which he knew to be rapidly spreading in the clergy of his diocese—and which, indeed, must have been prevalent already before, to have made it possible for the Society to effect so flagrant an insurrection against what was most indubitably the legitimate ecclesiastical authority. When the decision arrived at in Rome reached America it was found to be in favour of Palafox. Innocent X. had instituted a Congregation specially to consider the contention that had arisen between the Bishop of Puebla and the Members of the Society. This tribunal, after carefully hearing the advocates of both sides—and particularly the Procurator-General of the Society—gave its sentence to the effect: "That in the town and diocese of Puebla it is not lawful for the Religious of the Society to hear the confession of laymen without the approval of the Diocesan," and that, "inasmuch as they had not proved their having obtained such approval and licence, it was legitimate for the Bishop or his Vicar-General to enjoin on them, under penalty of Excommunication, to abstain from hearing confession and preaching; for this reason it was not lawful for these Religious to have elected Conservators as if in this matter there had been done them patent wrong and violence, and the Excommunication, which, according to what has been related us, was fulminated against the Bishop and his Vicar, was therefore null and unlawful." This sentence was promulgated in a Papal Brief, which, after having been transmitted to the Royal Council in Spain, was duly forwarded to Palafox, and by him intimated to the Jesuit Provincial. Though at first professedly accepted with reverence, this Papal decree was practically set at nought. The Jesuit Fathers presented protests to the Bishop, in which, while avowing themselves ready to respect his individual authority, they pleaded various reasons—mostly technical—for not considering the document in question a formal Papal Brief. The Provincial

Rada, however, ventured on a far more serious plea, namely, that the text presented to him was not the genuine text of the Pope's Brief; and that it could not be legitimately enforced until a further appeal to the Holy See had been heard. The influence of the Society in Rome was able to secure that it should be heard in argument against the Brief at the same time that in Spain it exerted itself to make the Crown intervene. It is characteristic, that in each quarter the Society took up a different ground for action. In Spain the Fathers sought to induce the Crown to exercise its veto on the Brief as having been obtained surreptitiously, and by false representations; while in Rome they petitioned for a new hearing on the ground that there had been a failure in the evidence. The whole case was, therefore, reinvestigated by a Congregation of Cardinals; and, on November 19, 1652, a new Brief was promulgated, solemnly confirming the previous one, and dismissing as frivolous the allegation that this had been issued in error. Accordingly, the sentence ran, that the Brief was fully justified, and that "its execution must in no manner be obstructed or retarded." The translation of Palafox to another See may be taken as evidence that, though defeated in principle, the Society still retained sufficient influence practically to mitigate the severity of the censure inflicted. It is, anyhow, on record that when, after a long interval of time, the Beatification of Palafox came to be entertained by the Holy See, the decree was prevented by the action of those who earnestly represented that it would necessarily involve a distinct slur on the Society.

There cannot be a doubt that the conduct of the Fathers towards the Bishop of Puebla was characterised by a spirit wholly at variance with every ordinary obligation of Church discipline — quite irrespective of that special vow of obedience to the Pope's commands which professedly should constitute so distinctive a feature in the engagements of a Jesuit. The outrageous licence that broke out in the mock procession on the Feast of St. Ignatius is a secondary incident. This might plausibly be represented as the unauthorised burst of boyish wantonness. The Society may plead that it was not identified with the regrettable proceedings, in the person of any responsible representative. No such plea can, however, be maintained, in relief of the Society, from the charge of having glaringly striven to disown the organic authorities of the Church, when it found that the exercise by these of their Faculties, in a particular case, would tend to hamper its members in the exercise of certain powers which they had been in the habit of usurping, with advantage to their influence. Nor is it a point of slight significance for the position, which the Society had secured, that it should have been able to carry on a contention of this nature, for years before the ecclesiastical tribunals of Rome, when it is remembered with what vigilance and sharpness the utterances of the Holy See are there ordinarily enforced.*

---

* Crétineau Joly, in his 'Hist. de la Compagnie de Jésus,' vol. iv. p. 85, insinuates that Palafox's retreat from Puebla was a spontaneous act, and in no degree due to violence. For this statement he refers cursorily to a manuscript relation on Palafox's administration, drawn up as late as 1815, by Don Guttierez de la Huerta, and said to be in the Madrid Archives—a document that, from its date, can have no value as direct evidence. It is noteworthy that notwithstanding his excessive partiality Crétineau Joly does not venture to exonerate the Jesuits entirely. He admits that they exhibited a mutinous spirit. "Les Jésuites, selon l'appréciation du même Bref, n'étaient pas restés dans cette position, que la prudence leur a si souvent conseillée. Ils en avaient appelé à des juges conservateurs, dans un cas où l'injure n'était pas plus évidente que la violence. Ils auraient dû se soumettre à une décision peut-être inique à leurs yeux, et attendre le jugement du Saint-Siège." There are many books which treat of the history of Palafox; but the facts with the evidence will be found given with clearness and fulness in the fourth volume of 'La Morale Pratique des Jésuites,' 1690.

CHAPTER XIV.

The plea of special privileges advanced by the Jesuits—Pius V.'s Brief barring revocation of privileges by the Holy See—*Oracula vivæ vocis*—Exemplified by action after suppression of the Order—Jesuits betake themselves to Prussia and Russia—Articles in the 'Cologne Gazette' hostile to Holy See—Their authorship by Father Feller—Vainly denied in the 'Month'—The evidence brought forward has demonstrably no bearing on the articles in question—Erastian propositions publicly submitted to discussion at Heidelberg—Statement by Nuncio Garampi—Two spurious Briefs circulated—Their authenticity affirmed by Father Curci—Allegation in like sense by writer in the 'Month'—Examination of his statement—Despatch from Cardinal Corsini to Nuncio Garampi—Clement XIV.'s Briefs to Archbishop of Gnesen and others—Reference in 'Month' to Pastoral by Bishop of Mohilew—Explanations as to this Prelate's position—Acquisition of White Russia by Catherine—Jesuit establishment in that region—Attitude of the Fathers—Vice-Principal Czerniewicz sent to St. Petersburgh—Becomes *ex officio* representative of Society—In reply to an obsequious Memorial from Jesuits, Catherine forbids publication of Brief *Dominus ac Redemptor*—The Fathers acquiesce—Constitution devised by the Empress for the Latin Church in her dominions—See of Mohilew instituted, and Siestrenciewicz appointed thereto—His antecedents—Catherine's intentions as to his sphere of duties—The writer in 'Month' does not pretend that the Pope confirmed his Pastoral—Positive evidence to the contrary—Papal Brief addressed on this subject to various Catholic sovereigns—Benislawski's unfounded statement—Distinct disapproval of Bishop of Mohilew's doings in Pius VI.'s Brief—This no proof that Pius VII. was not differently disposed—It is disingenuous to mix up the proceedings of the two Popes—Question of clandestine revival of Order through *Oraculum vivæ vocis*—Stated to have been affirmed by Father Roothan, when General, in an Encyclical—Importance of the allegation in such document, and of the declaration by the writer in the 'Month' that the *Oraculum* would be perfectly legitimate.

THE plea in support of contumacious disregard of Pontifical censures, which the Jesuits rested on their being possessed of special faculties, cannot fail to recall that remarkable

Brief by which Pius V. secured the privileges of the Order against revocation, even by a Pope, and of the acknowledged conveyance of Faculties through the medium of *Oracula vivæ vocis*. In regard to both points, the action pursued by the Order on its suppression by Clement XIV. is well deserving of notice. No Papal sentence could be more emphatic than that which was promulgated in the Brief *Dominus ac Redemptor*. Also the Society appeared to bow before it, and its members made a show of quietly dispersing in obedience to the dissolution pronounced by the Pope. But before long it became known that a considerable number of Fathers had betaken themselves to Prussia and to Russia, where, under the anomalous protection of heretical and schismatic Sovereigns, they continued, in contravention to the Pope's Brief, their previous association, and even on some occasions ventured on demonstrations glaringly hostile to the Holy See and in manifest contradiction to the professed principles of the Society. In Cologne there was published a Gazette of wide circulation. In it articles appeared which with much bitterness and point were directed against the ecclesiastical authority of the Holy See, and breathed the spirit of rank Gallicanism. From the position of the journal, these compositions attracted much notice, and thus bespoke the attention of the Papal Nuncios at Cologne and Vienna. It was hoped that the secular arm would interfere to stop their publication; and the official correspondence of these Pontifical representatives furnishes distinct information regarding the individual responsible for their appearance. On July 22, 1773, the Nuncio informed the Cardinal Secretary of State how he had found technical obstacles in the way of restraining "the editor, who is the ex-Jesuit Feller." Again, in October of the same year, the Nuncio at Vienna, in addressing to the Chancellor of the Empire a formal request to bring the paramount action of Imperial authority in arrest of their publication, makes this distinct allegation: "Since several months the privileged Gazetteer of Cologne, the Abbé Feller, ex-Jesuit, allows himself to insert in his journal most bitter and seditious reflections on the Holy See, in reference to the suppression of the Society of Jesus." It has, however, been attempted boldly to deny the fact that Father Feller ever gave expression to sentiments of disrespect for the Holy See. The critic in the 'Month' makes the statement that "as to the assertion about Feller, it has been completely refuted by Binterim in a letter which appeared in the *Ami de la Religion*, and cited by the Pères de Backer in their *Bibliothèque des Ecrivains de la Compagnie de Jésus*."* The letter referred to, however, has no relation whatever to the matter in question. It bears on the authenticity of a publication which appeared twenty years after the period we are treating of, and dealt with a wholly different subject from the Brief for suppression of the Society.

In April, 1794, Pius VI., by the Bull *Auctorem Fidei* condemned the Synod, which under the guidance of Bishop Ricci had assembled at Pistoia. A few months later there appeared strictures on this Bull in a pamphlet which by some was attributed to Feller, who had taken up his residence at Dusseldorf. This allegation Binterim has contested, and in the article, under the heading of Feller, the Editors of the Dictionary of Jesuit Writers incorporated his statement of grounds against Feller's supposed authorship.† It must be

---

* 'Month' for November, 1874, p. 392.

† In De Backer, *sub voce* Feller, we read, "On attribue, mais injustement, à Feller quelques notes sur la Bulle *Auctorem Fidei*, publiée à Rome à la fin d'Août 1794 contre le Synode de Pistoia; ces notes auraient paru à Dusseldorf sous le titre de Rome en 1794. . . . Les notes ne furent pas même imprimées à Rome, comme le prouve le savant Binterim dans une lettre insérée dans *l'Ami de la Religion*." This letter is then given, and it contains the following passage: "La Bulle *Auctorem Fidei* fut publiée à Rome à la

manifest, that however convincing may be the evidence in demonstration, that in 1794 Feller could not have been the writer of a particular treatise, hostile to the attitude taken up by the Holy See, in regard to the action of the clergy participating in the Pistoia Synod, such evidence cannot in any possible manner bear on the point, whether or not Feller did take part, some twenty years earlier, in the composition of writings sharply criticising the sentence pronounced by the Pope against the Society of Jesus. The fact is indisputable, that if the assertions by the Papal Nuncios in regard to the authorship of the articles in the 'Cologne Gazette' are to be disproved, this can be only through other evidence than that adduced by Binterim's letter in the *Ami de la Religion*, which deals with a wholly different matter.*

Feller's case does not, however, stand alone. There are other instances of Jesuits who at this period propounded strange opinions. On August 20, 1774, there was held in Heidelberg University, according to custom, a public disputation on prescribed theses. A Jesuit Father presided on the occasion, when amongst several very Erastian propositions which the young men were called on to make good was the following:—All property owned by the Church is subject to the rights of the Sovereign, ecclesiastical immunity being due in origin, not so much to the Pope as to the favour of Princes. It stands quite to reason that very excellent Catholics may subscribe

fin d'Août 1794; elle ne parvint sans doute à Dusseldorf qu'en Octobre suivant; mais alors le pays était envahi par les Français, la ville était assiégée, et Feller n'y était plus."

* Several of the articles from the 'Cologne Gazette' are given in Theiner's 'Life of Clement XIV.' It is interesting to note that in some the power of any Pope to suppress the Society is disputed on the ground that its existence was secured by superior guarantees.

such a proposition, but for Jesuits to propound the same and make scholars defend the principle embodied therein, was to act in open contradiction to the principles which they had at least universally professed to assert. The Jesuits in Russia went, however, beyond this; they did not shrink from knowingly countenancing the dissemination of absolutely false statements, and even from seeking to accredit these by forgeries, with the view of having a plea for not obeying the Brief of Suppression.

In November, 1773, Monsignor Garampi, Nuncio in Warsaw, wrote these remarkable words in a ciphered despatch:*—" No conceivable error against true doctrine exists which there is not ground for apprehending that we may see professed by persons who are exasperated, licentious, irreligious, and the worshippers of might." Facts speedily established the correctness of this appreciation. Two spurious documents were put in circulation, that purported to be Briefs, bearing respectively the dates of June 9 and June 29, 1774, the one expressive of the Pope's joy at the position the Order had secured in Russia, the other intimating the repeal of the Brief *Dominus ac Redemptor*. It was not merely in the heat of excitement—in the struggle for existence—that the Jesuits allowed themselves to be hurried into this reprehensible stratagem. The authenticity of these forgeries has been gravely re-affirmed by Jesuit writers of high standing in the face of overwhelming evidence to the contrary. No less eminent a man than Father Curci—the starring preacher at the Gesù Church in Rome, and amongst the most prominent contributors to that *Civiltà Cattolica*, on which Pius IX. has conferred the unprecedented distinction of being declared by an Apostolical Brief the specific organ of truth and holy doctrine—has not

* See Theiner's 'Hist. de Clément XIV.,' vol. ii. p. 409.

refrained from repeating the glaringly false statement that with acquiescence of the resident Nuncio this supposed Brief was published in the ' Warsaw Gazette,'* while quite recently these gross fabrications have again been made to do service.

The writer in the ' Month,' already referred to, makes the statement that Father Curci, "in affirming the approval given by Clement XIV. to the maintenance of the Society in Russia, was only speaking in accordance with what is certified by no small authority." The authority brought forward is two-fold. First comes a quotation from some manuscript apparently kept at Stoneyhurst, and written, it is said, in 1783-4, by Father Plowden, wherein this passage occurs: " Some months before the death of Clement the Fourteenth, the Bishop of Warmy, being at Braunsberg, declared to the Russian Jesuits, on June 7, 1774, that he had received despatches from Monsignor Garampi, Nuncio at Warsaw, containing a very favourable answer of Clement the Fourteenth in their respect, allowing them to remain *in statu quo* till further orders be issued."† Is it the case that one so intimately at home in all that appertains to the Society as the author of this article can have been unaware who this Bishop of Warmy‡ was whom he has brought forward as a witness? This Prelate, by name Krassinski, besides causing much scandal from his mode of life, acquired notoriety by prominently abetting the contumacious action of certain Fathers who flagrantly set at nought the injunctions that came from Rome. To quote him as one whose word can serve as a guarantee for the mind of the Holy See in reference to the matter in question is, to say the least, a

---

* See his ' Una Divinazione sulle tre ultime opere di V. Gioberti.' Paris, 1848.

† The ' Month,' November, 1874, p. 391.

‡ Bishop of Ermeland would be the proper designation.

strange piece of criticism. What really was the mind of the Holy See in regard to this matter stands written in records of unimpeachable authenticity, which are public and easy of access. On March 16, 1774, Cardinal Corsini, Prefect of the Congregation *Pro Rebus Extinctæ*, wrote officially thus to the Nuncio Garampi, "Their Eminences have had the pain to learn that the members of the extinguished Society, who are residing in the Russian Empire, still decline to submit to the Brief of Suppression, on the plea of inhibitions from the secular authority (inhibitions to which they themselves doubtless are not strangers) with the view of cloaking their rebellion from their comrades of tenderer conscience. You likewise inform us that Monsignor Siestrencicwicz, named Bishop of all Catholics in the Russian Empire by the same secular authority, also refuses to defer to the commands of the Holy See."* These words establish conclusively that from Rome there had not been issued any warrant at that date for initiating an underhand revival of the Society. On the contrary, in September of the same year, consequently two months after the date of Bishop Krassinski's statement, Clement XIV. expedited no less than five Briefs to the Archbishop of Gnesen and fellow prelates, holding out certain assurances to the Jesuits, subject, however, to the express condition of their punctually obeying the Brief of Suppression. What possible weight can then be attached, as against evidence of this nature, to a scrap of unsupported statement picked out of a manuscript written by some Jesuit, and that has never been submitted to criticism?

The same writer, in the 'Month,' however, points to a second authority in support of his allegation. He refers to a Pastoral from the Bishop of Mohilew, Vicar-General of White Russia, in 1779, sanctioning the erection of a

* See Theiner's 'Hist. de Clément XIV.,' vol. ii. p. 501.

Jesuit Novitiate, and wherein this Prelate stated that at the desire of Clement XIV. he had forborn to carry into execution the Brief *Dominus ac Redemptor*, and that the then reigning Pope, Pius VI., "suffered the Clerks Regular of the Society of Jesus to return to their state, their habits, and their name in the dominions of her Majesty (the Empress Catherine) notwithstanding the said Brief." The authenticity of this Pastoral may be readily accepted and yet the truth of the statements contained therein may well be open to question, when it is known who was this Bishop of Mohilew, and what was the very equivocal position he assumed in his capacity as the appointed ecclesiastical superior of the Catholic congregations in White Russia. It is necessary to give a few preliminary facts to enable the reader to appreciate at their exact value an allegation of the above nature when resting on the mere authority of an utterance by this Prelate.

Through acquisition of White Russia the Empress Catherine first found herself Sovereign over a considerable Catholic population. In these regions the Society of Jesus had long been largely and powerfully established. No less than six Jesuit Colleges existed in White Russia besides missions and other settlements. In presence of Russian occupation, and the memory of the treatment to which their body had been exposed at the hands of Peter the Great, the Fathers not unnaturally became alarmed at what might befall them from a Sovereign of such enigmatical temperament as Catherine. Accordingly they resolved by every possible means to seek to propitiate the favour of the new ruling power. In marked contrast to the backwardness shown by the Catholic nobles, and by other religious bodies of the Church, the Jesuit Fathers not only in their chief College at Polotzk made a showy ecclesiastical demonstration of loyalty to the Russian Empress on her name's-day, but the Vice-Principal, Father Czerniewicz, with two other members, was deputed to St. Petersburgh, there to swear to the Empress loyalty in the name of all Jesuits, even of those outside her dominions. By this proceeding these Fathers plainly proffered themselves as pioneers for the promotion of Russian interests in the Catholic, that is the Polish, provinces not yet acquired, and this circumstance did not escape the observation of Catherine, whose desire was to constitute the Catholic Church in Russia, so as practically to make it derive its privileges directly from the Sovereign will. If the Society of Jesus would lend itself to be an instrument to this political end, she, in return, would afford it the benefit of special favour, as was soon rendered manifest. When the Brief of Suppression became known, the Provincial of Lithuania acquiesced in the Papal sentence, and, abandoning his position, retired from the scene. Thereupon Father Czerniewicz, as Vice-Provincial, became *ex-officio* the representative of the Society in White Russia. This dignitary now addressed a memorial to the Empress, expressive of the professed desire of himself and his companions to execute the Pope's commands, and entreating her Majesty, "with whom rests the granting permission for execution of the decree," to allow the Order to obey his Holiness. The result of this singular appeal was, it may be affirmed, in harmony with what its authors had anticipated. The Empress forbade publication of the Brief on the ground that, as it had not been officially submitted to her by the Holy See, it could have no force in her dominions, and she directed the Fathers to continue in White Russia as heretofore, inasmuch as in all points, but those of dogma, they had to regard only what was enjoined by the Sovereign will. The Fathers saw no ground for finding fault with this sentence, and accordingly accommodated themselves to its endurance.

Simultaneously, or nearly so, with these incidents, the constitution of the Latin Church in the Empress's new dominions was in course of arrangement. Until then the spiritual jurisdiction had appertained to the Prince-Bishop of Wilna. On separation from Poland, Catherine desired to have a new circumscription of dioceses, with the view of ensuring an organisation independent of authorities outside her dominions. By assuming a very decisive tone, and in some respects an arbitrary action, she carried her point more rapidly than is generally the case in ecclesiastical matters. A new See was instituted at Mohilew, by an Imperial Ukase of May 23, 1774, which was to be administered by the Prelate Siestrenciewicz, already alluded to, who had been previously created Bishop of Mello *in partibus*, and was now invested with jurisdiction as Vicar-Apostolic over all Catholics in that province. This Prelate was a remarkable man and a handy instrument. Originally a Protestant, he had acquired much experience of the world and its intrigues in the tangled web of Polish politics. He now entered with intelligence and promptitude into the special views of Catherine in regard to Church government. The Catholic body was to be allowed entire liberty as regards ceremonial and points of doctrine, but the Bishop of Mohilew was to act as chief dignitary appointed by, and having to look to, the Sovereign, who gave very precise directions, as to what should and should not be done. In the latter category was included the promulgation of the Brief *Dominus ac Redemptor*. Peremptorily the Empress enjoined that this should not be. " I hinder in my Empire the exercise of no religion, any more than your relations with Rome, but as I know that this Court makes serious pretensions, my will is that you do not divide your obedience; that is my will," said Catherine to Siestrenciewicz on his nomination.* It would therefore be quite in character if an unscrupulous, time-serving ecclesiastic of this stamp, having accepted preferment on these terms, should issue a Rescript in the sense of the quotation given by the writer in the 'Month.' What would not have been in character is that the utterances in question had received the approval of the Pope, and had been confirmed from Rome. The writer in the 'Month' has, however, not made the slightest pretence of even remotely implying the existence of any such confirmation, and herein he has shown his good faith. But where he has been wanting, at least in completeness of statement, is in the circumstance that he has omitted to point out how documentary evidence of the most irrefutable force exists to show that Pius VI. emphatically reprobated and disowned this particular action of the Bishop of Mohilew in White Russia.

Exception might be fairly taken to the tone of Father Theiner's narrative in his history of Clement XIV. by those who are friendly to the Society. No one, however, can venture, or has ever ventured, to question the genuineness of the documents which as an Appendix form the contents of the third volume. In it the reader will find Briefs addressed by Pius VI. in 1783 † to the Sovereigns of France, Spain, Portugal, and Sicily, in reference to a report that he had expressed his approval of the proceedings in White Russia, under the auspices of the Bishop of Mohilew. A Father Benislawski, then on a mission in Rome, had circulated the

---

* The facts relating to these matters are nowhere stated more fully than in the second part of the second volume of Bernhardi's excellent 'Geschichte Russlands,' pp. 351-60.

† The date assigned to the Pastoral of the Bishop of Mello is June 29, 1779.

statement that the Pope had to him expressed approbation of his fellow Jesuits in these words: "Approbo societatem Jesu in Alba Russia degentem, approbo, approbo." This story having been widely put about, Pius VI. deemed it incumbent to give it an emphatic contradiction in these Briefs, and at the same time to stigmatise as unauthorised that very Pastoral which the statements made by the writer of the 'Month' would lead inadvertent readers to accept as convincing testimony to the fact that Pius VI. had sanctioned the reversal of his predecessor's sentence. The Pope, on the contrary, informed the King of France and the other Sovereigns addressed by him that, on the first intimation of what the Bishop of Mello had ventured to do in White Russia, on the strength of his Faculties as Vicar-Apostolic, misinterpreted and strained beyond their true bounds, he had taken care to chide and curb this Prelate's licence. Accordingly the Pope desired to assure the French Monarch, that he utterly dissented from, and disapproved of, the acts of the Bishop of Mello, which were in contradiction to his predecessor's Brief of July 21, 1773—the one suppressing the Society. "Readily do we give this Brief to your Majesty," wrote Pius VI., "and expressly affirm therein, that the things reported to have been done, be it in White Russia or elsewhere, contrary to the Brief of Clement XIV., above referred to, are held by us as abuses, and are deemed to be wholly illegitimate and void." * This

* "Carissimo in Christo Filio Nostro Ludovico Francorum Regi Christianissimo Pius Papa VI., Romæ, 29 Jan. 1783. Cum primum nunciata nobis erant ea, quæ in Alba Russia Episcopus Mallensis agere cœperat, ex facultatibus (ut ipse in edicto suo die 30 Junii 1799 dato vulgaverat) sibi ut Vicario Apostolico per nos concessis, perperam tamen ab ille interpretatis, et ultra veros consuetæ formulæ limites extensis, statim, quæ nostræ partes erant, hanc ejusdem licentiam arguere, et coercere, exposita ipsi nostra voluntate, et præfixis facultatum finibus curavimus. Ut ea et tuæ, et Catholicæ Majestati referri possent, ac item cetera, quæ deinceps consecuta, omnium

was the Pope's utterance in Rescripts spontaneously addressed to Catholic Princes four years after the Pastoral quoted by the writer in the 'Month' as evidence of Pius VI. having given his Apostolic sanction that the Clerks Regular of the Society of Jesus in White Russia "should return to their state, their habit, and their name, notwithstanding the said Brief" of Clement XIV. It is impossible to have a more perfect demonstration than is given in these words of the falseness of the whole story.* Of course these remarks do not apply to allegations as to action taken at a later period by Pius VII. The immediate revival of the Order by this Pope on his restoration to power is the public record of the sentiments he came to entertain towards it; nor can there be a question but that during the reign of Paul he was already a party to certain operations, and sanctioned a partial revival of the Society in Russia. It is, however, a disingenuous arrangement to mingle the two sets of incidents together, so as to make the utterances of Pius VII. do misleading duty for entrapping an unwary reader into the impression that here he has got evidence that can prove the truth of alleged

---

certiores fieri voluimus tam Venerabilem Fratrem nostrum Cardinalem de Bernis tuum Plenipotentiarium apud nos administrum, quam Dilectum Filium Nobilem Virum Ducem Hieronymum Grimaldi Hispaniarum Oratorem, perspicuoque ipsis sensus nostros aperuimus *plane abnuentes, improbantesque illa Mallensis acta, quæ Apostolicis fel. rec. Clementis XIV., Prædecessoris nostri in formâ Brevis Litteris die* 21 *Julii datis adversarentur*. . . . Libenter ad Regiam Majestatem tuam has damus litteras, iisque expresse profitemur, *haberi a nobis tamque abusus, atque illegitima ac nulla prorsus reputari, quæcunque vel in Albâ Russiâ vel alibi acta esse feruntur illis contraria, quas superius memoravimus, Clementis XIV. Litteris.*"—Theiner's 'Hist. de Clément XIV.' vol. iii. p. 379.

* The writer in the 'Month' refers to statements resting on allegations in regard to expressions dropped by Pius VI. to Father Pignatelli, but these are of no more value than Benislawski's. It is merely a repetition of the story which Pius VI. himself declared without foundation in his Briefs.

events which if they had occurred at all, would fall in the period of his predecessor.*

A further curious question, however, is connected with the assumed secret revival of the Order by the Pope at some period anterior to its declared restoration in 1814. Dr. Huber makes a statement calculated to throw a new light on the relations between the publicly suppressed Society and the Holy See. According to him there exists a printed Encyclical, under date of December 27, 1839, by Father Roothan, then General of the Order, in which it is affirmed that the Society had been clandestinely revived by Pius VII. through an *Oraculum vivæ vocis*. It has not been our good fortune to obtain sight of the Encyclical in question. The allegation of its existence rests, therefore, on Dr. Huber's authority. Such a statement made in a document of this character, promulgated under the very eyes of Rome, and, as we are assured, never challenged from that quarter, would furnish an astounding illustration of how much, in the opinion of the most competent authorities, it is held to be within the faculty of a clandestine instrument to effect. Even if it were to turn out that the particular allegation made by Father Roothan were erroneous, and that Pius VII. never did give any verbal sanction for the revival of the Society, the significant fact would still be there, that the General of the Order has solemnly declared it in conformity, with the system and practice of the Society at the present time, to consider an impalpable instrument of this nature a sufficient warrant for the most radical action. As-

* The Brief " sent to Father Gruber, Superior-General in Russia, March 7, 1801," is pointed to in the ' Month ' as if it were evidence in confirmation of what is represented to have been done by Clement XIV. or Pius VI., without the reader being warned that the document emanated from a different Pope.

suming it to be correct that the statement in question was put forth by the General in a solemn document to which the Holy See must have been privy, without remonstrance or protest having been raised by it, then it must be necessarily concluded that an *Oraculum vivæ vocis* has been expressly affirmed to be an instrument by no means obsolete, but still actively operative, and as unlimited in the scope of its faculties as it is inscrutable in its nature. It is therefore not without interest to observe that the writer in the 'Month' is far from treating this allegation about Father Roothan as without foundation. On the contrary, he not only asserts all Jesuits to be perfectly familiar with the existence of such *Oracula*, but he further declares it must be a matter of easy comprehension that Pius VII. should have adopted on this occasion a mode of procedure enabling him " to refrain from openly rousing the antagonism of the Bourbon Courts." We have it, therefore, here clearly given under the hand of this experienced authority, that in the opinion of those intimately acquainted with the present spirit of the Society, it would be deemed perfectly justifiable with the view of obviating embarrassments, to make in public a very solemn disavowal, which in practice should be set at nought in virtue of an impalpable warrant,*

---

* "The author is very amusing in his speculations on a dreadful bugbear which he has discovered, the orders of the Popes, which, being unwritten, are called *Oracula vivæ vocis*. Very terrible indeed it must be, that the Pope, like other rulers, may order or sanction a thing without writing it. Yet we never heard that the British army at Waterloo waited for the Duke of Wellington to write his order for the final charge on the French. We beg to inform this writer that not Jesuits only, but all Catholics, are perfectly familiar with the sort of orders or sanctions of which he speaks, and consider themselves bound to obey them. To 'the inscrutable medium of the *Oraculum vivæ vocis*' the Society owed its first approval, given by Paul the Third. That Pius the Sixth should refrain from openly rousing the antagonism of the Bourbon Courts, and from condemning the judgment of his predecessor, Clement the Fourteenth, can be readily understood, and it is a matter of

that from its nature can defy the process of tangible detection.

history that many of his Court were, from interested or other motives, strong upholders of the ruthless and complete suppression of the Society. *That in such a conjuncture the Pope made use of the by no means exceptional form of a verbal approval, which, while it satisfied the consciences of the Fathers of the Society, shielded him from the exigencies of the Spanish Court, is also quite natural.*"—The 'Month,' November, 1874, p. 390.

CHAPTER XV.

No foundation for attributing death of Clement XIV. to poison—Evidence relied on for the report—Theiner wholly exonerates the Jesuits—Story about antidotes found in Pope's apartments—Important testimony by Tanucci to Pope's natural death—Account given by Dr. Huber of incident in conference on Grace in Clement VIII.'s presence—Rests on no authority—Sorry does not bear out the statement, nor is it warranted by Lemos—Statement of what really occurred on the occasion.

THE death of Clement XIV. has been ascribed to poison administered by the Jesuits. That such an idea should recommend itself to a certain class of writers is natural, but it is matter of astonishment to find Dr. Huber giving countenance to a story so manifestly unsupported by any but the flimsiest evidence. No one who gathers his knowledge of the circumstances surrounding Clement's death from Dr. Huber's narrative can well acquire any other impression than that, notwithstanding Dr. Salicetti's medical statement after a post-mortem examination, the indications of a mysterious cause of death are still serious, and that the fact of the Pope having been poisoned was believed in at the time by some who were in a position to have the best means of knowing what happened inside the Vatican. We wish we could remain under the impression that Dr. Huber has here been merely guilty of carelessness; but there is an arrangement in his apparent references and in his statements which savours strongly of studied intention. According to Dr. Huber, the Spanish Ambassador, Monino, reported his firm persuasion that the Pope had been poisoned; this belief was credited at the Court of Spain and generally in the Cabinets of

Europe; and "it is a fact" that antidotes were found after the Pope's death in his room. It is noteworthy that Dr. Huber omits all but a passing reference to Father Theiner's 'Life of Clement XIV.,' not only the capital work on the subject, but one written in a spirit decidedly hostile to the Jesuits. The reason may possibly be found in the circumstance that Father Theiner, despite his unfriendliness towards the Society, is clear in wholly exonerating the Jesuits from having poisoned the Pope. But Dr. Huber does refer, in support of his allegation, to another historian of standing, Ginzel, and therefore it may fairly be demanded of him to have carefully read and faithfully given the statements of his cited authority. We have seen Dr. Huber affirm "as a fact" the discovery of medicines in the Pope's apartments that were antidotes. On turning to Ginzel,* we find the following words: "Of these pills the Pope made use, at the advice of Dr. Bianchi, as a means to promote perspiration, and by no means as an antidote."† Is this a statement confirmatory of Dr. Huber's glib allegation? Far more important, however, than the opinion of any modern writer, would be the proof that at the time Foreign Ambassadors, such as the Spanish and Neapolitan, with their excellent means of information, had been led to the conclusion that poison had been administered, and on this head direct evidence is afforded in a book Dr. Huber never seems to have heard of, Ferrer del Rio's 'History of Charles III.' What a leading position was occupied by the Neapolitan Minister Tanucci amongst the political influences brought to bear against the Society of Jesus, is notorious. He, at all events, can never be reckoned as a witness whose testimony in favour

---

* Ginzel, 'Kirchenhistorische Schriften,' vol. ii. p. 246.

† This Dr. Bianchi was a personal friend of the Pope's from his youth, and a native of Rimini.

of the Order must be considered liable to the imputation of partiality. Yet on two occasions Tanucci expressed his clear conviction, in confidential letters, that there was no shadow of foundation for the charge of poison, and in one addressed to King Charles,[*] he even referred to the very Monino whose authority is invoked by Dr. Huber in support of the statement which he has not scrupled to introduce into his text. There cannot be a doubt that the charge against the Jesuits of having accelerated the death of Clement XIV. by poison is substantiated by no tittle of valid evidence, and it is lamentable to find in a book like Dr. Huber's allegations, though in part veiled and rather insinuated than directly expressed, which are wholly unworthy of an author who lays claims to critical faculties.

This is not the only instance where Dr. Huber has been led into making very grave statements which can be characterized only as being without the shadow of foundation. A notable example occurs in his account of what passed on the occasion of the discussions in presence of Clement VIII. in reference to the doctrines about grace, represented by Molina. Dr. Huber's narrative is as follows: " In the History of these Transactions, where both parties carried on their causes, it is related how the Jesuits made expressly for the occasion an edition of Augustine, in which they altered or expunged all the passages contrary to their doctrine. Thus,

[*] 'Hist. de Carlos III.,' por Don A. Ferrer del Rio. Madrid, 1856. Vol. ii. p. 505. Tanucci escribió á Centomani el 8 de Octubre : " La recibida confidencial con que V. S. I. me ha favorecido el 4 del corriente concluye lo que yo creia del decantado veneno; esto es, que no es veneno criminal, sino veneno dialéctico el orígen del deplorable suceso." A Carlos III. el 11 de Octubre: " Monino habrá referido la conjetura y la fama del veneno por obra de los Jesuitas. Seria sumamente prolijo el discurso con el cual, despues de haber considerado y leido muchas cartas y minutas voluminosas de Roma sobre el asunto, ha venido á la opinion de que ningun otro veneno han dado los Jesuitas y tantos agentes suyos en aquella corte al buen Papa sino el de hacerla creer que estaba envenenado."

in 1603, Valentia, in presence of Clement VIII., affirmed, in the teeth of the Dominican Lemos, who had cited a passage of Augustine, that the same did not exist in his writings. Thereupon Lemos demanded that the works of this Father should be fetched. But Valentia had them quite ready to hand and read, out of the falsified edition prepared by the Order, the very contrary to what the Dominican had affirmed. Taken wholly aback at this, Lemos asked that the works of Augustine be fetched out of the Pope's library, and Clement VIII. was then able to convince himself with his own eyes that the Dominican had quoted correctly. On the fraud being thus disclosed, the Pope said to Valentia, 'Is it in this manner that you seek to deceive the Church of God?' Whereupon the latter fainted, and two days later died." *
For all this Dr. Huber refers, as his one authority, to Serry's 'Historia Congreg. de Auxiliis.' In the first place, it may be asked why refer to a second-hand authority? Serry was merely a compiler, who very fairly, in his account of this capital discussion, refers to and quotes quite accurately the narrative by Lemos, himself an active participator in the debate, and one of the principal parties in the supposed transactions narrated by Dr. Huber. It will seem hardly credible that neither in Serry nor in Lemos is there one word which justifies the astounding statement, that the Jesuits had expressly printed a falsified edition of Augustine, and brought it forward during the discussion in support of the views which they sought to affirm. It is narrated with dramatic effect that Valentia, in the course of his spoken argument, did cite a passage out of the 'De Civitate Dei'— that Lemos, taken at first aback, nevertheless happily remembered the passage; and, recognising the quotation to be garbled, appealed to the Pope to have it looked up — and

* See Huber, p. 282.

that thus he convicted the Jesuit doctor of misquotation.*
What, therefore, stands on record is the fact of a garbled
reference — one, doubtless, of capital importance for the
matter under discussion, but still garbled only in spoken
reference, and not at all such a most elaborate and portentous
trick as would have been the deliberately falsified edition
which Dr. Huber explicitly alleges to have been printed by
the Jesuits, with the express view of misrepresenting St.
Augustine, and making him appear to have held views in
conformity with their favourite theology. Dr. Huber's reputation is too high to let it be thought possible that he should
have knowingly given currency to a sheer invention—an
absolute myth. We do, however, believe him culpable of
negligence and hastiness. As he was content with a passing
reference to Serry, instead of looking into Lemos, so we can
understand that he satisfied himself with a mere glance at
his authority, without reading through the very detailed
account which is given of the incidents attending this
remarkable controversial duel.

* The passage can be found in Lemos, 'Hist. Congreg. de Auxiliis.'
Lovaniæ, 1702. P. 279.

PART II.

CHAPTER XVI.

Mechanism of the Society its mere skeleton—Mystic letters A. M. D. G.—
Signification thereof—Guarantee involved in official *imprimatur*—
Faculties of Examiners—General alone sanctions publication—The same
casuistry inveighed against by Pascal still prevalent in Jesuit schools—
Authorities for this allegation—Father Gury.

WONDERFULLY supple as may seem to be the Mechanism of the Society of Jesus, it yet constitutes the mere skeleton of a system that derives animation from essences of doctrine too subtle to be compressed within the bounds of palpable provisions. Of such essences there exists but one visible symbol, the mystic letters A.M.D.G. (*Ad Majorem Dei Gloriam*) conspicuously emblazoned as a sacred sign on the frontispiece of every work, structure, or creation, with which the Order acknowledges itself to be identified. Through the motto abbreviated into these four initial letters the Society of Jesus ostentatiously advertises itself as being in possession of a superior knowledge in divine things, that can furnish means of specific efficacy for ensuring the upward progress of humanity towards such a state of purified existence as will be capable of reflecting the bright imagery of God's enhanced glorification. No other religious corporation has ever put forth the like pretensions. It will be our endeavour to inquire what particular lights of thought and doctrine mark off this Jesuit illumination from that ordi-

L

nary enlightenment which can suffice (as is to be gathered from the Society's motto) only for an inferior glorification of God. For the knowledge we are in quest of we shall turn exclusively to the writings of Jesuit Fathers who are fully qualified to be considered authoritative spokesmen of their Order. It is however well to establish first the degree of guarantee implied by the Society's official *imprimatur* affixed to a book by a Jesuit writer; for, in his rejoinder to Pascal, Father Daniel pleaded that it could not fasten on the Order any responsibility for the opinions set forth in such publication. This plea is wholly untenable. In the 'Constitutions' it is written that "no differences of opinion are admissible, neither by word in discourses or public lectures, nor by written books, which last it is not allowable to publish without approval and consent of the General, who, however, may confide their examination to three men endowed with sound doctrine and eminent judgment."* Again, the Faculties of these Examiners are absolutely limited to the examination of writings transmitted by the General, and to the draughting of an opinion, on which "the General can take such decision as may to him seem suitable." The Father Revisors have merely consultative powers; they never can sanction publication; they are not even permitted to receive a book for review from any one but the General; in every instance the sanction for publication expressed by the word *imprimatur* must emanate directly from the General himself at his absolute discretion.†

---

* Const. Tertia Pars, cap. i. Inst. S. J., vol. i, p. 372.

† See 'Regulæ quæ a Patribus Revisoribus in recognoscendis nostrorum Libris observandæ sunt,' 1650. Reg. v., "Absolutis cujusque libri consultationibus tam ejus libri approbationem, tam censuras, Patri Nostro subscriptas exhibebunt ut de his statuat quod convenire videbitur." Reg. x., "Nullum librum scriptumve a quoquam recognoscendum accipient præterquam a P. Generali aut ejus nomine a P. Secretario."

It would be a labour of supererogation to show what has been proved over and over again, that certain Jesuit Fathers in former days did broach gravely questionable opinions. No interest could attach to a repetition of work that has been done for all times by Pascal. But interest may attach to the demonstration that the spirit of casuistry, so keenly riddled by his pungent invective, still flourishes with unimpaired vigour, and that the same maxims, which it might have been deemed the shafts of Pascal's wit must have banished for ever, are being inculcated at the present day in every Roman Catholic School, College, and Seminary where Jesuit doctrine prevails, and this comprises the vast majority. The works whereon we shall rely for evidence cannot be open to challenge on the score of authority. No modern treatise can show a more formidable array of guarantees than Father Gury's 'Compendium of Moral Theology.' It has been appointed, in Roman Catholic seminaries in all lands, as the standard Manual of Moral Theology. It has been printed in every country, and translated into every tongue. In the new issue of De Backer's 'Dictionary of Jesuit Writers' there are enumerated no fewer than twenty-four editions. The one we quote from was issued in 1872 from the presses of the 'Propaganda' at Rome—the highest possible voucher for the entire approval of every line and every word in the book by the supreme representatives of the Roman Catholic Church. The volume on 'Cases of Conscience,' by the same author, is a commentary in practical elucidation of the larger work.*

* Father Gury was born at Mailleroncourt in 1801; for thirty-five years he was Professor of Moral Theology, first in the Seminary at Vals, and then in the Collegio Romano. He died in 1866 while on a mission at Marcour in Auvergne. 'Compendium Theologiæ Moralis.' Auctore P. Joanne Petro Gury, S. J. Romæ, ex Typographiâ Polyglottâ, S. C. de Propagandâ Fide. 2 vols. 1872.—'Casus Conscientiæ.' Auctore P. J. P. Gury, S. J., Theologiæ Moralis Professore, Editio in Germaniâ Prima. Ratisbonæ, 1865.

The 'Compendium,' by Moullet, first appeared in 1834, at Freiburg, in Switzerland, and was largely used as a text-book in Jesuit Seminaries, though the author was not a professed member of the Society. It was particularly recommended by the Bishop of Lausanne "to the whole clergy of the diocese," on the special ground that the author's conclusions were eminently distinguished for their happy mean between "rigorism and laxity." The edition before us, printed at Prato in 1846,* again enjoys the episcopal endorsement of its contents, while Gury brings the cumulative weight of his recognition to the value of Moullet, by referring to him as a decisive authority for the soundness of a particular opinion.

* 'Compendium Theologiæ Moralis ad usum Theologiæ Candidatorum.' A. J. P. Moullet. 2 vols. Prati, 1846.

CHAPTER XVII.

Three cardinal propositions in Jesuit system — Probabilism — Mental Reservation — Justification of Means by Ends — Definition of *opinio probabilis* — What is sufficient to render probable an opinion — Its justificatory range — *Extrinsic* probability — Confessor shall not impose his opinion — Pascal's *Adoucissements* — Principle of dispensations — Latitude vested in Pope — Rulings by Gury that meet Jesuit proceedings in China — As to wearing Pagan vestments — Explicit belief in Trinity and Incarnation not indispensable in a Christian — Invincible Ignorance — Its operation according to terms of Jesuit definition — Case of Jesuits in China as judged by foregoing sentences.

ADVOCATE and antagonist will alike admit that the system of lax opinion popularly charged against Jesuit divines rests on three cardinal propositions — of Probabilism, of Mental Reservation, and of Justification of Means by the End. We shall begin by examining whether those who now speak as approved organs of the doctrine of the Order have at all abandoned, as to these three heads, the sentiments which caused so great scandal when propounded by former Jesuit celebrities. "Je vois bien que vous ne savez pas ce que c'est que la doctrine des opinions probables; c'est le fondement et l' A. B. C. de toute notre morale," says Pascal's imaginary Jesuit in the 'Provinciales;' a statement amply corroborated by Father Gury. The first section in his ponderous volumes is devoted to an analysis of human actions and of their constituent motives. In the chapter on Lust we come across this axiom: "Temptation, when greatly protracted need not be *positively* withstood continuously, inasmuch as that would be over-irksome and render one liable to innumerable scruples."* We then have definitions of conscience in various conditions, and of the moral facts from which it would be justifiable to derive elements for its guidance and satisfaction. Prominently amongst such moral facts is ranked the *opinio probabilis*, which is explained to be "any judgment resting on some really grave motive, though with fear of the opposite."† This means that, notwithstanding an irrepressible inward impression that truth is really in opposition to a given *opinio probabilis*, yet any opinion, in behalf whereof there can be adduced what is technically termed a "grave motive," may be safely accepted as full warrant for action in its sense. It is of such essential importance to grasp the import, as expounded by the Father himself, of this doctrine which is the corner-stone in his system, that we must request the reader's attention to some illustration on the matter.

We have had probable opinion declared an adequate justification for conscience to act upon it; but we have not yet learned what are the tests for an opinion to be probable. Father Gury is explicit on this head. If a person be of "learning and uprightness," then for any opinion he may entertain to become "assuredly probable" for his *own guidance*, it suffices that he "should be conscious of having thought it out diligently" and persuaded himself to his own satisfaction of its correctness;‡ for *the general public* one single author "of exceptional superiority" is capable of rendering probable any opinion he may express, "even though his teaching be contrary to what is commonly held;"§ while in the case of a *person* "*unversed in letters*" it is enough that he can point to a particular opinion as having fallen from any one whom "he

---

* Gury, vol. i. p. 15, Resol. 6.   † Id., vol. i. p. 36, Cap. 4.   De Conse. Prob.
‡ Id., vol. i. p. 38, Conclusio 4.   § Id., Concl. 7.

himself deems to be possessed of learning and insight," for his confident acceptance of such opinion as a rule of action.* As in the immediately subsequent line the efficacy of probable opinion is declared " to ensure its rendering the dictate of conscience practically confident," that is, to remove it beyond the reach of disturbing scruple,† it is evident how far-reaching must be a doctrine which makes it justifiable to act on the authority of opinions, notwithstanding conscious misgivings as to their correctness, on the mere ground that they can be pointed to as standing in type in some book, which for some reason is affirmed to be the production of a man of learning, or that they have been uttered by a person who declares that he has clearly argued himself into their truth. But this is not all we are taught in reference to probable opinions. Father Gury affirms, in a special proposition, that the fact of *extrinsic* probability, which consists in the merely clerical circumstance of a particular opinion being within the literal sense of terms employed by a particular writer of reputed authority, of itself gives to that construction all the value of probability ;‡ and this even though, by another ruling of the Father, the justificatory range of probable opinions reaches to points of divine as well as of positive legislation.§ Accordingly we

* Gury, vol. i. p. 39, Concl. 8.

† Id., p. 39. Filliucius says : " Dico licitum esse sequi opinionem probabiliorem, relictâ minus probabili, etiamsi sit magis tuta . . . licitum esse sequi opinionem minus probabilem, etiamsi minus tuta sit."—Quæst. Morales, Lugduni, 1633, tom. ii. p. 12. And Moya, " Quamvis opinio sit falsa, potest quilibet tutâ conscientiâ illam practicè sequi propter auctoritatem docentis."—Opusculum, p. 27.

‡ Id., vol. i. p. 53. Amongst the authorities cited in support of this proposition is a decision of the Congregation of the Holy Penitentiary that the material fact of an opinion being in St. Liguori's writing is amplo warrant for its adoption without any need to weigh the reasons.

§ Ib., vol. i. p. 52, Quær. 78. " An licitum sit, uti probabilitate, non tantum in materia juris positivi sed etiam juris divini et naturalis ? "

are instructed that it is no part of the duty of a spiritual adviser to disturb peace of mind derived from opinions the probability whereof is to him gravely doubtful. "Is it lawful or incumbent on a Confessor," asks the Father, "to absolve a penitent bent on following an opinion, probable indeed, but contrary to the judgment he himself holds?" And his reply is in the affirmative, on the ground "that the penitent has the right to follow any opinion truly and wholly probable, while the Confessor has no right to impose his own opinion even though it be more probable. For a Confessor is no judge of the opinions his penitent should follow, but is only a judge of his disposition."* Do we not here become instinctively conscious of being in presence of those *adoucissements*, which were so scornfully lashed by Pascal?

The foregoing propositions are so many applications of the principle of dispensation, and the latitude involved therein acquires a range absolutely unlimited, when brought into correlation with the supreme depositary of sacerdotal essence. The query, "whether the Pope can dispense from God's precepts," is thus solved: "He can dispense therefrom for a just cause in cases where divine law comes into action through human will, as in vows and oaths. In other cases the point is one of controversy, whether he is empowered *actually to dispense for some very grave causes or only to declare God's law suspended for the time*." "But," adds Gury, not a little significantly, "in *practice* the *difference* is of *small consequence*."† Without, however, bringing into play the

* Gury, vol. i. p. 52. This ruling is repeated, vol. ii. p. 360 : "An possit absolvi pœnitens qui vult sequi opinionem sententiæ Confessoris oppositam? Resp. Affirm. si sit vere probabilis."

† Id., vol. i. p. 77. It should be noticed that in the section on Laws and their binding force, every Papal utterance or Brief, even though not inserted in the Corpus Juris, is declared to be possessed of the full force of law (see p. 89), a statement which would cover the *oracula viva vocis*.

supreme agency of Pontifical plenitude, many concrete cases are given by Father Gury, in which a notable departure from the received acceptation of the law is justified, and some of these cover precisely points in the history of the Order that have caused much controversy. Thus we are told that it is certainly not unlawful to adopt the symbols and vestments of Pagans if only these be considered by the wearers in the character of prevalent national customs, and therefore not necessarily *per se* referable to a particular worship.* But even " if they should be the vestments and symbols of religion," Father Gury sees a way to justify their adoption by Christians; they might be lawfully worn if only " the vestments were not exclusively distinctive between sect and sect, for then their primary use would be to cover the body, and only their secondary use to distinguish the sect "—a ruling that very appositely meets in part the case of the Chinese rites. The Jesuit missionaries were, however, besides accused of having modified articles of Christian doctrine to suit the Chinese intellect, so as even to have put out of sight such points as the Incarnation and Crucifixion. If they did so, they did only what Father Gury distinctly affirms to be quite legitimate. The query is gravely mooted, whether "*explicit* belief in the Mysteries of the Holy Trinity and the Incarnation be indispensable in a Christian,"† to which Father Gury replies, that opinions are divided on this head; but, says he, " the one which is the more probable is in the negative, for the reason, that a merely *implicit* belief sufficed before Christ, and, therefore, should also suffice after his coming."

He then considers whether " absolution can be obtained by

---

* Gury, vol. i. p. 124.
† Id., vol. i. p. 125. "An requiratur fides explicita mysterii SS. Trinitatis et Incarnationis de necessitate medii?"

one who ignores the Mysteries of the Trinity and the Incarnation;" and, again, after some circumlocution, his conclusion is, " that according to the more probable opinion, he can be *validly* absolved if only he be living in invincible ignorance."* Here we have met with a term of first-rate importance in the system of our Jesuit divines, but also of singular elasticity, the bearing of which it is essential to grasp. Let an individual be surrounded by preachers straight from heaven, speaking with tongues of divine persuasion, and yet, according to the terms employed in the definitions given of what constitutes invincible ignorance, he might, with impunity, withhold acquiescence, alleging moral inability to comprehend what was spoken, while in fact he was obdurately bent on not expressing assent, with the inward design to establish a plea that would warrant his indulgence of a selfish purpose. Invincible ignorance should be a natural malformation of the intellect (except in cases where physical means of knowledge are positively absent), which prevents a point being recognised and a truth being felt, just as insanity in the eyes of the law exempts an individual from its consequences, as being thereby incapacitated from discriminating between right and wrong. There is, however, this capital distinction between the methods by which the relative pleas are established, that, whereas civil tribunals apply objective tests to confirm the existence of insanity, it is enough, according to Jesuit definitions, that invincible ignorance should be persistently alleged by a party for it to become admitted by Jesuit divines, with all its consequent exemptions. The scope of a rule can be found only within the terms in which it

---

* Gury at least puts his proposition as admitting of some controversy. Moya's language is even more positive : " Fides explicita de Mysteriis Incarnationis et Trinitatis non est medium necessarium ad salutem."—' Opusculum,' p. 36.

is laid down; and our contention is, that in the definitions and exemplifications given by Father Gury in regard to invincible ignorance, no term can be found which must render it necessary, before the validity of this plea is admitted, that there should be aught adduced in its support besides the obdurately persistent insistance of the party interested in not acquiescing in a particular proposition, or in not admitting a particular point. No language can be more precise than Gury's as to the degree of relief from obligations ensured by invincible ignorance. "Invincible ignorance," says he, "wholly removes all voluntary element, for nothing can possibly be voluntary where there is no cognition .... according to the axiom, Nothing can be willed unless it be previously contemplated. Therefore, *no deed proceeding from invincible ignorance can ever be made the ground for accusation against the doer.*"*

The case of the Jesuit Missionaries in China, judged by these grave sentences, would, therefore, stand thus: For Christians to adopt Pagan customs, when to omit doing so might be attended with some inconvenience, is quite legitimate; only they must say to themselves inwardly that they mean merely to conform to a local practice, irrespective of its intimate relation to heathen observances. Again, it is not at all essential for a Christian to believe explicitly in the Trinity or the Incarnation; should, therefore, missionaries boast of numerous converts, none of whom have been indoctrinated in these dogmatic points, there would be no ground for charging the missionaries with laxness, as they would only have omitted to teach what was not essential, or for denying to these neophytes the character of thorough Christians, their ignorance on these points of established secondary importance being plainly invincible; consequently

* Gury, vol. i. p. 13.

in all they did in China the Jesuit Fathers must be held wholly beyond reproach. *

* Gury reverts to this matter in the 'Casus Conscientiæ' (p. 60). "Can a missionary," he asks, "for purposes of concealment assume the dress of ministers of a false religion so that he may seem one of them?" which is answered in the affirmative, the same qualifying grounds of distinction as above being adduced: "for dresses primarily serve for covering the body, and are not merely declaratory signs of some sect." This ruling meets the case of the Jesuit who in Sweden occupied a chair of Protestant divinity.

CHAPTER XVIII.

Mental Reservations—The Jesuit in the 'Provinciales' on them—Two kinds of Reservation according to Gury—Broadly mental reservations on occasions lawful—Condition *sine quâ non* for said lawfulness—Gury's doctrine as to force of solemn promises—Oaths not necessarily binding—Conditions that sanction repudiation—Statements by penitents to be accepted even though doubts exist as to their truth—Scope for equivocation—An illustration given by Gury—Another afforded by proceedings in reference to Suarez's '*Defensio Fidei Catholicæ*'—Acquaviva's alleged general prohibition of its objectionable maxims: only special to France as results from *Juvencus*—Reprints of Suarez's volume without censure—Modern propositions about Pope's Supremacy—Possible bearing of Mental Reservation on clandestine affiliations—'*Cusus Conscientiæ*' stated by Gury—Single limitation apparently considered as of propriety—Note about Stark's affirmed secret conversion to Roman Catholicism.

LET us now see what we can learn in reference to Mental Reservations, the second capital count in the popular indictment against Jesuit principles. "Une chose des plus embarrassantes qui s'y trouve," exclaims our Jesuit of the 'Provinciales,' "est d'éviter le mensonge et surtout quand on voudrait faire accroire une chose fausse. C'est à quoi sert admirablement notre doctrine des *équivoques*. Mais savez-vous bien comment il faut faire quand on ne trouve point de mots équivoques?" "Non, mon père." "Je m'en doutais bien," dit-il; "cela est nouveau; c'est la doctrine des *Réservations Mentales*." Father Gury carefully points out that Mental Reservations are of two kinds, the *strictly* and the *broadly* mental. The first are absolutely unlawful, as involving the use of terms from which the hearer never could infer the concealed sense of the speaker. But "for grave reasons" it is declared "lawful at times to make use of broadly mental reservations, as also of equivocal terms;" it being quite essential, however, that the terms employed be such "as may make it possible for the listener to understand a matter as it really is, and not as it may sound."* In other words, it is a condition *sine quâ non* for this device to pass muster, that it should be carefully constructed out of terms into which a double meaning can possibly be imported. Consistently with this ruling, we learn that no oath need be binding, of which it can be alleged that a sense of pressure conduced at the time to its having been sworn. Coercion may very fairly be taken as an extenuating circumstance for departure from an engagement; but it is startling to find it enunciated as a principle, in the standard Handbook for the instruction of Roman Catholic youths in Moral Obligations, that an oath may be repudiated with perfect impunity, if only the person who has sworn will plead to having been at the time influenced in his mind by some apprehension of possibly injurious consequences to himself, unless he had so sworn.

It is well to follow out Gury's doctrine as to the force of solemnly contracted promises. In the section about Contracts we find this query: "If a donation has been promised on oath, but has not yet been accepted, is it still binding?" which is answered negatively,† on the ground that, as the deed is incomplete, it is void in substance, and consequently no oath in reference thereto can be held to have binding force. Father Gury—and he is in accord with the divines of his Order—has, however, more to say in limitation of the obligations following on oaths. He lays it down, that according to more probable opinion no oath is binding "if made with the intention indeed of swearing, but not of

* Gury, vol. i. p. 280. "Quomodo præcisè distinguatur restrictio latè mentalis a restrictione strictè mentali?"   † Id., vol. i. p. 483.

binding,"* though he admits that to go deliberately through the semblance of an oath without any intention whatever to keep it does involve "a venial sin amounting to a lie, with a taking in vain of God's name." To remove all doubt as to what is implied, this explanation is added: "The binding force of an oath has to be interpreted according to the tacit conditions either included or implied (*subintellectas*) therein; which are: 1st, if I could have done so without grave injury; 2nd, if matters had not notably changed; 3rd, if the rights and will of the superior were not contrary; 4th, if the other had kept his faith; 5th, if the other does not waive his right." Whatever may be said for several of these relieving conditions, the first virtually puts it within every one's power to repudiate his oath whenever he sees fit to allege that its observance would be accompanied by what he himself thinks to be serious disadvantage; for here again, no qualification limits the faculty of the interested party to impart, of his own mere will, a justification to the action that may suggest itself as pleasant for adoption.

The prohibitions against spiritual advisers interfering to make so-called penitents, who are of a restive temperament, entertain a rigid sense of duty are elaborately explicit. Though he might have grounds to entertain "doubts as to the sincerity of the penitent,"† the Confessor is yet simply to accept his statements. Even in the case of "having certain knowledge that a sin has been kept back or denied," the Confessor is not to extract its admission unless in a roundabout manner, but he shall grant absolution because the penitent must be believed, whether

* Gury, vol. i. p. 200. "Non valet probabilius jurmentum factum cum animo quidem jurandi sed non se obligandi, nec vice versa."

† "Quid agere debeat confessarius in dubio de sinceritate pœnitentis? Regula hæc communis est, et axioma receptum in hoc tribunali: Credendum est pœnitenti, tam pro se, quam contra se dicenti."—Gury, vol. ii. p. 355.

speaking for or against himself; and "if he really did commit the sin in question, it may be presumed he has forgotten it, or confessed it to another, or has some great cause for keeping it secret, or that the informers were deceived."* What room for equivocation is afforded by this ruling the following exemplification will show. "Anna having been guilty of adultery, and being interrogated by her husband, who has formed a suspicion, answers, the first time, that she has not violated wedlock; the second time, having in the interval obtained absolution, she replies, *I am guiltless of such crime*. The third time, she absolutely denies the adultery, and says, *I have not committed it*, meaning within herself such particular adultery as I am bound to reveal, or, I have not committed an act of adultery that has to be revealed to you. Is Anna to be blamed?"† Gury's reply, too long to give here, justifies each answer of the adulterous woman, supporting his ruling by a grave array of authorities, amongst which figure the Jesuit Suarez and St. Liguori.

In illustration of the equivocation that has been practised by the Order in its corporate capacity, the facts relating to the purported condemnation by its General of the doctrines on Tyrannicide, and the Supremacy of the Pope over Princes, as maintained by Suarez in his treatise, '*Defensio Fidei Catholica*,' are of interest. The first edition appeared at Coimbra in 1613; and in September, 1614, Paul V. conveyed to Suarez, in a Brief, his Pontifical approbation of its contents. Despite this august sanction, the treatise excited controversy, and in 1618 was even condemned by the Parliament of Paris to be burnt by the public hangman. Thereupon the Jesuits came forward with a Brief alleged to

* Gury, vol. ii. p. 355.
† Ibid., 'Casús Conscientiæ,' Restrictio Mentalis, p. 129.

have been issued by their General Acquaviva, as early as August, 1614—that is, a month before the Pope's congratulatory Epistle—prohibiting all public discussion by members of the Order on the two points that had given rise to the objectionable propositions. This Brief has been reprinted in the Institutes* and reads there as a general instruction to all Provincials not to tolerate within their jurisdictions any disquisition as to the Pope's Supremacy or Tyrannicide, without special authority from Rome. But Juvencus, in his History, printed with official approval a century later in Rome, informs us incidentally that this Brief never was a general instruction, but was addressed to France alone, having been written solely to allay the unpleasant controversy there awakened by Suarez's propositions.† This statement at once deprives the document of the character sought to be given it by Jesuit apologists. There is, however, something more to be observed. By this document most certainly all publications on the said topics are professedly prohibited for the future, without special permission from Rome. Suarez's volume has been re-issued, —in 1619 at Cologne, in 1655 at Mayence—without a trace of such special permission, and without disapproval from the General. Had the special sanction then been given clandestinely? If it had not, why did the Order never reprove the new issues? It is certain that at no time has the Order levelled a word of public censure against Suarez. On the contrary, he is proclaimed as a light of the first magnitude

* Inst. S. J., vol. ii. p. 5. 'Præceptum Provincialibus circa editionem Librorum.'

† "Abunde jam provisum fuerat a Præp. Gen. Societatis ne tractarentur a nostris scriptoribus hujus generis argumenta . . . Exstabat editum ante annos quatuor, super eâ re decretum, quod *in Hispaniam tamen et in Lusitaniam non perlatum erat, quia nulla ibi lis ejusmodi movebatur, atque decretum Acquavivæ a Patribus Gallis fuerat procuratum, sic ad eos, proprie putabatur*."—Juv., p. 88, lib. xii. Romæ, 1710.

M

in the firmament of doctrine by Father Gury, in his most recent editions :—" Inter Theologos post D. Thomam eminens, a Paulo V. et Bened. XIV. *doctor eximius* nuncupatus, et apud omnes ingenio, *doctrinâ* et *sapientiâ* admodum commendatus." We shall have occasion to advert to certain propositions of quite modern date as to the Pope's Supremacy over Princes; and then it may possibly be deemed that the principles embodied in the objectionable propositions, on account of which Suarez's treatise was publicly burnt, are to be found at the present day in the approved writings of the great organs of Jesuit learning and doctrine.

We have before dwelt on some matters which apparently countenance the allegation, that clandestine affiliation is a thing not absolutely repudiated by the Society. It is not without relevancy to this point, and specially to Mental Reservation, that clandestine conversions to, and protracted clandestine professions of, the Roman Catholic faith, are declared quite permissible practices under certain circumstances. At page 60 of the 'Casus Conscientiæ,' we read the following interesting case:—" Paternus, a Protestant clergyman, and in extreme peril of death, having come to believe the Catholic religion to be alone true, has requested a priest to be called in, but that he should come dressed as a layman, to avert all suspicion of the convert's being about to abjure heresy. To this priest Paternus opens his mind, attaching however two conditions : that in the event of his succumbing to the illness, he be allowed to die concealing the Catholic faith and the baptism he had received; and that, in the event of recovery, he be allowed to postpone his public profession until such time as this could be done free from any injury to his estate. To both conditions the priest assents readily." The question is, Was the priest justified in doing so? and Gury's argumentation is eminently typical of the spirit pervading all Jesuit doctrine—which finds expression in the apparently emphatic affirmation of a rigid principle, coupled with the immediately subsequent introduction of terms which practically make the observance of the affirmed principle a matter of option at the dictate of expediency. With stern rigorism our Father begins by declaring it hardly conceivable how the first condition could be conceded, " for Paternus was bound before death to profess the true faith and recant the errors he had taught, otherwise as one not properly disposed he could not be admitted to the grace of baptism. Besides every true believer is bound to profess his faith, no matter what injury may confront him, whenever the glory of God and the salvation of his neighbours demand this, and in the given circumstances, the glory of God and the salvation of his neighbours did alike demand a public profession from Paternus as tending towards the extirpation of the errors he had been teaching." At this point our moralist breaks abruptly away from this prelude of rigorism, couching the remainder of his utterances in a very different tone. "Should, however," are his words, "despite every possible effort, Paternus prove incapable of being persuaded [to waive his conditions], as a last resource, he might be induced to attest before several witnesses that he professed and wished to die in the Catholic religion, or he might at all events affirm that he had entrusted some secret of great moment to the priest, to be declared after his death. In this manner he might satisfy his obligations. *A fortiori* this transaction would be feasible, should Paternus be not a clergyman, but a simple heretic. But," adds the cautious Gury, " it would be prudent in the priest not at once to manifest the entire obligation, but first to declare only the lighter portion, so that this having been accepted the penitent might be led on to the greater."

There, remains, however, the condition as to postponement of a public declaration, in the event of recovery, until such time when the convert may consider himself secured against all risk to his worldly interests; and to this condition Gury distinctly asserts there can be no objection, provided a fairly serious motive can be adduced. "for it is lawful to dissemble the true faith for a while in consideration of very *severe inconveniences* that might accrue from public profession."* The only limitation on this indulgence, which Gury considers proper, is that a clergyman, after clandestine profession of the Catholic faith, should avoid the direct performance of any sacerdotal offices connected with the service of his secretly disowned Church. With this single exception, we are unable to gather from Gury (and he cites in concurrence two great luminaries of Jesuit doctrine, Elbel and Tamburini), that there can be any material obstacle, should some motive of expediency recommend the proceeding, against a convert being admitted to embrace the Roman Catholic faith in strict secrecy, and being afterwards allowed for an unlimited period to go about the world, carefully concealing from its sight the fact of his profession. It is true that the grant of indulgence seems limited to cases where specially serious consequences would be entailed on immediate public profession. But to any one familiar with Gury's terms this qualifying limitation reduces itself to nothing, as it is dependent on no other standard than the stubborn insistance of the neophyte himself to exact the concession, and the

* "Conditio altera Paterno concedi potuit urgente gravi ratione quia licet veram fidem ad tempus dissimulare ob maxima incommoda quæ ex professione publicâ sequerentur."—'Casus Conscientiæ,' p. 61.

appreciation of the priest as to which is worth more to the
Church—the proffered accession of a particular neophyte
on his own terms, or the stern enforcement of a rigid principle.*

* There is curious record of one supposed instance of clandestine conversion,
which if authentic would exactly illustrate the case put hypothetically by
Gury. In the latter part of the last and the first quarter of the present
century, there existed in Germany a Protestant divine, by name John
August Stark, who acquired great reputation by his writings and his preaching.
Stark was born in 1741 at Schwerin. His talent having been early recognized,
he came to be thrown into various relations of life, which ensured connec-
tions in divers countries. After filling some subordinate posts—amongst
others that of Conrector at Wismar—he resided for some years in St. Petersburgh
as tutor in a nobleman's family. He then visited England and France, after
which for a considerable period he occupied the pulpit in the principal
church in the University of Königsberg, until in 1781 his fame obtained for
him nomination as Court preacher and Councillor in the Consistory at
Darmstadt. These offices he held till his death in 1816. But though the
continued object of Court favour—for instance, Stark was ennobled—his conduct was not a little canvassed. Stark was a voluminous writer on questions
connected with religion. At this period there existed, principally at Berlin,
a knot of men, amongst whom Nicolai was conspicuous, who were distinguished for morbid perception everywhere of an organized Jesuit conspiracy.
They were popularly known as the "*Jesuitenriecher*." By them Stark was
denounced openly as a Crypto Jesuit. An action for libel which Stark
threatened to bring in the Berlin Courts came to nothing, and the charge
was therefore neither withdrawn nor disproved. On the contrary, new fuel
was heaped on the flame of controversy by the discovery that Stark was the
author of an anonymous publication, entitled the 'Symposium of Theodul,'
which had a decidedly Catholic tone. Nevertheless Stark retained his preferment at Darmstadt till his demise, when, it is affirmed, that on his death-
bed he declared himself not merely a Catholic, but a formally-received member
of the Church since many years. A story of this nature can be accepted only
with much caution. The utterances of heated partisans like Nicolai and
associates could never be deemed of sufficient authority to accredit it. That
a posthumous book of Stark's undoubted authorship—a continuation of the
beforementioned 'Symposium'—plainly defends Catholicism is a fact. It is
also indisputable that on his demise, amongst persons not liable to the
imputation of foolish credulity, it was believed that evidence had come to
light of Stark's having been in long standing connection with the Church of
Rome. The matter was indeed sought to be hushed up, but its recollection
did not pass away from the memory of those who then lived in Darmstadt.
Nor has the story been left unnoticed by writers of a serious stamp. The
grave character of Herzog's 'Realencyklopädie der Theologie' is too well
known to need testimony. In the notice of Stark occurs this explicit state-

ment authenticated by the name of the contributor—H. Mallet. "When he died in 1816, there was found in his house a room completely arranged for performance of mass, and in accordance with his direction he was buried in the consecrated earth of the Catholic churchyard in frock and tonsure (in Kutte und Tonsur). It is said he had declared his conversion already during his Paris stay of 1766 in the church of Saint-Sulpice, though, according to others, this happened later at Dresden." So far the writer in Herzog's 'Cyclopædia.' That, however, does not exhaust the evidence in regard to Stark's clandestine conversion. In the 'Biographie Universelle' (Michaud, Paris, 1825), there is a notice of Stark which is very remarkable for the precise and detailed statements in regard to the circumstances attending his conversion which are given by the writer. This was Picot, and it is well to add that he wrote with a manifestly strong Catholic bias; he deplores more than once that Stark should have seen cause to conceal his convictions. "His design," Picot says, "at first was to go to Rome, where he had got into relations with Cardinal Castelli, Prefect of Propaganda; but the Marquis de Bausset, Ambassador of France in Russia, persuaded him to go in preference to Paris, where he would find more assistance for devoting himself to study. This envoy gave him letters of recommendation to the Bishop of Orleans, M. de Jarente, his kinsman, who disposed over royal patronage; to the Abbé de Bausset, the Agent of the Clergy, and soon after Bishop of Frejus, and to the Abbé Barthélemy. Stark reached Paris in October, 1765, and after proper instruction and preparation he pronounced his abjuration on February 8, 1766, in the church of Saint-Sulpice. This is what is shown by a register of abjurations received in Saint-Sulpice from 1686 to 1791—a manuscript register still preserved, and which we have had under our eyes. The deed of abjuration, besides the signature of Stark, has those of the Abbé Joubert of Saint-Sulpice, of the Abbé Bausset, and of the Abbé Chazal de la Morandie, Vicar. In addition we have seen a Mémoire, written by the hand of the Abbé Joubert, which made express mention of this abjuration. Stark became closely allied with this ecclesiastic, who, himself a learned Orientalist, took a keen interest in the young stranger, and seems to have directed his instruction. The Abbé Joubert drew up a Mémoire, in which he petitioned for a place for Stark, laying stress on his knowledge—on the sacrifices exacted by his decision—and on the advantageous proposals which were then being made to him, even from Germany and Russia. . . These steps were unsuccessful, and Stark, still insufficiently confirmed in the faith, pressed by relatives and friends—driven perhaps by want—returned to Germany and took up again the practice of the Protestant religion. His abjuration in Paris had been secret and remained always unknown to his enemies, who would not have failed to reproach him with it in their numerous writings against his person or his works; but the fact is incontestable; the Mémoire of the Abbé Joubert is still in existence and leaves no doubt whatever." Nothing can be more explicit than these very circumstantial allegations, which it seems impossible to dismiss as unworthy of credit, except on the assumption that Picot was a deliberate concoctor of impostures.

CHAPTER XIX.

Justification of Means by their End, third count in indictment against Jesuits—Has been affirmed by Jesuit divines of high authority at all times—Proofs of this—Busenbaum—Layman—Wagemann—Voit—Fathers Liberatore and Gury—Force of limitation contained in the term *media per se indifferentia*.

WE now come to the third great count in the indictment against the teaching of the Jesuits, namely, that they have affirmed the maxim of means being justified in virtue of the end to which they are applied. No charge has more powerfully tended to raise popular prejudice against the Jesuit Fathers. The champions of the Order have indignantly denied that this maxim has been broached. They challenge the quotations in support of this allegation, as marked with misprision or prompted by a spirit of misconstruction. It is essential in a review of Jesuit doctrine, however summary, to arrive at an understanding in reference to this point. We believe it to be demonstrable that the maxim has been broached by an unbroken chain of Jesuit divines of first-rank standing, from Busenbaum down to Gury and Liberatore. In substantiation of this allegation we submit a series of quotations from writers whose authority cannot be disowned by the Order.

The first is from Busenbaum (who may be called the Patriarch of the Maxim), whose 'Medulla' has gone through more than fifty editions, and, by its reprint not many years ago in Rome at the press of the 'Propaganda,'* can claim the continued and solemn approval of

---

* The plea that no responsibility is implied by permitting such reprint is confuted by the course adopted in another case. Emmanuel Sá, having given

the supreme authority of the Church. "Cum finis est licitus, etiam media sunt licita," are his words, and again, "Cui licitus est finis, etiam licent media" (pp. 320 and 504, ed. Francoforti, 1653). Amongst Jesuit luminaries of first magnitude ranks Layman, of whom Gury says, "Inter maximos theologiæ moralis doctores sine dubio referendus." In his 'Theologia Moralis' (Munich, 1625) we meet with the same proposition in almost the identical formula, "Cui concessus est finis, concessa etiam sunt media ad finem ordinata." In 1762 the Jesuit Wagemann, Professor of Morals at the University of Innspruck, published a Synopsis of Moral Theology, duly authenticated by official approbation, in which occurs this passage: "Is the intention of a good end rendered vicious by the choice of bad means? Not if the end itself be intended irrespective of the means," a proposition which he thus exemplifies: "Caius is minded to bestow alms, without at the time taking thought as to the means; subsequently, from avarice he elects to give them out of the proceeds of theft, which to that end he consequently commits;" and so Caius is declared entitled to the merits of charity though he has aggravated the offence of violence by the motive of avarice. Wagemann is not a doctor who deals in obscure words, for he says: "Finis determinat probitatem actûs," a definition of neat preciseness.

Our next extract is taken from the widely disseminated treatise on 'Moral Theology,' by Father Voit. He puts the following case:—"Arcadius kills Caius in some city where the law inflicts capital punishment on a murderer.

---

expression in his 'Aphorismi Confessariorum' to some opinions which in Rome were deemed objectionable, these had to be expunged in subsequent editions. Why has this not been done, at all events, in the recent editions of Busenbaum, issued as they are from the Propaganda press, if any portion of his doctrine had been taken exception to in Rome?

Arcadius is delivered up and condemned to death, but he escapes, forcibly breaking out of prison, though foreseeing that he may render his gaolers liable to grievous injury. The question is whether Arcadius, by escaping after sentence had been pronounced, has done wrong. My answer is in the negative. . . . Has Arcadius then done wrong by rupturing his chains and forcibly breaking out of prison? . . . He has done no wrong, *cui enim licet finis, ei et media permissa sunt.*"* The estimation in which Voit is held would be sufficiently evidenced by the fact of the edition we quote from being the twelfth; but there exist three other editions of modern date—one printed at Rome in 1838, another at Ancona in 1841, and the last at Würzburg in 1860. Indeed, the soundness of his language has received a crowning illustration in the fact that his formula and his exemplification have been adopted almost textually by the two most signally honoured modern luminaries of Jesuit teaching—Fathers Liberatore and Gury.

In an essay, originally inserted in what has been proclaimed by Pius IX. the special organ of true doctrine, the *Civiltà Cattolica*, Father Liberatore, after an elaborate argument in support of the indefeasible title of the Church to press into her service the agency of physical means, thinks to strengthen his position by the maxim "that from the obligation to attain an end arises the right to procure the means needful and useful for obtaining the same."† Finally, amongst Gury's hypothetical problems is one as to the justification for an individual guilty of a gross theft first to deny his guilt, and then, after condemnation, to escape from prison by violent means, such as perforating walls and

---

* 'Theologiæ Moralis a P. F. Voit, ed. duodecima, accurate emendata curâ et studio Domini M. Gauthier.' Parisiis, 1843, voL i. p. 99.
† 'La Chiesa e lo Stato,' 2nda Edizione, p. 185.

breaking open doors. By common consent it is declared, that before condemnation a guilty party is certainly entitled to escape, while, though there is controversy as to whether this is lawful after sentence, Gury adduces the opinion of "several" who hold it to be always lawful to break away from very stringent imprisonment, "*carcerem durissimum,*" on the ground "that it would be an act of heroism to undergo very severe punishment when it was possible to escape easily."

Be this as it may, of one thing Gury, however, speaks with confidence:—" In all cases where it is not unlawful for a guilty individual to escape, he does no wrong in breaking open doors and perforating a wall, *quia ubi licitus est finis, etiam licita sunt media per se indifferentia.*"* No doubt there appears here to be introduced a qualification through the introduction of the last term; but if the reader will accurately weigh its import, he will find the limitation involved in this term shrink into infinitesimal proportions. Unless we grievously misunderstand Father Gury, his test for the *indifference* of an act resides exclusively in the question, whether or not it must necessarily be wicked under all conceivable circumstances. For instance, an act of adultery could never be indifferent, though an act of stabbing can be so considered, inasmuch as the operation of plunging a knife into a living human body need not be, under all conditions, hurtful, but might possibly be beneficial, as in a case of surgery. This will become clearer when we come to what Father Gury says as to evil intentions not rendering wicked an indifferent act. Here we confine ourselves to the opinion—and we assure those who challenge our view that we have arrived at it not hastily—that, according to Father Gury's definition, the words "per

---

* Gury, 'Casus Conscientiæ,' p. 332.

se indifferentia" cannot be held to limit of themselves in any effective degree the licence involved in the other terms of the proposition. We submit, therefore, that the quotations given establish that the maxim of the end justifying means has been broached by a successive chain of eminent and approved Jesuit divines, and that the approbation of the said maxim has been continued to our day, as evidenced by the repeated recent issue, with authoritative sanction, of the works by former writers containing the doctrine in question, and the reiteration of the same by Fathers Liberatore and Gury.

CHAPTER XX.

Practical application of the foregoing cardinal principles—Two distinct groups of cases—Jesuit definition of Charity—On whom Acts of Charity are incumbent—In what cases, and to what extent, according to Gury—Evil intention does not make a deed wicked, though designed for compassing death—Reparation not obligatory on those by whose unjust deed harm has been wrought—Amazing exemplification—Extraordinary character of Jesuit maxims regarding Mine and Thine—The red thread running through all Jesuit doctrine—Absence of all test for grounds said to justify invasion of a neighbour's property—Communistic proposition—*Extreme* and *quasi* extreme necessity: what they are held to sanction—An imaginary case put—In extreme necessity all things become common.

HAVING satisfied ourselves as to the views held by those best entitled to represent the actual teaching of the Society in regard to these three main principles — Probabilism, Mental Reservation, and Justification of Means by the End —we proceed to some consideration of their attested application, as far as this can be gathered from positive rulings by the same high authorities. This inquiry falls aptly into two divisions, corresponding to the two groups into which cases arrange themselves naturally: one comprising the dealings between Man and Man which arise out of the relations of individual life, the other comprising points that touch the relations between Man as a Citizen and the Community as a State. We commence with the first category.

Amongst not a few Christians it has become an accredited notion that Charity is a virtue of capital merit; but if we accept Father Gury's ruling, we can hardly avoid looking upon it as a trivial, if not a downright silly practice. In

the section devoted to a definition of what is demanded by "Love of one's neighbour"* we find the following canon:—
"First Rule—Every one is bound *simply* and *absolutely* to love himself more than his neighbour, for the reason that every one stands nearer to himself than does any one else. Hence, love of oneself is by Christ laid down as the standard for love of a neighbour—*Love thy neighbour as thyself*. This, besides, is clear from the natural and insuperable disposition to love oneself more than one's neighbour; whence the common maxim—*Charity, well understood, begins at home*." In Montaigne or La Rochefoucauld such a sentence would have sounded not out of character, but in an approved 'Handbook of Morals,' it falls on us with a rather startling ring. Yet the terms are perfectly normal according to Jesuit theology. If we refer to Moullet we meet with these words: "In the order of *effective* charity, it is our duty to love ourselves more than a neighbour."†

To clear away all ambiguity, Father Gury explains that acts of charity are incumbent only on those who "are tolerably well off, and either the absolute lords or administrators of their properties;"‡ and that in cases of "ordinary necessity," the obligations of charity cannot involve more than certain assistance "out of superfluities, to the extent of some privation of pleasures."§ Even in cases of "ex-

* 'De Amore Proximi,' Gury, vol. i. p. 1319.

† Moullet, 'Comp. Theol. Mor.,' De Charitate erga Proximum, vol. i. p. 244. This is a maxim of old standing. Maldonatus ('Summula,' Coloniæ, 1605) already says, "Quod attinet ad affectum, nemo tenetur præcepto tanto affectu alios diligere, quanto se."

‡ "Quinam debeant, aut possint eleemosynam facere? Illi soli generatim qui sat commode vivunt, et sunt veri domini vel bonorum suorum administratores."—Gury, vol. i. p. 145.

§ On the same page (vol. i. p. 144) we have some curious calculations as to the proportion, not of gross income, but of what remains over outgoings—of loose pocket-money—that need be bestowed in alms to fulfil all ordinary obligations of charity. According to the opinion best entitled to acceptance

treme necessity . . . no one is bound to lay out any large sum of money for relieving a poor man from peril of death."* Only in cases of the gravest necessity does a call exist for some contribution "out of the strict necessaries for the donor's station," which are enumerated as comprising not merely "what is needful for the education of the family, but also the maintenance of servants, the reception of guests, the cost of fitting presents, and of customary entertainments." † It seems to us that in virtue of this definition of "necessaries," any one disinclined to charity might escape its calls on the plea of impecuniosity, while this had been artfully incurred by deliberately wasteful expenditure on lavish feastings, with the express view of securing a plea, which would be held valid by a Jesuit confessor, for shirking an irksome obligation. For Father Gury lays it down distinctly, that no evil intention can render wicked any deed which in itself must not by nature be necessarily evil ‡—a proposition illustrated by various remarkable exemplifications. A judge is declared free from blame who may have condemned a murderer to death, though he was actuated in pronouncing the sentence by personal hatred, because the sentence was within his legal attributes. The same rule is held to apply to a landowner, who, with the deliberate intention of injuring his neighbour, diverts a stream into a particular channel, if only he can allege that in its old

one-fiftieth is said to be ample, and even this proportion need not be so expended where the superfluous sum is very large. Some doctors, indeed, he adds, as, for instance, Concina, characterised as "sententiarum rigidarum fautor" (vol. ii. p. 631), are disposed to claim for the poor a twentieth, and even possibly a tenth.

* "In necessitate gravi vel extremâ . . . nemo tamen tenetur magnam pecuniæ summam erogare ad pauperem a periculo mortis liberandum."—Gury, vol. i. p. 144.

† See various definitions, Gury, vol. i. p. 144.

‡ "Ad injuriam non sufficit mala intentio." Gury, vol. i. p. 405. See also p. 366.

course it had caused some annoyance to himself, as he would be merely availing himself of a faculty within his strict right.

Father Gury does not shrink from extending justifications under this head even to acts designed with the view of compassing death. "An individual sets poison or a snare in a locality where his enemy, though very rarely, passes, with the express intention that he might perish if he should chance to come by. A physician applies the degree of attention he is bound strictly by his calling to exercise, but out of hatred is resolved to apply none beyond, in order that the patient's death might ensue." Gury asks whether these men should be held guilty of having wrongfully caused death, if this actually came about from circumstances prepared with so much deliberation. His answer is, that according to the *more accredited* opinion they should be held exempt from guilt, "because, on the one hand, the external act is not unjust, inasmuch as, in human dealings, the mere possibility of another man's injury has not to be taken into account, and on the other hand an internal act is not rendered unjust in virtue of intention, for intention has influence neither for the efficacy of a cause, nor for peril of injury. Consequently, the result must be said to have happened by mere accident, and of this an evil intention does not change the nature."* No one who has thoroughly drunk in the essence of Father Gury's teaching—and it cannot be too often repeated that his teaching is now systematically administered in most Roman Catholic seminaries—need ever be disturbed in his conscience as to any moral liabilities being consequent on intentions, however wicked, if these have only been artfully connected with agencies of which,

---

* See for all this Gury, vol. i. pp. 366-7.

by some ingenuity, it could be plausibly pleaded that in some conceivable contingencies they might prove harmless.

It must be admitted that Gury is elaborately precise when dealing with points of conscience that arise out of transactions which, to unsophisticated minds, seem acts of fraud or theft. It may perhaps cause surprise to hear it gravely questioned, in a Handbook of Moral Duties, whether "you are bound to make any reparation for the harm that has befallen another in consequence of your unjust deed, as for instance, if the theft were imputed to him of that which you yourself had stolen." Father Gury will not even admit the possible probability of this notion, and he gives three grounds, respectively *probable*, more *probable*, and *certain*, against such obligation, "even though you should have expressly striven to get your own action imputed to him;" the basis of his argumentation being laid in a casuistic distinction between what is accidental and what is inherent, and in the assumed inefficacy of evil intention to render evil any action of which the possible indifference can be pleaded.* Astounding as this may sound, the following exemplification of what roguery may perpetrate, with every security against disturbance of conscience, will probably seem yet stranger. "Quirinus, with the intention to steal a piece of cloth, breaks into a shop at night and lights a candle, taking due precaution to guard against the danger of fire; but, by some sudden chance, for instance the leap of a cat, the candle is pitched into the straw; quickly the whole shop is

* Gury, vol. i. p. 404, Resp. 2 and 3 ad Quæst. 13. "An tenearis reparare damnum alicui obveniens occasione injustæ tuæ actionis, v. gr. si furatus fueris et furtum ipsi imputetur. . . . Imo probabiliter etiam negandum est, *licet de industriâ egeris*, ut actio tua ipsi imputetur, quia semper hæc actio est tantum causa damni *per accidens* et non *per se;* non enim in illud ex naturâ suâ efficaciter influxit. Prava enim intentio non efficit ut injustum sit illud opus, quod ex se respectu tertii injustum non est."

in flames, and the thief taking flight only just gets off safe. What about Quirinus? Why *he is liable for nothing*, inasmuch as he never contemplated the danger. He is certainly not liable for the cloth it was his intention to steal, even though he had laid his hand on it, for its destruction also is involuntary; neither is the seizing of the cloth the cause of the injury, nor did the carrying of the candle create the immediate peril of conflagration, sufficient care having been employed." * The necessary conclusion from this exemplification is, that should some one have broken into a dwelling, with deliberate intentions of burglary, and should he have become the direct agent of an occurrence which but for his unlawful presence at that very time never could have happened, involving intensely aggravated injury to the already wronged owner of the invaded dwelling, nevertheless this burglarious individual would be entitled to dismiss from his conscience all idea of his being under obligations of reparation (provided he himself has also lost the goods on which he had laid burglarious hands)—as regards the consumed dwelling, because his instrumentality has been unpremeditated,—as regards the purloined articles, because they had subsequently slipped out of his hold.

The whole theory which is propounded by our Jesuit divine, in regard to the laws that should regulate distinctions between Mine and Thine, departs so widely from what are generally held to be fundamental principles, that we must say a few more words on a matter so intimately affecting the capital relations of society. Although we were told that not even the direst distress could establish an obligation to make any such disbursement in charitable relief as would encroach on our comforts, we learn that not merely a sense of pinching necessity, but the bare apprehension of its

* See Second Case. Gury, vol. i. p. 406.

imminence would entitle an individual to help himself out of his neighbour's property. Here again we encounter that capital feature which, like a red thread, runs through the whole system of Jesuit doctrine, providing the unfailing sanction for laxness in the application of principles—namely, the unlimited discretion accorded to the individual in assertion of justificatory pleas. Just as for the probability of opinions and the invincibility of ignorance, so also the determining test for the plea authorising an invasion of other people's property rests wholly on the *ipse dixit* of the party interested in exemption from established law; for who can verify the existence of an inward apprehension as to necessity being *imminent?* All that is wanted in the eyes of Gury is, that a person should vehemently affirm his having been prompted by some inscrutable dread of threatened distress. Of necessity itself, however, a definition is given. It is of three degrees: "ordinary, in which pauper mendicants as a rule find themselves;" "grave, in which life is kept up with great labour;" and "extreme, in which life itself is in risk." An individual in this last plight is pronounced to be entitled "to make use of as much of another person's property as may suffice for relieving himself from the said necessity, on the ground that *division of goods, however it may have been made, never can derogate from the natural right appertaining to every one to provide for himself, when suffering from extreme necessity. In such circumstances all things therefore become common, so that any one receiving another person's property for his own succour receives a truly common thing which he converts into his own, just as if this were happening before the division of goods. Consequently, he commits no theft.*" * The allegation often heard in Germany that the strength of the Communistic movement lies there amidst a

* For all this see Gury, vol. i. pp. 371-5.

population prone to priestly influences, will hardly lose in weight when we find propositions enunciated by such high ecclesiastical authority, that embody maxims of the rankest Communism.

Even this does not exhaust the pleas advanced by Gury in justification of proceedings which unskilled Christians would consider acts of reprehensible violence. "All that has been said about *extreme* necessity," says Gury, "is also applicable to *quasi* extreme or very grave necessity, such being deemed to have occurred when there is *probable* peril of incurring death, or of losing an important limb, or of lasting imprisonment, or of *undergoing the penalty of the hulks (pœnam triremium)*, or very serious or enduring illness."* Let it be noted that in the schedule of justificatory circumstances, no qualifying term makes the application in reference to the hulks dependent on the justice or injustice of the sentence. In foreign countries condemnation to the hulks — technically termed the *Bagnes* — has been freely awarded to those considered dangerous revolutionists. We need only call to mind the Neapolitan Liberals of 1848 — Poerio and his comrades, who for so many years had to drag the galley slaves' chains. Again, recently, we have seen deported first to the *Bagnes* on the French coast, and then to penal settlements, large convoys of so-called Communard prisoners as men too dangerous for society to tolerate. We should like to have it from the lips of a skilled Jesuit Father, how he would have borne himself in the following case. We assume our Father to have been Almoner in the prison of Poerio or of Rochefort, and that it had come to his knowledge that either was planning evasion, and cunningly contriving to procure through robbery the means for seducing the gaolers, so as to effect his escape from that convict

* Gury, Resol. iv. p. 375.

condition which is affirmed by Father Gury to constitute the kind of necessity which justifies recourse to such practices. Would the Father Almoner have spoken words of encouragement to the plotting prisoners as engaged on a meritorious enterprise, or would he have informed the governor of the intended evasion, and if so, on what ground would he have justified that proceeding in the face of maxims confirmed by the highest authorities of the Church, through the sanction accorded to Gury's book? Father Gury himself candidly admits that what is lawful to the principal is lawful to an accomplice, so that a friend breaking into a bank, to procure the money for facilitating the escape of a confederate out of the *Bagne*, would be simply "showing that he loved his neighbour as himself."* Lest the reader should fancy that these rather startling propositions flow from a train of thought peculiar to Gury, we subjoin a kindred passage on the same subject from that other eminent teacher, Father Moullet: "Whoever, in extreme necessity, takes another person's property for the needful sustenance of his own life or that of his belongings, does not commit theft. For in that condition, *all things become common*, especially as *to enjoyment*." †

* Gury, vol. i. p. 375.   † Moullet. Comp. Pars 1, p. 274.

CHAPTER XXI.

Case of Jean d'Albe in the 'Provinciales': fully approved by Gury—Servants entitled to recoup themselves for over-work by clandestine compensation, which means robbing their employers—Gury's difficulty in fixing a figure up to which abstractions are merely venial offences—Provides a sliding-scale—Nice question in connection with this—Gury's thoughtfulness in devising exculpatory pleas—Case of woman robbing her second husband for benefit of son by first marriage—Every one justified in helping himself to his rights if recourse to legal means involves scandal or expense—The secreting of assets by insolvent—Informal death-bed gifts—Pope's right to alter their destination—Stories of pressure on dying persons to make bequests on Church—System of simulated donations sanctioned by Gury.

Those familiar with the 'Provincial Letters' will remember the story of Jean d'Albe, serving-man in the Jesuit College, who, having robbed his masters, pleaded that he had only practised the doctrine he had heard them broach, as, under the conviction that he had been made to work in excess of what he was paid for, he had simply helped himself to what he was convinced to be his due. This story, which reads like a squib of Pascal's invention, would be strictly in harmony with Gury's doctrine. "Can servants," is his query, "who are of opinion that their wages are inferior to the work done by them, make use of *clandestine* compensation?"— *occulta compensatio*, which is defined as consisting "in the recovery of what is due by invasion of another person's property."* The Father replies that, speaking generally, such a proceeding cannot be approved; but, he adds quickly, "I say, *speaking generally*, for not a few make exceptions," which he enumerates; amongst them being the case of

* " Recuperatio debiti per rei alienæ invasionem." Gury, vol. I. p. 376.

servants who have contracted for inadequate wages, under physical constraint or moral fear or the strain of necessity, or who are conscious of being overweighted with labour; all such being declared entitled to help themselves to what they deem their rightful due, for, says the Divine law, "the labourer is worthy of his hire."*

With perfect consistency, the lawfulness of this operation is extended to all cases in which any wrong charge has been made. Should a judge, by error of judgment, sentence a man to payment of moneys never received or already paid, the suffering party would be justified, says Gury, in recouping himself by an exercise of *clandestine compensation*, though we are puzzled to understand against whom in particular the letter of licence is to hold good, if no moneys had been received.* Is there to be a right of general raid on society? It is, however, right to note how our Jesuit is at pains to impress that appropriations of other people's property are not tolerated to an indefinite extent. Father Gury admits the difficulty in fixing a figure, which could be a hard-and-fast point to mark off in all cases grave from trivial thefts, but he gives the best sliding-scale he has been able to calculate, according to the rank in fortune of the parties mulcted, for distinguishing between the two degrees of offence, and the figures range from one to twelve francs.† In connection with this tabular estimate, there arises, however, a very nice question: how far can a person consummating thefts, that amount in the aggregate to what is "grave," still permanently enjoy the privileges of merely "venial" offence, by guardedly apportioning the heavy total into successive pilferings, each kept within the limit of triviality? If practised on the same party, Father Gury is clear that these acts must

---

* See Gury, vol. i. p. 378. Quæst. 4. This opinion is given as *general*.
† Gury, vol. i. p. 369. 'De Naturâ Furti.'

roll up into "gravity;" and he is disposed to think this might also happen though several persons were victimised, unless an adequate interval were allowed to elapse between each act of pilfering. What period must elapse for a protection against this inconvenient aggregation of peccadilloes, has been matter of not little controversy, but Gury considers *two* months amply sufficient, " even though the matter might verge on something grave." *

The Father's thoughtfulness in devising exculpatory pleas for thieves extends even to unnatural complications. He discusses the case of a son who has robbed his father of eight francs at one time, and then of ten francs on successive occasions, pronouncing him not guilty of a grave offence, because as regards the first theft, "according to general opinion, a grave matter for the son of a well-to-do family should amount to at least ten francs;" and as regards the second, " because if about ten francs are needed, though the money be taken at one time, the value of fifteen francs will be necessary in thefts that are in driblets." Gury also puts the case of a woman, with a son by her first marriage, for whose benefit she robs the second husband (on whom this son can have no claim), and this proceeding Gury is prepared to justify, if only the wife be moderate in her abstractions, and will profess an inward disposition at some future time to make them good. It follows † that " he who has caused grave injury through various deliberately perpetrated venial offences," is held free from all obligation to make good that injury "in the total," if he has been only shrewd enough to scatter the injury over various victims; or, in the case of its perpetration on one, if he has been careful to leave the proper interval

---

* Gury, vol. i. p. 371.

† See Gury, 'Casus Conscientiæ,' 'De Furtis Filiorum et De Furti Uxorum' (the particular case is headed ' *Uxor Provida*'), pp. 172–3.

between the stages of the operation,* while an incendiary who has burned down a stranger's house, in the mistaken belief that it belonged to one he hated, is free from obligations of compensation "because such action was unintentional towards the sufferer." † Can it then create surprise to hear it emphatically affirmed, that everyone is justified in helping himself to what he considers his rights, rather than have recourse to legal procedure, whenever this might be attended with difficulties, or the prospect of scandal, or even merely heavy cost?‡

Maxims of this nature must gravely modify the best established rules of life. An insolvent, who secretes any portion of his assets, is, by civil law, deemed guilty of fraud. Father Gury holds it distinctly lawful for an insolvent to guard himself from "great poverty"—manifestly something short of "*extreme* necessity"—by clandestine abstraction of such an amount of property as he may deem needful for his maintenance, the fact of such "great poverty" being, as usual, determined by the insolvent himself.§ The same process of abstraction is likewise held justifiable in the case of one satisfied in his own mind of a legacy having been mentally intended for him, but which has not been bequeathed in a due legal conveyance.

Informal deathbed gifts—*donatio manualis ab ægroto facta* —are also declared strictly valid, as are likewise "testamentary deeds, in favour of pious bequests, though defective in legal form," while absolute power is allowed to the Pope to alter at discretion the special application of such last

---

* Gury, vol. i. p. 402. † Idem.
‡ Id. vol. i. p. 378. "An graviter, et contra justitiam peccet qui se compensat, quin prius ad judicem recurrere possit? Nullo modo peccat, si valde difficilis sit recursus ad judicem, ob scandali periculum, sumptus extraordinarios, etc.; quia tunc recursus est moraliter impossibilis."
§ Id. vol. i. p. 471. ' De Obligatione Contractus.'

wishes.* Indeed it would appear that every priest is empowered to divert at discretion the application of a pious legacy. Gury puts the case of an individual who bequeathed a sum for endowing with a wedding portion some orphan girl to be designated by the parish priest. The latter sees fit to select a girl who is not an orphan, no ground except his pleasure being assigned for this manifest departure from an explicit condition, and yet the priest is summarily declared liable to no blame. Elsewhere Gury, in concurrence with St. Liguori, pronounces "a donation affirmed by oath, but not yet accepted, to have no binding force." † It will be observed here that the repudiation is general, so that it would appear to be inculcated that, whereas a sacred obligation of fulfilment does attach to any verbal instruction, however informal, perhaps whispered unintelligibly into the single ear of an interested party by a dying person only half conscious, whenever a so-called pious foundation is the object to be benefited, yet no obligation is held to attach to the fulfilment of informal donations for other objects, even though the intention to make them had been affirmed by a solemn oath.‡ Many unfounded stories have been afloat as to priestly pressure exercised on dying persons to extract bequests in favour of the Church. Nothing can be better calculated to confirm popular prejudice on this head than to find such propositions sustained as sacrosanct maxims by the most

---

* See for all this, Gury, vol. i. pp. 486, 494, and 496. The reason alleged in the first line as decisive of the validity of informal pious bequests is that, being a matter touching the Church, it is wholly beyond the pale of the civil power: "Piæ causæ ad Ecclesiam pertinent, ejusque subjacent jurisdictioni, porro Ecclesia *libera et immunis est a potestate civili in omnibus quæ jurisdictioni suæ directe subsunt*," p. 485.

† Gury, vol. i. p. 483.

‡ "An valeant in foro conscientiæ testamenta *ad causas profanas* formis legalibus destituta? . . . 2ᵈᵃ Sententia docet ex lege positivâ prorsus irritari." —Gury, vol. i. p. 485.

accredited organs of Church doctrine. In France a system of clandestine trusts and fictitious bequeathals has notoriously contrived to counteract the action of the law for preventing the growth of corporate properties. This practice is explicitly sanctioned by Gury, without the least attempt at reserve, in the following proposition: " Are clandestine trusts for pious causes valid, *in foro conscientiæ*, when made in the guise of *simulated donation* or of *fictitious testament*, or of legacy to some individual?" * Can there be a more open approval of a contrivance deliberately devised for driving a hole through a statute?

* Gury, vol. i. p. 498.

CHAPTER XXII.

Gury's maxims approve transactions ordinarily deemed immoral—Hush-money—Its extortion under false pretences—Bribery—Conditions under which it is practically sanctioned—Jesuit views on Courts of Justice—Judges can accept money if taken after delivery of sentence contrary to justice—Obligations to make restitution declared void by Physical or Moral inability—Latter defined as synonymous with grave inconvenience to the party in question—Illustrated by instance of a nobleman forced to reduce his establishment—The integrity required from witnesses—Cases in which the reproduction of documentary evidence would be excusable—Illustration how this maxim might have operated in a notorious suit—Bearing maxims of this kind may seem to have on the charge that Jesuits have not been foreign to forgeries—Relations between the sexes—Plighted troth may be broken for a fat inheritance—Seduction under promise of marriage involves no necessary obligation to wed—Exposure of offspring—Should wealthy parents, dropping their children at Foundling Institutions, make any payment?—Witchcraft—Black Art—Love philters—Sortilege.

BEYOND doubt the teachings of Gury's schools furnish ready justification for transactions which, by the light of ordinary insight, would be instinctively pronounced immoral. As an instance, let the following conclusion serve: "If you threaten an individual caught in the act of theft, that you will hand him over to the injured owner or the jailor or the judge, unless he promises you a particular sum, *the promise holds good, and you are not bound to return the received sum,* unless, perchance, in the opinion of a man of judgment (*viri prudentis*) it should seem excessive. This holds true, even though *you never meant to hand over* but merely to *frighten the individual, because you would be waiving spontaneously the power to do something which can be taxed in money value.*"*

* Gury, vol. i. p. 468.

Here we have an approval, in one breath, of hush-money and of its extortion under false pretences. Bribery is near akin to extortion, and Father Gury quite naively admits himself at a loss to know why so natural a proceeding should be stigmatised. "Can a price be lawfully accepted for a matter of duty, not indeed on the score of justice, but of some other virtue; for instance, if you were to take money for observing your fast in Lent?" and the conclusion is, that the money can be rightfully taken, "it being considered as a strictly gratuitous gift, bestowed out of sheer generosity."[*] Accordingly, it is quite lawful to accept money for the performance of a prescribed duty, only the person receiving such reward must plead that the prospect thereof was not his direct motive for acting up to his duty. It would be unfair, however, to conceal that the lawfulness of such acceptances is nicely limited to cases in which the service rewarded is of a kind "that can be taxed in money." For instance, any one would be bound to make restitution "who exacted money for showing the road to a passer-by, *if this could be done without trouble or loss of time*, as he would be bound to this act of love, and such action could not be taxed." It is well to note the qualification smuggled in by the words put by us in italics, for it ensures the plea for payments otherwise disallowed.

We are told, also, it is by no means decided that a judge is bound never to accept money gifts from a party to a suit before him. If the gift were proffered with the view of influencing a prospective judgment, contrary to justice, the judge should, indeed, sternly refuse acceptance; "but the sentence having been already pronounced, it is matter of controversy" whether he may not retain what might then seem a mere offering of gratitude from one benefited by

[*] Gury, vol. i. p. 454.

the delivered sentence, *even when this had been contrary to justice.** Decisions of this character subvert fundamental notions as to right and wrong. Let us take the case of a person knowing all about a theft, and accepting hush-money from the guilty party. According to received ideas, the compact would be criminal. Father Gury, however, decides that, provided the person bribed be not *ex officio* bound to give information, the bargain would be quite lawful, " as without injustice he might keep silence about the thief, in deference to his entreaties . . . therefore, *e pari*, without injustice, silence might be observed in deference to gifts given or promised."† The problems raised by such maxims strike at the whole order of our ideas. Some are of a nature that will not bear discussion here, and we can but glance at one important subject in a note.‡

Two grounds are distinctly recognised as valid pleas of excuse from restitution, " Physical disability . . . and *Moral inability*, or serious difficulty, in making restitution; that is, if restitution be inseparable from grave inconvenience to the debtor, for instance, that through making restitution he should be notably reduced in his fairly acquired station or

---

* Gury, vol. ii. p. 8. ' De Obligationibus Judicum.' † Idem, vol. i. p. 418.

‡ A "contractus turpis" being an immoral bargain (as for murder or prostitution), Gury is distinct that viewed prospectively it never can be justified. It is by its essence null, and any benefit received in consideration of future execution must be returned. But how about a benefit received after execution? Will it be impossible to retain it? Here comes in the side plea already dwelt upon. Besides the capital subject matter, other matters may be collaterally involved in the execution of the bargain as labour, risk, &c., which being in themselves legitimate, are assessable in money, so that after execution a gratuity can be accepted if taken as in remuneration of these secondary elements. A woman may not take money for her honour, but for risk or personal inconvenience, or loss of position, " An semper restituenda sit res ex turpi contractu accepta? Ante positionem operis turpis, affirm. Post operis positionem acriter controv. . . Quia licet actio turpis, quasi illicita, nullo pretio digna sit, *pretium tamen quatenus laboriosa, ignominiosa, periculosa agenti, vel utilis alteri, meretur.*"—Gury, vol. i. pp. 455–6.

fall into serious need . . . for then there is a real impossibility to make restitution, *inasmuch as in morals that is termed impossible*, which is *very hard*, and which cannot be done properly and *becomingly*. Thus *if a nobleman cannot make restitution, without depriving himself of servants, horses, arms*, or a *leading citizen without embracing a mechanical art to which he is unused*, or *an artisan without selling the tools he lives by or encountering severe loss, then restitution may be postponed and obligations discharged by degrees*."* It is unnecessary to dwell on the undisguised laxness of a definition, which makes moral inability synonymous with a sensation of inconvenience, and excuses a man of rank and wealth from the discharge of admitted obligations every time he can allege that such discharge might cramp his means for providing an ample supply of "servants and horses."

The administration of justice demands integrity, not merely in judges, but also in witnesses. Let us see how our Jesuit Divines fashion their teaching on this head. The first point laid down is, that no obligation to make reparation can attach to any one who has given false witness from invincible ignorance, inadvertence, or delusion, a proposition which, though not wholly free from objections, need not be canvassed. But Father Gury proceeds to consider the case of one who, with the view of supplying deeds that have been lost, and of promoting the success of indisputable right (the indisputableness of such right being left to the subjective test of individual appreciation), either reproduces, that is, forges, or tampers with a writing, a chirograph, or a deed of acknowledgment; and he concludes that, though a person acting thus "would, indeed, sin venially on the score of a lie, the document produced not being the authentic one, on the strength of which judgment should rest; and

* Gury, vol. i. p. 431. 'De Causis a Restitutione Excusantibus.'

though he might possibly incur a grave sin against charity toward himself by exposing his person to imminent peril of very severe penalties in the likely event of detection; nevertheless, he would be wholly free from all sin against mutual justice, and would consequently stand absolved from all obligations to make restitution."*

An illustration, suggested by a memorable case not likely to fade from the memory of the living generation, will bring out better than much argument the consequences which might follow, if this ruling were to hold good. Amongst the numerous witnesses who spoke confidently to the identification of the Claimant as Roger Tichborne, it is undeniable that many spoke in unimpeachable good faith. It is well known that in the tangled web of the evidence in this suit a sealed document, which had been deposited by the genuine Tichborne with a particular person, constituted a capital incident. Let us now assume that in the belief of Roger's death the paper had been destroyed, but that the depositary was amongst those who had persuaded themselves as to the Claimant being the true man. In this state of mind he blames himself as having imperilled, by premature destruction of the document, a claim the justice of which has become to him a matter of firm belief. That he is a witness testifying under invincible ignorance is beyond dispute, for his faith in the Claimant is the result of thorough delusion. What would be more natural than that, with so earnest a conviction as to the justice of the cause advocated, he should be overcome with remorse at the injury he believes himself to have wrought, and a burning desire to do whatever may be in his power to make it good? And now let us further assume that this depositary had sat at the feet of Father Gury, that he had penetrated himself

* Gury, vol. ii. p. 21. 'De Obligationibus Testium.'

with his teaching, and that at this conjuncture of severe mental trouble there flashed back on him the recollection of this particular ruling. He then exclaims to himself, Here is a man striving to assert "undoubted right," in the chain of whose evidence one link is alone wanting, and that link is wanting solely in consequence of my own unwarrantable hastiness; I know the goodness of the case; I am deeply sensible of my obligation to promote "undoubted right;" and most happily my memory recals the exact tenour of the rashly destroyed document; for I have it under the hand of that superlative master in morals, Father Gury, that in such circumstances, to reproduce a document, and palm off a copy on the judge, is no sin of gravity, but at most an act of fibbing or of exposing myself lightly to the inconvenient penalties of the law; therefore I will reproduce the document, and so do the one thing needful to ensure the triumph of struggling and "undoubted right." On what ground, we ask, could any Jesuit divine hold that such an act under these circumstances would not be exempt from all serious blame? Critics of authority have brought charges of apocryphal compositions and tamperings with texts against scholars either themselves Jesuit Fathers or under the influence of Jesuit training, and the evidence, already not slight in support of such charges, cannot but gain in force when we find the most accredited spokesman of the Order propounding maxims that deliberately countenance recourse to fabrication and forgery.*

* Lest it should be thought we are too hard on Father Gury, we submit another of his rulings. A will written in the testator's own hand, so that no outside witness to its contents can be forthcoming, has been made in exclusive favour of Adrian, who is aware of the fact. Immediately after the testator's death there occurred this mishap. As the joyous heir was feasting his eyes on the document ensuring his possession of fortune over the heads of the natural heirs, an untoward gust of wind swept it into the fire, and the precious deed was burnt. "Adrian was on the point of going into sheer despair, when

It is not possible in a review of Jesuit doctrine to avoid glancing at the delicate topic of its maxims in reference to relations between the sexes. The specimens of distorted speculation already given will afford an idea of how unfit for reproduction must be the problems which the imagination of these doctors conjures up in regard to this slippery subject. A few examples, carefully picked, we must however give. In the matter of plighted troth we learn from Gury, " that he who has sworn to a girl rich and healthy .... is not bound by his oath should she happen to have become poor or fallen into bad health." * Again we are informed that a probable opinion, countenanced by St. Liguori, allows an engagement to be broken off if a " fat inheritance " † should accrue, seriously modifying the status as to fortune of either party, and the case is thus illustrated:—" Edmund had betrothed himself to Helen, a girl of the same station and fortune as his own. As he was on the very point of celebrating his wedding, he acquired a fat inheritance from a deceased uncle. Wherefore he repudiates Helen, that he may marry another with a fortune to match. *It seems that*

---

a wonderful idea struck his mind. Lo and behold, he imitates perfectly the writing and signature of the testator, and thus puts things back exactly as they were." The question is whether Adrian did wrong, and how far he might be bound in justice to make any reparation to the natural heirs who would have come into possession but for his having palmed off his own handiwork as the testator's deed. Gury holds Adrian guilty of nothing more serious than a lie, and even this is not so positive, but that it has been gravely disputed. The same uncertainty, in the opinion of divines, attaches as to whether Adrian may have done what amounts " to a mortal offence against legal justice " by fraudulently reproducing a document. But whatever may be the difference of opinion on these heads as to any supposed moral duty of making some restitution to the natural heirs who by his successful trick are left without anything, Gury is clear and distinct that it cannot exist, for by the original will Adrian had acquired " a certain strict right."—See Gury, 'Casus Conscientiæ,' Testamentum casu destructum et arte redivivum, p. 260.

* Gury, vol. i. p. 204.
† Id., vol. ii. p. 412. Si sponso adveniet pinguis hereditas.

Edmund should not be disturbed for this." * Jilting is no unfrequent practice, but it is striking to find it justified in a Handbook of Morals, whenever " faith could be kept only by the surrender of a big advantage which would be tantamount to great loss."

Will it surprise the reader, that a string of rulings can be adduced in support of the opinion, that seduction under express promise of marriage need not involve a moral obligation to observe this promise? Father Gury puts the problem plainly: " Is the ravisher bound to wed the girl he has ravished under promise of marriage?" and after having stated an opinion affirmative of such obligation, except in " that practically most frequent case where it might be feared marriage would lead to bad consequences," he developes another opinion " having the intrinsic signs of adequate probability" in denial of any such absolute obligation.† Father Moullet is no less explicit on this head. " Whoever has seduced a maiden or a widow, under promise of marriage, ought to wed her, *speaking per se*, whether the promise was made in earnest or was feigned." But, he adds, ". . . . I say, *speaking per se*, for the seducer is not bound to marry . . . when the girl might easily have perceived that there must be deception, as for instance, from great disparity of condition; *in such case she has to impute the deception to her own self*." ‡

Next to seduction under assurances, followed by desertion, the exposure of offspring would probably be deemed by the majority of unsophisticated persons as the most heartless offence that could well be committed; yet from language held by our divine we must conclude that he at all events does not consider the proceeding as one very difficult

---

* 'Casus Conscientiæ,' p. 595.   † Gury, vol. i. p. 438.
‡ Moullet. 'Comp. Mor. Theol.,' par. i. p. 342.

of palliation, or which should be stigmatized as an offence of the first magnitude. Without expending one word of reflection on the character of the transaction itself, Father Gury inquires whether it might not be incumbent on wealthy persons, who drop at Foundling Institutions their children, be they simply illegitimate or born of an adulterous connection, to make some payment, rather than abandon them to public charity. The point is declared to be full of perplexity. One opinion very commonly accepted is in the affirmative; but the contrary is maintained in an opinion countenanced by St. Liguori, and given in detail by Gury, on the ground that as these institutions are intended for the indiscriminate reception of the illegitimate progeny of all classes, in protection against infanticide, payment would be contrary to the principle of public charity on which they are founded. Nevertheless, our Father believes that, on the whole, rich parents might be encouraged to make some donations; but, in his tender care lest they should be over mulcted, he calculates that a payment of 150 to 200 francs is ample for the fulfilment of all moral obligations on the part of profligates, however opulent, who might think it convenient to get out of sight their illegitimate offspring by clandestinely depositing them in a Foundling Home.*

The last point we would notice, in this division of our inquiry, is the fact that belief is inculcated by our divines in the grossest superstitions that can affect the mind of man—in Witchcraft and the Black Art. "Magic is of two kinds," says Moullet,† "natural and *superstitious* (*superstitiosa*, the

---

* For this see Gury, vol. i. p. 441. He did not originate these views. Layman has the following: "Fas est filios illegitime natos interdum exponere, si ita necesse sit ad gravem infamiam vitandam, adhibitâ tamen cautione, ne frigore moriantur et ut prius baptizentur, appositâ sedulâ, *nec cum periculo infamiæ tenetur parens filium sic expositum sustentare.*" 'Theol. Mor. Comp.,' Mogunt. 1637.   † Moullet, pars prima, p. 198.

technical term for the black art), which is the art of doing wonders by help of the devil . . . involving express or tacit invocations." Gury's words are, "Magic is the art of doing wonders which . . . can be done only through the devil invoked explicitly or implicitly." And, again: " Witchcraft is the art of working harm through intervention of the devil; it is of two kinds, *amatory* and poisoning; amatory witchcraft, otherwise a philter, is a devilish art, whereby lustful passion or aversion is inspired towards a person."* According to grave Jesuit authorities, it is within the faculty of the devil, working through these arts, to assume the phantom appearance of humanity in lovely shape; so that an irresistible passion for the Evil Fiend himself, lurking mockingly behind the phantasmagoric mask of a beautiful being, is held up before the imagination of those who are disciples of this teaching as amongst the horrible consequences that may befal them from these devilish drugs. As for the second kind of witchcraft, this is what Gury says in definition of it,—" Poisoning witchcraft is precisely the art of doing injury to your neighbour in various modes through help of the devil, or by disease, the causing idiocy, &c. Commonly witchcraft is called *sortilege*, because by it an evil lot is thrown on those against whom vindictiveness is exercised, through the operation of the devil." Such is the teaching which, at the present period of the nineteenth century, with the express approval of those who from Rome govern the Latin Church, is being studiously infiltered into the minds of that preponderating majority amongst the Roman Catholic youth who are being trained under the influence of Jesuit tuition.

* Gury, vol. i. pp. 172-3. 'De Magia et Maleficio.'

CHAPTER XXIII.

A second group of cases relating to demarcation between civil and ecclesiastical jurisdictions—The *Civiltà Cattolica*—Terms of Apostolical Charter conferred on it—Three noticeable points in this document—Maxims on obedience due by subjects—Father Liberatore—Question whether the wording is not artfully framed to warrant constructions not apparent at first sight—The only test for the bearings of Jesuit maxims to be found in application to them of the canons of Probabilism—" *Is it lawful to slay a tyrant?*"—Distinction drawn between rights of Sovereigns *de facto* and *de jure*—Emphasized in that between those of Sovereign Pontiff and all Princes—Distinct claim for Church of direct supremacy in civil matters—According to Liberatore, the State is strictly subordinate—Specially in all touching on Charity, Justice, or Morals—The Church has right to cancel all temporal arrangements not to its mind—This a peremptory article no true Catholic can presume to question.

WE shall now touch shortly two or three points of primary importance in connection with the questions which we have marked off as constituting a second category, and which group themselves around the central problem—where the line between civil and ecclesiastical jurisdictions is to be fixed. Here other assistance must be called in beside our previous guides. What is required is some organ as well attested in regard to genuineness of inspiration as Gury, and directly discussing the practical problems involved in the demarcation between Church and State rights. We must be safe against the charge of having picked out an inadequately authenticated guide, if we turn for instruction as to what is taught by sound Jesuit doctrine on these topics to the pages of the 'Civiltà Cattolica,' stamped as it is with the highest voucher for its orthodoxy by a Pontifical Brief *ad hoc*. That Brief is a document of exceptional, we believe of unique character. In it Pius IX., speaking in his Pontifical capacity, adopts the typical phrase which the Society puts forward as its specific motto. Again, the document is not merely a testimonial, but an Apostolical Charter conferring privileges on a body of writers exclusively confined to the Society of Jesus, for the grant whereof there exists no precedent. "In order that there may be at all times appointed men," it is said in this remarkable Brief " . . . capable of fighting the good fight, and continually defending by their writings the Catholic cause and sound doctrine . . . we here desire that the Religious of the illustrious Society of Jesus should constitute a College of Writers, composed of members of the Society, who by seasonable and apt writings . . . should prove *champions of the Catholic faith, its doctrine, and its right*, with all their powers. The said Religious, most zealously seconding our desires with every possible care and study, already in 1850 undertook to write and publish a periodical entitled ' La Civiltà Cattolica.' Following in the footsteps of their predecessors, and sparing neither care nor labour, these men had nothing more at heart than, through this diligently and wisely edited periodical, in writings learned and profound, to shield and defend manfully the truth of our august faith, the supreme dignity, authority, power, and right of this Apostolical See, *and to teach and propagate the doctrine that is true* . . . Wherefore it is our most earnest desire that so sublime a work should for ever prove stable and flourish. *Ad Majorem Dei Gloriam*, the salvation of souls, and the daily greater promotion of the right method of studies. Accordingly by these letters in virtue of Apostolical authority *we erect in perpetuity this College of Writers of the Society of Jesus* of the periodical popularly termed the ' Civiltà Cattolica,' *to exist in a house set apart for themselves*, and constitute it according to the laws and privileges possessed and enjoyed by other Colleges of the said Society, *under the express condition, that this College shall in all things depend absolutely on the General.*" *

Three facts are noticeable in this document:—1. Throughout it, the cause of the Church as a teaching body is identified by its acknowledged Head with that of the 'Civiltà Cattolica.' 2. The Supreme Pontiff, exercising his ecclesiastical prerogative in the most solemn form, calls into existence as a champion of "true doctrine" a special corporation, which by Apostolical Charter is restricted to members of the Society of Jesus. 3. That corporation is constituted not for a term but in perpetuity; and is therefore proclaimed to be an organic institution of the Church. In presence of so superlative a warrant, we should be justified in quoting indiscriminately from the 'Civiltà Cattolica.' We confine ourselves, however, to the writings of one contributor, Father Liberatore, for two reasons; because he is avowedly held in the highest estimation at Rome, and because we have a reprint of the author's contributions, which combines the triple advantage of matured revision—of issue subsequent to the Vatican Council,—and of renewed high ecclesiastical approval affixed to this reissue.†

At first sight, no maxims could seem more conformable to the personal interests of those clothed with temporal sovereignty, as regards the obligation of subjects to yield absolute obedience under all circumstances, than those propounded by our Divines. "At no time can it be lawful to rebel," says Gury, and he stigmatises, in the words of St. Liguori, as most pernicious, Gerson's opinion "that a

---

* The Brief, dated February 12, 1866, will be found in the 'Civiltà Cattolica' of April 17 of that year.

† La Chiesa e lo Stato del P. Matteo Liberatore, D.C.D.G., Seconda Edizione corretta ed accresciuta. Napoli, 1872.

monarch might lawfully be judged by the whole nation, in the event of his ruling in violation of justice."* On scanning closely, however, the propositions in Gury which bear on the relations between princes and subjects, we cannot dismiss the impression, that the terms wherein they are stated do not exclude the possibility of extracting a plausible justification, not merely for occasional insurrection but even, under specific conditions, for making attempts on the lives of those in possession of sovereign power, under no better warrant than the intimated assent of whoever may be looked upon as the legitimate claimant. Once more we impress on the reader that, in deducing inferences from propositions in Jesuit writers, we advisedly proceed upon the principle, that the terms, to be appreciated at their value, must be tested by every sense they can be made to bear without a glaringly forced strain. For, according to the doctrine of Probabilism, any opinion, that can be brought into apparent conformity with terms employed by any single writer of authority, may be safely accepted and acted upon by an individual, even in opposition to the mind of his spiritual adviser. Therefore, when engaged in fathoming the scope of a proposition, we are bound always to note carefully every construction which the terms employed might be physically capable of being made to bear—a point ever present also to the minds of a school of doctors, than whom there have been no more consummate masters in the art of weighing expressions.

Accordingly, in scrutinizing these particular propositions, there appears to us to run through all the terms employed a latitude, difficult to consider accidental, which affords ground for such mental distinction between those in merely physical possession of, and those with legitimate ownership of a throne, and of all that is assumed to appertain thereto in the

* Gury, vol. i. p. 248.

nature of rights, as might furnish to any one in search thereof the justification for assuming, at a merely verbal intimation from him who is considered legitimate, a mission to slay the individual who is considered an intruder. "Is it lawful to slay a tyrant?" asks Gury; and no answer apparently could be more distinct, " certainly it is lawful to kill neither a tyrannical governor (*tyrannum regiminis*) . . . nor a legitimate prince tyrannically governing and oppressing a people. No more is it lawful to kill a tyrannical usurper, when once in possession . . . nor a tyrant not yet in *complete possession, otherwise than with the sanction of the legitimate prince.*" *
The point to note is the proviso for drawing a distinction between what is due to the actual ruler and to him who is considered the legitimate prince, though no definition is given as to a test for establishing legitimacy. The mere assent of the latter—independent of any judicial sentence— is declared sufficient to justify an attempt on the intruder's life, the apparent qualification as to his not having attained complete possession being reduced to something merely nominal, inasmuch as there is nothing in the terms of the proposition which makes it indispensable to bring in evidence of incomplete possession, more than that half-a-dozen individuals were still mentally withholding allegiance.

The positive distinction drawn between the degrees of right vested in sovereigns *de facto* and sovereigns *de jure* becomes enhanced and emphasized when the relative attributes of the Sovereign Pontiff and of all princes, however thoroughly *de jure*, are discussed. We venture to maintain that the language of the leading Jesuit Divines, on this particular matter, is such as not merely to leave an opening for, but to constrain the construction, that they claim for the Supreme Pontiff all the same superior prerogatives

* Gury, vol. i. p. 252.

over princes, though perfectly *de jure*, which they consider these to possess over rulers *de facto*. Therefore we are compelled to conclude that, in so far as the terminology and reasoning of these Jesuit Doctors can be taken as the authentic expression of doctrine accepted by the Church, an order from Rome to slay a ruler would, under particular circumstances, be one that a faithful member of the Church could execute with a clear conscience. It would be simply monstrous to insinuate the probability of any order of this nature emanating from Pius IX. Whatever may be the untoward acts to which passion can impel those who direct, or will direct, the Church of Rome, of this we may be confident, that the present conscience of the age is too keen to let a Pope, like his sainted predecessor Pius V., send an assassin on a mission for slaying a contumacious prince. But, notwithstanding a confident assurance of this kind, the employment, by leading modern Jesuit Doctors, of language which by fair construction does express an assertion in principle of acts of this nature, is a circumstance as noteworthy as it is characteristic of the present spirit of their doctrine. Passing on, however, from what we are readily disposed to consider a dead letter and mere anachronism, we come to matter of far more practical importance,—the distinct claim set up, on behalf of the Church, to such direct supremacy in matters appertaining to civil existence as would constitute, if carried into execution, a very material encroachment on what in every modern polity has become the recognised domain of the State.

"The State," declares Father Liberatore, "must understand itself to be a subordinate sovereignty, exercising ministerial functions under a superior sovereignty, and governing the people conformably to the will of that lord, to whom it is subject."* Who that lord may be we are left in no doubt.

* P. 11.

It is that Sovereign Pontiff, "the visible monarch" of "God's realm on earth," to whom "every baptized person is more strictly subject than to any temporal ruler whatever."* Still a division is recognised in the immeasurable labour that would be heaped on the shoulders of the Pontiff if he were himself to administer directly this universal empire; and the definition of such division gives us a statement in clear terms of what functional attributes it is conceded shall fall within the jurisdiction of the State. Its independence of action, we are told, is to be absolutely restricted to "matters directly relating to the mere physical well-being of material life (finance, the army, trade, domestic peace, and relations with other nations), but in no wise can it be that in matters directly concerning *charity, justice, morals,* the State should be otherwise than bound to conform to the rules dictated by the Church, while even in the matters before mentioned as being within its competency, the State would be under the negative obligation to do nothing hurtful to the morals of its subjects or the obedience due to God. For where the *contrary has happened, the Church has clearly the right to remedy and cancel* whatever may have been appointed wrongly and immorally *in the temporal order of things.*" † "Therefore the civil ruler of a Christian people must be in subordination to the Christian priesthood, *and especially to the Roman Pontiff.*"‡ And, again, "The temporal sword, symbol of civil authority, has to be subordinate to the spiritual sword, symbol of priestly authority;" § all which, we are told a few lines further on, "is a *peremptory sentence to be called in question by no one who would be a true Catholic.*"

* P. 39. † P. 14. ‡ P. 22. § P. 23.

CHAPTER XXIV.

The advent of Christianity has narrowed bounds of State authority—The title-deeds for perennial maintenance of Pope's temporal sovereignty—Church can over-ride civil tribunals, and direct the employment of armed forces—Dogmatic character of Bull *Unam Sanctam*—Liberatore's demonstration of this character—Peculiar importance attaching to such utterance from Liberatore—Array of guarantees for the authoritative value of his opinions—Functions of State reduced to a police force at the command of Church—Application of coercion—"*The best form of government*"—Toleration to exist only under pressure of prudence—Right residing in a State that has apostatized—Force of any instrument concluded with a State that is Catholic—Affirmed existence of a legitimate power independent of public depositary of force—No Concordat binds Church—Vicomte de Bonald—Brief of approbation from Pius IX.—Concordats mere Indulgences—Revocable by Pope at will.

HAVING been made acquainted with these indelible principles, on which no compromise can be tolerated, that are to fix the line between the provinces of ecclesiastical and temporal powers, we are treated to the following theorems in completer definition of the respective natures of these two entities. We have it stated as of positive certainty " that, through institution of the Church, society has been subjected *by divine law to the rule of a new supreme power, sacerdotal authority*, which *is utterly independent of State authority*," and that, " by the advent of Christianity, State authority has been confined within narrower bounds," [*] a thesis which will be self-evident only to minds not startled at hearing it also affirmed that our Saviour on no occasion manifested indifference to a temporal estate, and "that, in very truth, his kingdom is here below, and will abide unto the fulfilment of time ;"[†] novel dogmatic versions of Christian

---
[*] P. 82.   [†] P. 37.

facts, which, after having been uttered with the oracular curtness of an infallible illumination, are then presented by Father Liberatore as indefeasible title deeds for the perennial maintenance of the Pope's temporal sovereignty as absolutely essential to the observance of what constitutes the spirit of Christ's doctrine! If any doubt be yet entertained whether it can really enter into the conception of this accredited organ of the "true doctrine" to claim for the Church the right, whenever this may suit its pleasure, to interfere with, arrest, suspend, and annul the faculties of State authority, even in a matter so wholly outside all conceivable affinity to spiritual agencies as the mode and manner for employment of the armed force, we submit the following passage—not dovetailed by selection, but standing consecutively in the text as it does here—and to which can never be denied the merit of clear language:—" The Church is empowered to *amend and to cancel the civil laws, or the sentences proceeding from a secular court,* whenever these may be in collision with spiritual weal, and she has the faculty to check the abuse of the executive and of the armed forces, *or even to prescribe their employment* whenever the requirements for the protection of the Christian Faith may demand this. The jurisdiction of the Church is higher than the civil. Now it is within the competency of a superior jurisdiction to control the action of the inferior, but in no manner can the inferior do this to the superior. In this matter of jurisdiction, what has to be done is to observe the *rule prescribed by Pope Boniface VIII. in his Dogmatic Bull Unam Sanctam Ecclesiam."* *

It is well known how much has been spoken and written, both before and since the decree of the Vatican Council declaratory of Papal Infallibility as a dogma, to define what

* P. 46.

really does lie within the range of this Infallible attribute. This is not the place to consider the various tests which different authorities have alleged to be alone conclusive for marking off fallible from infallible utterances, as they may drop from Papal lips. Thus much alone has been laid down with certainty; that whenever a Pope does speak *ex cathedrâ* he is infallible, and that whatever is thus spoken is dogmatic, and consequently partakes of the sacredness of an article of faith. What then deserves to be carefully noted is how it is here unequivocally affirmed by the organ of "true doctrine," that the Bull *Unam Sanctam*, admittedly the extremest expression, that ever fell from any Pope's lips, of Papal pretensions to direct and wholesale supremacy in temporal matters, is comprised amongst the Pontifical utterances of which the dogmatic sacrosanctness is open to no doubt. For it should be stated that this attribution of high character does not rest on what, if standing by itself, might be deemed an inadvertent expression. It is spoken to more than once, and the allegation is substantiated by a very precise enunciation of the grounds which, according to the writer, are conclusive as to the dogmatic character of this Bull. "Some liberal periodicals and writers will be shocked at hearing this Bull termed dogmatic. But that it is so is manifest, whether one regards the matter of its contents or the authority whence it emanates. In it the Pontiff addresses himself to the whole Church, and speaks in the capacity of a teacher giving instruction about most important doctrinal points, such as are of a certainty the relations between the Church and the State. Besides, the Bull ends with an explicit definition: 'Subesse Romano Pontifici, omni humanæ creaturæ, declaramus, dicimus, definimus, et pronunciamus, omnino esse de necessitate salutis.'" *

* P. 23.

Whether the declaratory allegations here made with such remarkable assurance will be implicitly acquiesced in by all who may claim to be every whit as sound Roman Catholics as Liberatore, we do not care to consider. Our particular purpose is to seek from perfectly trustworthy sources authentic evidence as to the teaching propounded by the most authoritative modern school of Catholic divinity; and evidence of this kind on a pre-eminently important point—the amount and extent of Pontifical utterances from previous ages, which will be retrospectively covered through the Dogma of Infallibility with a sanction raising them to the position of Articles of Faith—we here obtain from a writer who comes before us with a well-nigh bewildering accumulation of vouchers for his plenary inspiration in what he says on this head. For here is the formidable chain of guarantees that Father Liberatore can point to for the perfect soundness of his exposition; first, he is a Jesuit divine held in acknowledged estimation as a mouth-piece of doctrine by the heads of the Order; then he is one of that picked number drafted from the body of the Order, and erected by Pius IX. into a special brotherhood, entrusted with the delicate task of making the world to know what is true doctrine; thirdly, he comes before us with a revision of his original composition, combining the benefit of matured afterthought and the corrections derivable from the protracted reflections of his Superiors; fourthly (and in reference to the passage immediately before us this fact is of capital weight) the revision has been issued subsequently to the dogmatization of Infallibility and the serious controversy awakened thereby; and fifthly, to remove every shadow of doubt as to the complete concurrence of those who are at present entitled to speak in the name of the Church in the views expressed in this publication, there has been affixed thereto the (as far as the law of the land is concerned) perfectly superfluous stamp of episcopal approbation. In presence of this converging array of endorsements the fact must be deemed proven that, in the minds of the Society of Jesus and of Pius IX., the Bull *Unam Sanctam* is held to be an article of dogmatic utterance binding on the conscience of all who would be Catholics.*

The function of the State, measured by these definitions, would therefore amount merely to that of an organised police, instituted for the enforcement of the Church's behests and the vigilant repression of dissent. This interpretation is in strict accordance with the saying, that the duty of the State is centred in " protection of the Church," † and that (these words being adopted from the reputed Ultramontane Legist Phillips) " the primary condition of an efficacious alliance between the laws of the State and the laws of the Church lies in the *application of coercive means,* in every instance where spiritual penalty may be inadequate." ‡ This

---

* In 1826, one who then was looked upon as an ecclesiastical authority of high degree, Bishop Doyle, in his public appeal to Lord Liverpool on behalf of the claims for Catholics to Emancipation, wrote thus of this same Bull : " If the Bull *Unam Sanctam* . . . be objected to us, is it not reasonable to attend to us, whilst we say, that no Bull of any Pope can decide our judgment if it be not received and *assented to by the pastors of the Church, an assent which this Bull Unam Sanctam never has had ?* . . . The Bull was of a most odious kind, and should, therefore, according to a maxim admitted by all jurists, *odiosa sunt restringenda,* be restricted as much as possible to its sense." ' Essay on Catholic Claims,' p. 37. On January 25, in that same year, all the Irish bishops signed also, it is true, a declaration : " That it is not an article of the Catholic Faith, neither are Catholics required to believe that the Pope is infallible ; " amongst the names subscribed being that of Dr. MacHale, the living Archbishop of Tuam. Neither Bishop Doyle's emphatic statement nor this solemn Declaration was ever disapproved of by the Holy See. What then can be the permanent value attaching to any exposition minimising the bearing and possible effect on civil jurisdiction of the dogma of Infallibility, from however exalted a Prelate it may emanate, and however much it may appear to be acquiesced in at the present moment by the Holy See?

† P. 73.   ‡ P. 78.

obligation to coerce—in other words to persecute—all who may differ, though ever so slightly, from any opinion propounded by the authorities of the Church for the time being, is insisted upon by Father Liberatore with reiterated emphasis, as a duty deriving its sacredness directly from Christ's injunction. "The capital and substantial ground, wherefore liberty of conscience must be reprobated, is neither peace nor national unity, but in truth the obligation to profess the true faith, and thereby ensure the attainment of man's superior good. Peace and national unity may be invoked as a secondary ground (being likewise a benefit), but only on the supposition that the true faith is preserved. For *in the contrary case the saying of Christ holds good, I came not to send peace but a sword;* national discord being beyond comparison a lesser evil than persistence in some error regarding a point of faith"—words distinctly enjoining the enforcement of religion at the sword's point. And again: "Amongst the rights appertaining to a perfect society is that of coercing enemies, internal and external. Where between the State and the Church there is reciprocal alliance, there the right [to coerce enemies] is exercised by the latter through the agency of the former . . . But where this alliance happens to have been broken, manifestly this right of the Church cannot perish, inasmuch as it takes its rise in the essence of social order with which the Church has been invested not by the State but by God."* Accordingly "the best form of government, *i.e.*, the form best answering to divine conception and the happiness of mankind" is where the State acts as the executioner of the Church's fulminations; though, in presence of the glaring fact how schism has asserted itself in a large portion of the Christian world, and the physical impossibility of enforcing

* P. 77.

everywhere at once that action of sharp repression conformable to Jesuit notions "of the form best answering to divine conceptions," Father Liberatore admits that "out of regard to religious divisions which have already taken root" in some parts, "prudence may counsel civil toleration of all forms of worship."* Consequently the acquiescence, which in some countries the Church has apparently yielded to the toleration of other religious persuasions, is no more than a feint, put on under the pressure of emergency, and a stratagem adopted for so long only as it may seem the most appropriate method for warding off additional difficulties.

Here we find ourselves brought face to face with two points of the gravest interest—the view entertained by the Church as to what rights and faculties remain inherent in a State that may have apostatized from its communion, and as to the binding force on itself of any formal instrument it may have concluded with a Civil Power, be it Catholic or not. That the Church is credited with the right to impress into her service all the physical forces under the immediate direction of the State, we have been already told, as also that this right extends to the exercise of vigorous coercion through State agency against Dissenters. That this right, as emanating from a Divine origin, is affirmed not to lapse because a State, as represented by those in possession of governing power, may fall away from the Church, and thus deprive it of the means to set these forces in motion, this likewise we know. What we still have to be enlightened upon by him who has so far been our ready guide and instructor, is what degree, if any, of legitimacy the Church in its conscience may recognise as remaining vested in a State which has apostatized, and with which the Church may have contracted public relations of comity. It must be admitted

* P. 74.

that Father Liberatore glides over the general question with more rapidity than is his usual practice. His opinion on this important head is comprised in a few sentences introduced in the course of a long dissertation on the duties of the State towards the Church, but, though few, the sentences are pregnant. After having insisted on the absolute obligation incumbent on the State to expend its forces "in protection and defence of the Church," he goes on to say that, whenever the State has apostatized, and "ceased to fulfil this special duty, the same devolves of its own nature on the individual Faithful," and that "in this manner there arises in society a necessary disorder, namely the *existence of a legitimate power, which is independent of the public depositary of force.*" * That it will be within the faculty of casuists to give to these words an interpretation different from their plain sense, is what we must be prepared for. The conclusion we have arrived at is that, bearing in mind the whole context of the argument, these words, without any invocation of that merely *probable* interpretation which a Jesuit writer should not consider improper, do plainly express this doctrine—that in countries where the State in its corporate capacity does not make profession of the Catholic Faith, the Church, even though it might have adopted towards the powers that be an attitude of friendly understanding, will still consider the only depositaries of the faculties, which in its opinion appertain to the State, to be the congregation of those who have continued faithful to its communion; just as, according to the same authority, while the throne is occupied by one man, another can be held entitled to issue commands that are binding for the gravest action.

That no unnatural strain has here been put upon the sentiments of our author, is clearly established by his very

* P. 77.

explicit language as to the possible binding force upon the Church of any engagement, however solemn in form, which it may have entered into with any State, even an orthodox one. With an elaborateness of diction that closes all question as to his meaning, Father Liberatore affirms that from the very nature of things, no Concordat can ever bind the Church—that it is a mere concession for the time of rights which are indelible, and are only waived in deference to expediency, until the strain of exigency may have relaxed. This view was broached some years ago by the Vicomte de Bonald, who declared that "a Concordat cannot be likened to a contract ; for there is a radical impossibility that a contract can intervene between two entities (the spiritual and the temporal Power), whereof the one is sovereign, the other subject, the one presides, the other is subordinate."* For the publication containing this passage Pius IX. addressed to the author a Brief of approbation. Some Catholics, however, demurred to M. de Bonald's opinion, and a controversy ensued. Amongst those who concurred with him most vigorously were Father (afterwards Cardinal) Tarquini and Liberatore, whose strenuous arguments the reader, if so inclined, may peruse for himself in the volume we have been quoting from. We have space only for these few emphatic sentences:—" It is beyond doubt that Concordats, in whatever concerns matters spiritual and such *as have any connection therewith*, cannot have the character of bilateral contracts. . . . Concordats in this respect have the character of mere indulgences and privileges. . . . Whatever privilege may at any time have been granted, which might in any manner limit or curtail the exercise of Pontifical authority, is a mere indulgence, *revocable at any moment, when it may be the opinion of the Pope*

* 'Deux questions sur le Concordat,' Genève, 1871.

that the continued enjoyment thereof might be prejudicial rather than beneficial to the welfare of the Church. In short, the Pope's authority is unalterable, for it has been fixed by Christ, and by Christ has been maintained in him exclusively, just as the light of the sun in the atmosphere." Such, according to the doctrine of the choicest divines of the Society, and the declared concurrence of the present occupant of St. Peter's Chair, is the exact value of instruments that have been concluded by the Church with every formality of solemn engagement.

CHAPTER XXV.

Apparent harmlessness of such extravagant views—But Jesuits dispose of more practical weapons—Capital importance for State of sound fiscal and military systems—Jesuit maxims capable of imperilling both—*Casus conscientiæ* relating to payment of taxes—Systematic smugglers guilty of no serious offence—Admirably distinct exemplification given by Gury—Another about defrauding the revenue in the matter of dues—Jesuit rulings as regards a soldier's duty to prove faithful to his flag—What constitutes a justification to desert—Plea to sanction a medical man taking money for a false certificate enabling a conscript to evade his obligations—Reference to political situations of recent times where such maxims were calculated to effect serious mischief—Illustration from instructions issued by the Holy Penitentiary.

ALL this may well seem mere dreaming and a building of castles in the moon. If the Jesuits have nothing more effective for checkmating modern society, than rhapsodies about Boniface VIII. and the perfection of a State reproducing thirteenth-century policy, governments might safely afford to disregard them as harmless monomaniacs. These lucubrations do not, however, make up the practical weapons at the disposal of those who strive to ensure the realisation of their aspirations. The means whereby the Jesuits may hope to injure the machinery of modern governments exist in that not easily definable store of subtle functions and sacerdotal ministrations, which, by the essence of the Roman Catholic system, appertain to the order of the priesthood. A State will rest on weak foundations, unless it can confidently repose on a fiscal system carried out with integrity and regularity, and on a defensive system penetrated with a spirit of discipline and staunchness. Let a breach be made on either point, and manifestly the position of the State is exposed to danger. It can be shown that the artillery of Jesuit practice has been brought into positions whence it may fire against both points at any time that seems propitious.

In Gury's 'Casus Conscientiæ' (p. 40) occurs this passage, taken from St. Liguori. "Speaking generally of taxes, Lugo is of opinion that people should be exhorted to pay them; but that after the act they should not be compelled to make restitution of a duty they may have withheld fraudulently, if they have any probable ground, for persuading themselves that in so great a number of taxes they may have paid something not justly, or that they had contributed adequately to the public wants"—notions which will readily recommend themselves to not a few tax-payers. On turning to the 'Compendium,' we read that "as to restitution, there is absolutely no obligation" on those who habitually import "prohibited wares," while the question, whether some act of contrition might not be incumbent for the violation of a statute by such a practice, is answered with what, but for the grave character of the book, would sound like a joke. "Those who import prohibited goods in small quantities, and for their own benefit, especially if poor, are certainly not liable to blame. The others [the rich and the systematic smugglers], however, are in danger of sinning against their duty towards themselves, by running a risk of very severe penalties."* And this view is strictly in accordance with Moullet's. "What is to be held of those who import contraband goods and arts? . . . It is the *common opinion* even of more *Rigorist Doctors* that they commit no sin and are *bound to make no restitution*."†

---

* Gury, vol. i. p. 446. "Cæteri vero facile peccare possunt contra charitatem in se ipsos, pœnis gravissimis se exponendo."

† Moullet, pars prima, p. 345.

To bring out clearly the degree of fraudulent operations which these divines are prepared to countenance, we subjoin two exemplifications from Gury, which are admirably lucid. "Sapricius is in the habit of conveying and moving by waggon, sumpter animals, or other modes, grain, wine, articles of food and wares, on all of which dues are imposed. But he seeks by every means to evade payment of the same, as often as this can be done without peril of fine, by moving them at night, by taking out-of-the way tracks, by avoiding the revenue officers, or by deceiving them through manifold tricks. He is of opinion that he is not acting wrongly, partly because the taxes are very heavy and numerous, as well as often expended on what is not at all for the common advantage, partly because the law, in virtue whereof they are imposed, is a merely penal enactment. At Easter time, however, when about to perform his obligations of confession, being impelled by scruples, he asks whether he might not have done wrong? Has then Sapricius erred, and is he bound to make any restitution?" Gury replies that, though some theologians have been of an affirmative opinion, others distinctly say the contrary. Of the former he gives neither the names nor one word of their argument; but he quotes in the opposite sense the opinion of Sanchez, as summarised by St. Liguori, and then he solves the problem in these terms: "Sapricius is not at all to be disturbed."[*]

The second case is couched in terms that have a not in-

---

[*] Gury, 'Casus Conscientiæ,' p. 39. It will be admitted that the case of Sapricius, as stated by Gury, is that of a professed smuggler, and we draw special attention to the terms of the exemplification, because definitions to be found in the 'Comp. Theol. Mor.' pp. 433-4, might be pointed to as confuting the idea that Jesuit practice ever would countenance any habitual fraud. These definitions, too long for insertion, will be found marked all through with qualifying expressions, that practically afford as many loopholes for excepting cases from the principle apparently enjoined.

appropriate flavour of rogues' humour. "Forbinus sells Gibertus some land for 30,000 francs. The two would, however, willingly reduce the very heavy duty imposed by government on the sale of real property. The question with them is how they may best set about this? The trick is a noted one—yea, even most common. They agree to declare and insert only 20,000 francs as the price in the public deed of sale. Accordingly they go to a notary and make declaration of the inferior sum only. The notary, with a smile he cannot suppress—for he was aware of the true value—says to Gibertus, 'Oho! Zounds! This will be a capital stroke of business for you;' and then, without a word more, he draws up the deed." The questions that arise are, whether (1) "they do any wrong who, after a sale of land, falsely state a lower price in the deed in order not to pay the duty; (2) whether the notary who was cognisant of the fraud is under any obligation to effect restitution; and (3) what would be his position if it was himself who had suggested the trick to the parties."* After a little preliminary flourish concerning the duty of making true statements, we read— "the opinion, which seems the more probable, exempts the parties from all obligation to declare the true price, as *the law apparently intends merely to authenticate the deed and the transfer of the property* . . . so that no obligation of conscience is apparent for making a declaration of the price paid, or even of the lowest value at which a property can be appraised." As for the notary, he is declared free from all blame, even though he may have been the suggestor of this manifest fraud, on the ground "that though a public servant, he is not set over the taxes." Such are the maxims and examples to which, by superior Jesuit authority, spiritual advisers are referred for guidance, in the event of their having to deal with cases of conscience where ques-

* Gury, 'Casus Conscientiæ,' p. 232.

tions are raised about the observance of most undeniable obligations towards the State, and the employment of deliberate fraud to evade the same.

Let us now see the rules and principles inculcated for direction in cases affecting what is generally considered the primary duty of a soldier—faithfulness to his military engagement. It really does seem, when we peruse the section treating this subject of cardinal importance to the safety of the State, as if the thought uppermost in the mind of Father Gury could only have been how to devise pleas sufficiently elastic to make it easy for a soldier to desert with a safe conscience. In the first place, it is declared that every soldier who consents to serve in an unjust war will be *directly chargeable* with responsibility for every act of injury perpetrated by himself individually during its course, and *proportionally* for the total injury wrought by the army;* thus introducing a principle absolutely subversive of all military discipline, that at every call to arms each soldier is to make himself judge whether to obey it will be in accordance with his conscience. That there exists a general obligation on deserters to return to their colours, Father Gury admits; but he couples the admission with grounds of exemption, amongst which one alone is quite sufficient to afford an unfailing plea for whoever may be minded to abscond. Any soldier, we are told, is justified in deserting, if he will allege "great risk to his salvation—for instance, in the event of adequate provision not being made for access to the Confessional;"† so that, let only a Catholic soldier make profession of his having been obstructed in the desire to draw near a priest, and he may desert his duties with absolute impunity, according to the doctrine of Father Gury.

Nor is this the only proceeding sanctioned, which is cal-

* Gury, 'Comp. Theol. Mor.' vol. i. p. 447.   † Ibid.

culated to weaken allegiance to the State. We find, beneath the customary preliminary display of general rigorist views, a ruling which practically relieves from censure so gross an act of fraud as the grant, in return for money, of a false medical certificate, with the view of getting off from conscription a man both liable and fit to serve. "Trepidantius, dreading intensely to serve, but having been drawn by lot, bribes Armandus, a medical man, and, though perfectly well, obtains from him a certificate of ill-health, and so gets exemption from service. A case occurring a thousand times every year! Is Armandus bound to give back the money he has taken?" Thereto Gury makes this reply: "Armandus could certainly not retain the money, if it had been received from Trepidantius before he had declared him in ill health, for that is a contract *de materiâ turpi*, and therefore void. But the fraudulent declaration having already been made, the matter is one liable to controversy, as will be presently explained in the cases relating to the substance of contracts;"* and so, on the same ground on which we have seen the sanction of connivance extended to the acceptance of a money gift from a suitor by a Judge, when once the unjust sentence has been pronounced, it is ruled that, on the score of conscience, nothing stands in the way to make it uncomfortable for a medical man, with direct personal money advantage, to lend himself to the active promotion of a conspiracy for paralysing the defensive power of his country and for striking about the most treacherous blow that can well be struck at an institution essential for the safety of the State.

A very slight effort of memory will recall more than one political situation, within the last twenty years, where maxims of this seditious tenour, if spoken with the tone of

* Gury, 'Casus Conscientiæ,' p. 231.

authority by those clothed with the sacred character of sacerdotal essence, and addressed to an imperfectly cemented, an agitated, in part even an ill-affected, and in many respects, a superstitious population, might well have been fraught with grave danger to the State. The embarrassments that might ensue to Governments engaged in the laborious strain of organisation, amidst the still encumbering *débris* of ancient institutions and the but half-completed fabric of new constructions, from expressions of this insidiously subtle character (directly sanctioned as they are by the gravest living authorities of the Church), when dropped from the influential lips of a priesthood actively hostile (as certainly the priesthood was, with but solitary exceptions, in Italy, and as it is as certainly in part in Germany), are too evident to demand development. It is unnecessary to expand this vein of ominous reflection by conjuring up a vision of political complications looming in the more or less proximate future, on which this authorised application of principles, certainly not free from a treacherous character, if brought into the field, might tell with seriously disturbing effect. In England we may, indeed, discard the notion, however exaggeratedly Ultramontane the sentiments of those who here preside over the Roman Catholic Church may become, that disloyalty to the Constitution would infect the body of the priesthood to any extent. The thought might, however, present itself to minds not necessarily labouring under the hallucinations of an alarmist mania, that there are portions of this Empire at once mainly Roman Catholic and not quite thoroughly penetrated with the spirit of political contentment; and it may not be altogether indifferent to reflect how it would be if, in the unfortunately not impossible recurrence of a state of popular sedition, the rising generation of the priesthood were to be disposed to put in practice those peculiar maxims, with which their minds have now perforce to make themselves familiar through the course of study in Jesuit theology, which is enforced by the present authorities of the Holy See.*

* That Gury's maxims are no dead letter for the Holy See, the following affords convincing proof. In 1860, and again in 1865, the Holy Penitentiary in Rome issued secret instructions for the direction of priests in cases of conscience connected with recent political events in Italy, manuscript copies of which we obtained at the time in Rome. In these documents, the authenticity of which is vouched, occurs the following passage (the queries being in Italian, and the instructions in Latin): "What is to be done with those involuntarily enrolled and obliged to serve in the national force of the intrusive government? Posse tolerari milites civicos coactos, qui militiam absque gravi damno seu incommodo deserere nequeunt, *dummodo tamen animo parati sunt eam deserere quamprimum poterunt*. Datum Romæ in S. Pœnitent. die 10 Dec. 1860." "Absolvendi sub conditionibus expressis, . . . milites qui arma tulerunt et dimicarunt contra Pontificiam ditionem *dummodo tamen animo parati sunt quamprimum poterunt sine periculo vitæ injustam militiam deserere*. Romæ die 9 Martis, 1865." It is to be particularly noted that this *last* instruction is framed so as to include the *whole* army of the Italian kingdom, irrespective of whether the soldier was a native of the old Papal provinces, and therefore a rebel against the Pope-King. See Appendix No. II.

CHAPTER XXVI.

Increasing influence of the Society in Latin Church—Probabilism the essence of its teaching—Jesuit Divines recommend, indeed, strict observances—But through Probabilism their Rigorism is readily dissolved—Yet there is no deliberate purpose to corrupt—Desire to ensure influence alone has prompted the Society—Inevitable effect of such system—Instanced by the case of the priest Riembauer—State interested in the action on Constitution of the Church wrought by the spread of the Society—Substance of Absolutism precipitated by its agency—Independence of every kind hateful to it—Practical result of Jesuit Education—French clergy in seventeenth century—At present time no section of the Catholic community has ventured to do like it—Stealthy progress in destruction of ancient sanctuaries of Catholic sentiment—The culminating stroke dealt in the Vatican Council—Conversion of Latin Church into synonym with Jesuit Order—Proclamation of Pontifical Cæsarism, with the Society as Prætorian Guard.

Such is an outline, slight indeed, but still comprising the most essential features of the doctrine presently taught, with the express approval of the Head of the Church, by accredited organs of the Society, as directly conducive to that best possible governance of mankind, which will make the world radiant with the Greater Glory of God. Of the organisation of the Order a sketch has been given which we see no reason to consider incorrect in any material point. Taken together, the two furnish, it is believed, a not unfaithful account of the resources of this mysterious Corporation, and of the principles which are agreeable to its spirit. That it has been exercising an ever-increasing power in the Latin Church, is a fact too plainly written in the ecclesiastical history of the last three centuries to be for an instant called in question. What is not so conspicuous is the special element through which the school of Jesuit thought has been subtly working on the spirit of the Roman Catholic Church. This resides in the doctrine of Probabilism, wherein which lies distilled the sublimated essence of all Jesuit doctrine. The champions of the Order will say and have said, that to pick out passages of the character we have quoted, as typical of what its doctors teach, is to falsify the nature of their writings. It must be admitted that the Jesuit Divines never omit recommendations in favour of a strict observance of the Moral Code. Our contention is, that these expressions of rigorous sentiment are practically reduced to mere figures of speech through the all-covering action of the principle of Probabilism, which runs continuously through the volume of Jesuit doctrine like a gloss that wholly modifies the force of the text, exactly as the conditions laid down in the Constitutions with an elaborate display of stringency are practically cancelled through the faculties quietly lodged with the General. Through the slides of a side-proposition artfully masked, the Jesuit Doctors have provided a mechanism for converting at will the whole series of moral principles into a set of dissolving views.

Undeniably lax as is the tone of the Jesuit code, it would yet be a grave misconception to attribute to its framers the deliberate purpose of corrupting morals. The motive that has actuated the Society has been simply to secure influence, and the laxness in its doctrine has been consequent solely on a sense that, to acquire this influence over untamed natures, connivance might prove an efficient instrument. "Cui enim finis licet, ei et media permissa sunt," is the maxim, of which the practical application is worked out in the Jesuit Code. The dangers must be self-evident of a so-called moral system, that rests on the principle of enticing coy spirits by sweetmeats within a charmed area.* On the majority of mankind, labouring under innate frailty, a doctrine replete with justificatory pleas for self-indulgence can hardly fail to act in relaxation of moral restraints. Pascal's story of the serving man who robbed his Jesuit employers is not the only 'instance in point. In 1808 a Bavarian parish priest, by name Riembauer, murdered his mistress with revolting cold-bloodedness, because he feared she would make their intimacy public to the ruin of his position. Being brought to trial, Riembauer, who displayed

* The eminence attaching to the memory of Dr. Möhler, author of 'Die Symbolik,' as a Catholic divine and controversialist, is universally recognized. It is therefore interesting to note the opinion on the character of Jesuit doctrine, expressed by him in a passage all the more significant from its intensely Catholic sentiment: "It is a very remarkable phenomenon, that during a period of fifteen centuries, the Catholic Church never knew principles of the kind, asserted by many Jesuits, so that the question arises why they came to be circulated immediately after the Reformation? The Jesuits should be considered historically as the other extreme to the Protestants. Having sprung into existence at the period of the painful schism, the spirit of Opposition against the Schismatics entered into their life—into their whole nature—and even constituted an essential element in their history, so that, on the other hand, the Protestant has a natural horror at a Jesuit. But as extremes again touch, so there never was found in the Catholic Church anything more Protestant than the Jesuits. It lay in the nature of things, for whoever strove to encounter the Protestants with success, that he must have something of a like nature to them, that he must have mastery in their weapons, their art, their science—adopt their uncommon activity and mobility (Beweglichkeit)—in short, imitate the Protestants. But the Jesuits have likewise adopted from them what was bad, and to this belongs, besides much else, the point in question. With the view of reconciling people with the rigour of Catholic moral doctrine, and of preserving them for the Church, they gradually deemed it necessary like the Protestants to bring prominently forward everywhere the frailty of human nature, and came to hold it indispensable, with human nature as it is, to moderate the demands made thereon, so as to calm and comfort the same. But as in Catholic Dogma there was nothing to change, as the universal was firmly fixed, they sought through accommodating and lax treatment of individual cases to effect as much as possible, that which the Protestants had at one stroke proclaimed when they taught *that faith alone can save*." 'Neue Untersuchungen der Lehrgegensätze zwischen den Katholiken und Protestanten, von Dr. Möhler, ord. Professor der Theologie in München.' Mainz, 1835.

much morbid ingenuity, symptomatic of warped intellect, defended himself, on the plea that the deed was in strict accordance with the maxims he had been taught in the Seminary—that it was quite lawful to put out of the way any one from whom there was reason to dread a ruinous denunciation—and this he sustained by extracts from Stattler's 'Ethica Christiana,' at that time a standard manual.* No doubt this is an extreme case. Still this miscreant could appeal with perfect plausibility to maxims in divines of authority, which, without any strained construction, did seem to justify his deed.

Grave as is the demoralization that may be wrought by this system on the individual fibre, the State is still more interested in the action which its spread has exercised on the Constitution of the Latin Church. Before the confirmed ascendancy of the Order, there had been recurrent exhibitions of imperious Papal pretensions; but these had not become so infused into the system of the Church as to be dogmatically proclaimed particles of its life-blood. The action of the Society of Jesus on the Constitution of the Church has been that of a chemical agent which precipitates a substance previously present in solution. The substance precipitated by Jesuit agency has been the essence of pure Absolutism, the sublimated corrosiveness of which has been steadily gnawing away with deadly edge every element of

* This psychologically very remarkable case will be found in detail with Riembauer's pleas in Feuerbach's 'Aktenmässige Darstellung merkwürdiger Verbrechen.' Giessen, 1829, vol. ii. p. 86. How inoculation with Jesuit doctrines results in strange reproductions—of this the following is a striking instance. Weishaupt, the founder of the secret society of the Illuminati, which at the end of the last century exercised powerful influence in Germany, received his education in the great Jesuit College at Ingolstadt. In a letter written by him as Grandmaster occurs this passage: "Marius retains still something out of the Court Library. Let him communicate this to us, and make to himself no *casus conscientiæ* of this, *for only what brings harm is sin, and when advantage exceeds the harm, then it becomes even a virtue.*"

organic independence. For what is wholly incompatible with the nature of the Jesuit system is an element of independence. Much as has been said about the intellectual eminence of the Order, as shown in educational institutions, its scholastic efforts have uniformly been directed to substitute for the occasional irregularities attendant on a buoyant nature that monotony which accompanies stagnant life— the dead-level of mediocrity. Independence of character, of mind, of research, are objects hateful to the Society, which must be expelled, and in lieu of these it has evolved a system of pseudo-culture, studded with the counterfeits of science—playthings adapted to natures that are being carefully nursed to grow up with stunted strength. Accomplishments of a captivating order—talents of handy and specious character—have largely distinguished those trained in the schools of the Society; but in the long roll of Jesuit Fathers—men of undeniably busy and sedulous habits—it will hardly be possible to pick out one name, the bearer whereof admittedly takes rank amongst the great discoverers in the fields of science and of thought—amongst the men who have materially advanced the knowledge of mankind. A glance at the Ecclesiastical annals of the last centuries is enough to reveal the increasing sterility within the officially recognised area of the Latin Church.

In the seventeenth century, the French clergy, then eminent above all others for Catholic tradition and conviction, not here and there individually, nor yet under the mask of timid-hearted anonymousness, but in corporate declarations with their names appended thereto, over and over again protested against, and stigmatized as outrageous the theological maxims propounded by Jesuit divines.*

* See 'Avis de Messieurs les Curés de Paris à Messieurs les Curés des autres Diocèses de France,' Paris, 13 Septembre, 1656—'Requête présentée

From no section of the great Catholic community has there, however, been heard any protest in recent times against enforced innoculation with such doctrine. If some individual has spoken an occasional word in disapproval, he has been forthwith darted upon and ostracized as a rebellious sheep; but of collective protest from any quarter that might claim to represent an element of weight in the Church, there has been no sign.

This fact gives a measure to what degree that fibre of honourable self-respect, which was the best bulwark for both the grandeur and the liberties of the Church, has been crushed out. Silently, but ruthlessly, that stealthy organisation which calls itself the Society of Jesus—in grim pursuit of what it also calls the Greater Glory of God—has laid siege to, broken into, and razed those glorious and venerable sanctuaries, in Italy, in Germany, and above all in France, whence during generations there had beamed forth across the wide plain of the Catholic world, with the calmly luminous glow of purified light, the mellow gleam of a religious sentiment, which did not divorce the fervour of Catholic piety from candid learning and heartfelt attachment to liberties, any more than it considered it essential for the triumph of the Faith to propagate a belief in coarse superstitions, and to fortify the Church by a network of trickeries. Having succeeded step by step in outlawing every element that betrayed a feeling for organic freedom, the Society of Jesus, in our time, has set the cope-stone on their work by that momentous stroke in the Vatican Council,

par Messieurs les Curés de Rouen à Monseigneur leur Archevêque 28 Août 1656,' with the signatures of 28 parish priests—' Remonstrance de Messieurs les Curés de Paris à Nosseigneurs de L'Assemblée Générale du Clergé, 24 Novembre, 1656,' all which will be found in the Appendix to most editions of the ' Lettres Provinciales.'

which has dogmatically identified the Church with the Order, and has practically transformed, at all events for the present, the organisation of the former into an enlarged house of the latter.

This is not the place to enter upon the proceedings through which this result was achieved, and the consequences which it is reasonable to infer may flow therefrom. Amidst much that is controverted, one fact is positive. The outcome of the Vatican Council was wholly in accordance with what had been strenuously striven for by the Order. It was a signal and emphatic victory for the Society. But the very magnitude of this triumph instantaneously evoked peril in the alarm instinctively instilled into the Civil Power at sight of this inflation of ecclesiastical pretensions. In consummating the conversion of the Latin Church into a synonym of the Jesuit Order, in vesting in the Pope absolute direction over a universal organisation, and in having ensured through careful preparatory enervation that, at the critical moment, all the forces in this organisation acquiesced in becoming obsequious agents at the beck of the Pontifical Cæsar, the authors of this transformation wrought a modification in the Church's Constitution, that materially altered the aspect presented by it towards the Civil Power. In the instinctive sentiment of the Civil Power, that it is being confronted by an organisation bristling with menacing sentiments, is to be found the key to the state of public feeling—most marked in Germany, but unmistakeably running along the whole line of modern governments—which looks on the new Constitution of the Latin Church with uneasiness, and singles out the Society of Jesus as the Prætorian Guard of a dangerous ecclesiastical Cæsarism. How things may shape themselves during the course of the conflict that has been fairly joined, it would be vain to speculate. This much, however, may be affirmed, that the deed which consummated the mischief was rendered feasible only because the ever-increasing spread of the influences specially represented by the Society of Jesus had thoroughly saturated and made subservient those who needed only to have protested, firmly and persistently, in order to have saved the liberties of the Church; and that the recovery of what has thus been lost from failure of heart, can be hoped for only when there is in the body of the Catholic community a revival of the spirit now apparently quenched.

APPENDIX No. I.

The following Extracts are from the Letterbook of Francesco Contarini, Venetian Ambassador in Rome, which is in Mr. Rawdon Brown's possession, by whose kind permission the Transcripts have been made.

FRANCESCO CONTARINI, ROME, FEBRUARY 9, 1608 :—"Ser^{mo} Principe."

"Per la Congregatione Generale che debbono fare in questa Città li Giesuiti, sono fin hoggi comparsi tutti li deputati eccetto quelli di Polonia e alcuni d' Italia; fra li venuti vi sono delli huomini insigni e per sangue e per lettere. Ogni Provincia ha elotto tre, sicche nelle 19 Provincie che abbraccia tutta la Religione, devono essere al numero di 57 cioè Spagna, et Portogallo hanno 5 Provincie, Italia 5, Francia 3, Germania 2, Indie 2, Polonia una et Fiandra una. A questi si aggiungano il Generale, 4 Assistenti, il Procurator Generale, il Segret^{rio} della Congregazione et un Compagno sicchè in tutto arriveranno al numero di 65 in circa. Comminciera della Congregazione Generale il primo giorno di Quadragesima a 21 hora, così resta concertata, al qual tempo spirera l'autorita del Generale, la quale residiera tutta nella Congregazione Generale, perchè essa disponerà, in caso che morissero li Rettori, delli Monasterii, e di tutti le altre cose, di modo che pare, che il Generale in questi convocationi possa haver quella medesima displicentia, che si ha nella convocatione dei Concilii Generali, perche si puo trattar in essi, et del capo, et delle membre; ha pero il Generale procurato, che siano nominati, per tale effeto soggetti dipendenti da lui il piu, che sia stato possibile, particolarmente in questa provincia d' Italia. Questi Deputati doppo principiata la Congregazione mangiaranno sempre separati dalli altri del convento, e si bene alcuni alloggiano in altri monasterii, si ridurranno a desinare insieme, e dopo faranno la Congregatione ne si ridurranno mai la mattina. Et perchè nelli Capitoli Generali dell' altre Religioni si suoleno fare delle dispute, et delle prediche, in questa occasione non si faranno, ma si attendera solamente al negotio, che non si puo sapere quando sia per terminare, come anco non si puo precisamente intender çio che habbino a trattare, perche hanno sacramento solenne di non conferir quello che fanno, et credo, che vi sia anco la scommunica. Quello che finora è potuto capitar a mia notitia è che li Spagnuoli voriano divider le loro Provincie in maggior numero, ma presento, chè non lo otteneranno; li Francesi hanno la medesima intention, et a questi si potria forse dar satisfactione di una Provincia di piu; si sta congetturando anco di qualche rifforma, e che forse vorranno proveder a doi diffetti, che sono piu communamente osservati da tutti, et sono li maggiori, cioe di quello d' ingerirsi nelli negotii de' Principi, et di mostrarsi troppo interessati nella robba. Si sa anco, che sono stanchi del presente Generale, il quale è piu di 25 anni, che commanda, et dicesi si portano poco buona affettione, si che perçio potria nascer qualche dispiacere fra loro."

FRANCESCO CONTARINI, ROME, MARCH 1, 1608 :—"Ser^{mo} Principe."

"Continua la Congregatione Generale de' Gesuiti in apparentia quietamente et con grandissima taciturnita. . . . . . Per altre vie mi vien rifferto quello, a che io presto credenza, se ben non posso cosi sicuramente affirmarlo, che li primi giorni si siano impegnati a riveder, et a ligitimar lo procuro. . . . . . . terminato queste cose, pare che habbiano principiato a proponer certi punti, per i quali si restringe l'autorità al generale, per il quale, come ho presentito ha ottenuto de Pontefice un Breve, che proibisce di trattar alcuna cosa appartenente a regulation delli primi ordini del Padre Ignatio, perche haveva sottrato, che si pretendeva di abbreviare il tempo in certi carichi, con che si veniva a diminuir la sua autorita: La dimanda fatta al Pontefice del Breve dimostra esteriormente occasion giusta et legittima, ma mi vien detto che sia con fini particolari di sostentar la sua riputatione et commande. Si aggionge alle cose detto che li Francesi dimandano, che nel numero delli 4 Assistenti, li quali risiedono del continuo in Roma, appresso la persona del Generale, debba esser uno della loro natione, ..."

Francesco Contarini, Rome, March 22, 1608:—"Ser^{mo} Principe."

"Nella Congreg. di Giesuiti è riuscito, quanto gia io haveva inteso, cioe, che ad instanza de' Francesi, oltra li Assistenti, che ordinariamente risiedono in Roma, appresso la persona del Generale, ne fosse eletto un altro della medesima Natione, cosi è stato eseguito ad approbato anco da S. Sta. Il nominato è il Padre Ricomes (Richeome) soggetto stimato fra loro di gran dottrina, et che ha messo in stampa diversi libri composti da lui in lingua lattina et francese; di modo che alle 4 Assistenti, che ordinariamente sono stati fino a questi tempi, si aggiunge il quinto, il quale si trattenira in Roma, colla medesima autorità delli altri, e per l'avvenire s'indricieranno adesso tutti li negotii, che occorreranno della Francia, anzi si procura, che sotto di quello siano compresi anco quelli d' Inghilterra, che per il passato erano sottoposti ad un Assistente fiammingo, come erano medesimamente quello di Francia."

Francesco Contarini, Rome, April 5, 1608:—"Ser^{mo} Principe."

"Li Giesuiti hanno terminato la loro Congreg. Generale, la quale per quanto sono informato, è stata chiamata in apparenza, per riformar diversi abusi della Religione ma in effetto era con fine di diminuir l'autorita del Generale. Quelli che havevano questa intentione, vedendo il poco fondam^{to} che havevano, et li gagliardi preparamenti contra i loro tentativi, sicuri, che non havevano in alcun modo potuto riuscire sono dechinati, ne hanno havuto ardimento di promuover alcuna provisione, e se ne sono del tutto astennuti, non solo per conto del presente Generale, ma ne anco per il venturo, come vi era per qualche disegno, si che il Generale, chi è soggetto di gran valore, et chi ha saputo reggersi in altre borasche, ha saputo anco ben governarsi in questa, et è restato vittorioso con maggior auttorita, che mai; anzi diversi particulari proposti in Congreg^{ne} sono stati rimessi tutti alla sua libera dispositione. Li Provinciali venuti da parti lontane si sono stancati ne vedevano l'hora di partire, et che si terminasse, per diverse incommodità, che ricevevano, e vogliono che in cio uno si sia stato usato dell' artificio, perche il patimento desse occasione di desiderare la mutatione della stantia; pero alcuni di loro hanno detto, che non torneriano piu per qualsi voglia causa. Et essendosi di prefinir il tempo di ogni tanti anni, per ridur la Congregatione, è stato deliberato di non farlo, ma rimetterla, per quando la necessita, et il bisogno la riccreasse. . . . ."

APPENDIX No. II.

I.

SACRA Poenitentiaria cum noverit plurimos animarum Pastores, ob praesentes rerum vicissitudines, non paucis urgeri anxietatibus, dubitantes multis in circumstantiis quomodo gregem sibi commissum consilio juvare, vel quid ei praescribere, aut prohibere teneantur, opportunum censuit nonnulla Locorum Ordinariis communicare responsa, quae, dubiis jamdiu expositis data ab ipsa S. Poenitentiaria, fuerunt, ut unam eamdemque doctrinae regulam in docendo grege sibi commisso prae oculis habere possent, hisce praesertim temporibus, in quibus hostes infensissimi, filiique degeneres Ecclesiae Matri suae bellum movent amarissimum, et in agro Domini zizania superseminare omni studio conantur. Id vero ex parte jam praestitit S. Poenitentiaria per Litteras datas Locorum Ordinariis die 6 Octobris, nuper elapsi, in quibus praeter facultates peculiares ad consulendum Christifidelium necessitatibus concessas, plures etiam dubiorum resolutiones continebantur. Verum cum hujusmodi Litterae ad omnes Locorum Ordinarios, ad quos missae fuerunt minime pervenerint, et plures interea supplices libelli S. Poenitentiariae porrecti fuerint, quibus vel super novis dubiis explanationes quaerebantur, vel circa nonnulla in iisdem Litteris disposita Apostolica venia postulabatur, hinc ipsa S. Poenitentiaria per praesentes Litteras eadem responsa, quorum aliqua attentis peculiaribus circumstantiis, ex SSmi. Domini Oraculo moderata, alia vero ampliata fuerunt, de novo transmittere, pluraque alia adiicere quae subinde prodierunt opportunum similiter judicavit. Hujusmodi autem responsa sunt quae sequuntur.

DUBIA ET RESPONSA.

1° Se sia lecito cantare il Te Deum in occasione della proclamazione dell' intruso Governo, o di altra analoga circostanza.

R. Negative.

2° Se possa recitarsi nella Messa o nelle altre Sacre funzioni la Colletta *pro Rege*, qualora venisse ingiunta dal Governo invasore.

R. Negative.

3° Se sia lecito prendere parte alla funzione religiosa ordinata dalle leggi subalpine nell' anniversario dello Statuto.

R. Negative.

4° Se sia lecito illuminare la propria abitazione in occasione dell' inaugurazione del nuovo Governo, o di altra analoga circostanza, e parimenti, se sia lecito indossare segni del nuovo Governo come Coccarde, fascie tricolori, ecc.

R. Negative: dummodo non immineant gravia damna et absit scandalum.

5° Se possano invitarsi dal Clero le Autorità Governative alle funzioni Ecclesiastiche. E qualora, non invitate, intervenissero, se il Clero possa prestar loro gli atti di onore secondo il Cerimoniale.

R. Negative, et quaetenus non invitati interveniant, Clerus passive se habeat; hoc est abstineat ab actibus honorificis in Caeremoniali praescriptis.

6° Se possono riceversi in Chiesa i Magistrati Municipali, e prestar loro gli atti come sopra.

R. Affirmative: dummodo tamen Magistratus non peregerint actus reprobatos per Litteras Apostolicas diei 26 Martii 1860, secus, ut in praecedenti.

7° Se sia lecito arruolarsi alla Guardia Nazionale o Civica, che dal Governo intruso viene ordinata a suo sostegno nelle Provincie usurpate.

R. Negative.

8° Che debba dirsi intorno a quegl' individui che contro la loro volontà sono ascritti e vengono costretti a far parte della medesima Guardia.

R. Posse tolerari milites civicos coactos,

qui militiam absque gravi damno seu incommodo deserere nequeunt, dummodo tamen animo parati sint eam deserere quam primum poterunt, et interim abstinere ab omnibus actibus hostilitatis in subditos et milites legitimi Principis, et ab actibus contra bona, jura, et Personas Ecclesiasticas.

9° Se sia lecito ai Parrochi dare gli elenchi chiesti dal Governo intruso per la Guardia Nazionale e Leva militare nelle Provincie usurpate.

R. Negative, et quatenus per vim libri auferantur, passive se habeant.

10° Se sia lecito prendere parte alla votazione, per comporre i Consigli e Rappresentanze Municipali, e se gli Eletti possano ritenere l' ufficio di Consigliere e Magistrato Municipale.

R. Dummodo Municipales non adigantur ad ea, quae adversantur Legibus Divinis et Ecclesiasticis, et se abstineant a praestando juramento juxta formam a Gubernio invasore propositam, posse tolerari.

11° Se sia lecito concorrere ai Magisteri ed accettarli, quando alcuno vi sia chiamato da qualche Comune, ed anche dal Governo, sempre astenendosi dal presentare adesione al Governo intruso, e dal far qualunque atto che tenda a riconoscerlo.

R. Affirmative, remoto scandalo, si adsit, et sub conditionibus in quaesito expositis; praesertim vero sub conditione ut in docendo sint omnino conformes Doctrinae Catholicae.

12° Se giusta l'Indulto già trasmesso dalla S. Penitenzieria gli Amministratori dei Luoghi Pii occupati dal Governo invasore possano essere dagli Ordinari abilitati non solo a continuare nell' Amministrazione, ma ancora ad accettarla coloro che venissero eletti nuovamente dalla illegittima autorità.

R. Poenitentiaria de speciali et expressa Apostolica auctoritate omnibus et singulis Locorum Ordinariis quorum Territoria a Gubernio invasore occupata fuerunt ad sex menses duraturam facultatem concedit, praefatis personis, ut officium Administratoris dummodo exinde non requiratur adhaesio Gubernio invasori, aut juramentum fidelitatis juxta formam ab eodem Gubernio propositam et ad effectum et sub conditione curandi utilitatem Locorum Piorum, et abstinendi omnino ab alienatione bonorum et cum dependentia ub Episcopo seu ab Ordinario Loci, cui rationem reddere teneantur retinere et de novo assumere et exercere licite valeant Apostolica expressa Auctoritate Indulgendi. Porro quisque curabit scandalum removere caute manifestando se id peragere de Licentia Apostolica; Episcopi vero et Ordinarii in Administratione Locorum Piorum passive se habeant, nullumque positivae conniventiae argumentum quoad Gubernium exhibeant et eidem dumtaxat si fuerint interrogati respondeant.

13° Se possano ritenersi ed assumersi gl' impieghi sotto il Governo intruso.

R. Dummodo non agatur de Officiis, quae directe et proxime influunt in spolium vel in ejusdem spolii manutentionem, et exerceri possint absque periculo laesionis Legum Divinarum et Ecclesiasticarum posse tolerari, in praxi vero quilibet ex dictis Officialibus aut Personis Ditionis Pontificiae qui paratus sit stare mandatis S. Sedis caute moneatur ut consulat Episcopum seu Loci Ordinarium, qui in singulis casibus decernet juxta mentem SSmi. Domini.

14° Se sia lecito il giuramento proposto dal Governo intruso nei seguenti termini od altri consimili che comprendono una ubbidienza illimitata : " Giuro fedeltà ed ubbidienza a Vittorio Emmanuele Re d' Italia e suoi Successori. Giuro di osservare lo Statuto ed ogni altra legge dello Stato pel bene inseparabile del Re e della patria Italia."

R. Juramentum prout exponitur non licere; tolerari autem posse juramentum obedientiae mere passivae in iis omnibus, quae legibus Divinis, et Ecclesiasticis non adversantur juxta formam a s. m. Pii VII. approbatam et hisce verbis expressam, scilicet "prometto e giuro di non aver parte in qualsivoglia congiura, complotto o sedizione, contro il Governo attuale, come pure di essergli sottomesso, ed obbediente in tutto ciò che non sia contrario alle Leggi di Dio e della Chiesa."

15° Come debbono gli Ordinari regolarsi intorno al Regio Placet ed Exequatur che il Governo pretende intorno alle Bolle, Brevi e Rescritti Pontifici.

R. Non esse inquietandas privatas personas, quae ut se servent indemnes a Gubernium pro Regio Placet, seu Exequatur recurrunt; verum Ordinarii hac in re quantum poterunt, passive se habeant, et, si a Gubernio super hujusmodi petitionibus interrogati fuerint, juxta leges justitiae, et ad formam S. Canonum sententiam suam patefaciant."

16° Se gli Ordinari, i Parrochi, i Beneficiati ed altri amministratori di Beni Ecclesiastici, qualora sotto gravi pene fossero richiesti, possano consegnare al Governo l'inventario delle respettive rendite.

R. Permitti, emissa tamen in scriptis protestatione in singulis actis a respectivis Administratoribus super necessitate traditionis ad evitanda **maiora mala, et pro** tuitione jurium Ecclesiae. Mens autem est SSmi. Domini, **ut Ordinarii ante** vel post traditionem **si fieri possit super** praemissis collectivam **faciant** protestationem reverenter quidem **sed** cum evangelica libertate.

17° Come debbono regolarsi gli Ordinari intorno a qualche Sacerdote, il quale caduto nelle censure non si curasse di essere riconciliato colla Chiesa, nè potesse dichiararsi sospeso a Divinis dall' Ordine senza timore di gravi scandali ed inconvenienti.

R. Curandam pro viribus ejusdem Sacerdotis resipiscentiam prout boni, ac prudentis Pastoris, officium exposcit, et si vocem Ordinarii non audierit, recurrendum **esse** ad S. Concilii Congregationem.

18° Come debbono i Parrochi regolarsi nella celebrazione dei matrimoni di coloro che notoriamente fossero incorsi nelle Censure Ecclesiastiche.

R. Curandum pro viribus, ut Ecclesiasticis Censuris innodati debito modo **cum** Ecclesia reconcilientur: at si reconciliari recusent, et nisi Matrimonium celebretur gravia inde damna imminere videantur, Parochus Ordinarium consulat qui habita rerum et circumstantiarum ratione omnibusque perpensis, quae a probatis auctoribus, et praesertim a S. Alphonso (Lib. 6. Tract. 1. **Cap. 2.** N° 54) traduntur ea declaret quae **magis** expedire in Domino judicaverit, **exclusa** tamen **semper** missae celebratione.

19° Come parimenti debbano regolarsi i Vescovi ed i Parrochi, se alcuno dei sopradetti Censurati si presentasse a far da Patrino nel Sagramento della Cresima o del Battesimo.

R. Ut in praecedenti.

20° **Se** possa amministrarsi la SSma. Eucaristia ai notoriamente Censurati senza essersi prima debitamente riconciliati **con** la Chiesa.

R. Negative.

21° Se venisse a morte alcuno dei menzionati incorsi notoriamente nelle Censure e secondo i S. Canoni e le regole assegnate in proposito dai Dottori dovesse assolutamente privarsi della Sepoltura Ecclesiastica, e d'altronde con gravi minaccie si chiedessero pertinacemente le esequie, e la **stessa** sepoltura Ecclesiastica, come dovrà **in** tale circostanza regolarsi **il Parroco**?

R. Curandum, **ut** cuncta ad normam Sacrorum Canonum fiant; quatenus vero absque turbarum et scandali periculo id obtineri nequeat, Parochus neque per se, neque per alios sacerdotes ad exequias et ad sepulturam ullo modo concurrat.

22° Se possa il Vescovo approvare i Predicatori, che venissero presentati dalle attuali autorità municipali.

R. Posse Episcopum támquam ex se eligere praesentatos, dummodo in eis concurrant omnes qualitates necessariae.

23° Se gli Esattori e Cursori possano escutere gli Ecclesiastici ed i Luoghi Pii **morosi** per l'esigenza delle imposte **tanto** Camerali che Comunali e con quali **norme** e cautele.

R. Sacra Poenitentiaria de speciali **et** expressa Apostolica Auctoritate, benigne **sic** annuente SSmo. Nostro Pio PP. IX., omnibus et singulis Locorum Ordinariis quorum Territoria a Gubernio invasore occupata fuerunt, ad sex menses duraturam facultatem concedit, sive per Se, sive per aliam Ecclesiasticam Personam ad hoc specialiter a quolibet ex dictis Ordinariis deputandam Apostolica auctoritate habilitanda Cursores et Exactores ad exequenda mandata tum contra loca pia, **tum** contra personas Ecclesiasticas, petita **et** obtenta prius in singulis casibus venia a respectivo Ordinario, et remoto prudenter scandalo: contrariis quibuscumque non obstantibus.

24° Se i Parrochi e gli altri Ecclesiastici, i quali sono stati danneggiati per l'abolizione delle Decime fatte dal Governo, possano percepire i compensi assegnati dallo stesso Governo.

R. Posse juxta oraculum SS. Domini titulo merae compensationis pro damno sibi a Gubernio illato ob impeditam Decimarum exactionem percipere pensiones a Gubernio assignatas, facta tamen prius sive ab Ordinario Loci in communi, sive a quolibet ex dictis Parochis seu Ecclesiasticis in particulari protestatione per hujusmodi perceptionem nullo modo recognosci aut adprobari Decimarum abolitionem a Gubernio factam, et caute monitis earumdem

Decimarum debitoribus eos non esse vi legis a Gubernio latae ab onere easdem solvendi liberatos.

25° Se possono i Parrochi chiedere al Governo quei sussidi che il medesimo Governo promette a quei Parrochi i quali hanno una popolazione maggiore di cinquecento anime, ed una rendita minore di ottocento franche.

R. Non expedire.

26° Se i Confessori debbano riputare incorsi nelle censure coloro che hanno dato il voto per l' unione dell' Italia, sotto di un solo Re, indotti da timore, da inganno o da ignoranza; coloro che diedero simile voto in altre Provincie fuori dello Stato Pontificio, ovvero diedero il voto negativo, o nullo ed insignificante: quei che illuminarono la propria casa, indossarono coccarde, ecc. non indotti da grave timore o per leggerezza si portarono al Canto del Te Deum; finalmente le Donne ed i Minorenni che firmarono indirizzi, lavorarono bandiere, ecc.

R. Censuras Ecclesiasticas juxta litteras Apostolicas dici 26 Martii 1860 incurri ab iis qui formaliter cooperantur vel adhaerent rebellioni Ditionis Pontificiae, quare ad dignoscendum in foro conscientiae utrum quis Censuras incurrerit discutienda est per confessarium uniuscujusque conscientia. In praxi vero satis provisum per facultates Locorum Ordinariis transmissas sub die 16 Novembris 1860.

27° In qual maniera dovrà ripararsi lo Scandolo publico dato da quei che dimandano di essere assoluti dalle censure incorse in questi tempi, nei quali una tale riparazione è difficile e pericolosa.

R. Reparationem scandali esse necessariam de jure divino eamque faciendam esse meliori modo quo potest prudenti iudicio Ordinarii seu Confessorii.

28° Se coloro che dimandano l' assoluzione debbano prima di essere assoluti assoggettarsi alla rifazione dei danni sofferti dal Governo Pontificio per gli attuali svolgimenti.

R. Sufficere ut animo sint stare mandatis S. Sedis desuper ferendis.

Datum Romae in S. Poenitentiaria die 10 Decembris 1860.

Firmato = A. M. Card. Cagiano, M.P.

II.

Sacra Poenitentiaria animarum saluti semper intenta, eisque meliori modo, quo potest in Dno. consulere cupiens, de specialis, et expressa Apostolica auctoritate benigne sic annuente SSmo. Dno. Pio PP. IX. Dilecto in Xto. ad annum . . . . infrascriptas duraturas concedit facultates, quibus sive per se, sive per confessarios sibi benevisos intra fines suae Dioecesis pro foro conscientiae uti licite valeat.

1° Absolvendi Apostolica auctoritate a Censuris et poenis ecclesiasticis omnes, et singuli Poenitentes, qui rebellioni Ditionis Pontificiae cooperati sunt, vel adhaeserunt, aut quocumque modo operam suam, vel favorem praestiterunt, sive votum pro unione Italiae sub unico rege dederunt, aut Immunitatem ecclesiasticam violaverunt, dummodo tamen prius verae resipiscentiae signa exhibuerint, illatum scandalum meliori modo, quo poterunt, prudenti judicio Ordinarii, seu Confessarii reparaverint, et obedientiam S. Sedi Ejusque mandatis desuper ferendis juramento promiserint, nec antea, nec aliter injuncta singulis pro modo culparum congrua poenitentia salutari, aliisque injunctis de jure injungendis. Exceptis tamen rebellionum magistris, Coriphaeis, ac officialibus publicis, et exceptis illis, qui violaverunt Immunitatem Ecclesiasticam per manuum injectionem in Cardinales, Episcopos, aut alios Ecclesiasticos in Dignitate constitutos, pro quibus omnibus recurrendum erit in singulis casibus ad S. Poenitentiariam.

2° Absolvendi sub praefatis conditionibus, et exceptionibus Ecclesiastici, si qui in praemissis culpabiles extiterint, ibique saltem per mensem exercitiis spiritualibus vacaverint; et cum eisdem super Irregularitate ex violatione dictarum Censurarum quomodocumque contracta Apostolica Auctoritate misericorditer dispensandi; injuncta singulis congrua poenitentia salutari, et injunctis de jure injungendis; exceptis tamen semper Personis in N° 1 exceptis.

3° Absolvendi similiter sub conditionibus expressis sub N° 1 a Censuris et Poenis Ecclesiasticis Milites, qui arma tulerunt, et dimicarunt contra Pontificiam Ditionem dummodo tamen animo parati sint quamprimum poterunt sine periculo vitae injustam militiam deserere, et interea abstinere ab omnibus actibus hostilitatis in subditos et milites legitimi Principis, et ab actibus contra bona, jura et Personas Ecclesiasticas injuncta pariter singulis pro modo culparum congrua poenitentia salutari, et obligatione reficiendi damna, prout de jure, si quae alicui certo suo privato **ausu** intulerint, aliisque injunctis de jure **jungendis**; exceptis tamen Ducibus, **et officialibus**, qui sine vitae, aut alterius **gravissimae** poenae periculo se dimittere et **militiam** deserere **poterant, et exceptis, ut** supra, illis, qui **Immunitatem Ecclesiasticam** violaverunt **per manuum** injectionem in Cardinales, Episcopos, **aut** alios Ecclesiasticos in Dignitate constitutos pro quibus omnibus recurrendum erit in singulis casibus ad S. Poenitentiariam. Contrariis quibuscumque non obstantibus. Datum Romae in S. Poenitentiaria die 9 Martii 1865.

III.

SSmus. Dnus. Noster **Pius PP. IX.** vices **gerens illius** Boni Pastoris, qui deperditam **ovem** peramanter quaesivit, eamque repertam atque suis humeris impositam gaudens ad ovile retulit, majori in dies sollicitudine agitur inveniendi illos Ecclesiasticos, qui studio novarum rerum abrepti, ac proprii officii immemores magno Christifidelium scandalo, ac propriae salutis discrimine a via veritatis aberrant. Quamvis enim maxima pars eorum praesertim, qui timore aliquo compulsi aut fallacibus verbis decepti perduellium doctrinis adhaeserant, aut supplicibus libellis pro inducendo Romano Pontifice ad dimittendum temporale dominium captiose ab aliquo militiae ecclesiasticae desertore speciatim exarata subscripserant, cognita fraude, errorem **suum** sincere ejuraverit, facilemque viam **ab** Apostolica Sede jam assequuta fuerit: **nonnulli** tamen adhuc remanent, qui **ambulantes in** vanitate sensus sui, tenebris intellectum obscuratum habentes, et alienati **a** viis Domini non vident, quod est omnibus perspicuum; infensissimos scilicet SSmae. Religionis nostrae hostes sub vanae libertatis specie, ac nationalis independentiae praetextu, humana quaeque ac divina subvertere, Ecclesiaeque Catholicae bellum inferre teterrimum, eique extremam, si fieri posset, moliri ruinam. Cum iis porro, qui pertinaciter adhuc propugnare contendunt, quod jamdiu fuit a Sede Apostolica et ab Episcopis Catholicis solenniter reprobatum, severius agendum foret: verum SSmus. Dnus. Christi Charitatis memor, et humanae fragilitati, quantum **fas** est, indulgere cupiens jussit, ut Locorum Ordinarii, remisso paulisper rigore poena**rum**, quibus hujusmodi Ecclesiastici mul**tandi** essent, **eos** adhuc benigne ac chari**tative** pertractent, mediisque omnibus, quae zelus animarum, et prudentia suggesserit, in bonam frugem, et ad debita officia revocare, ostensa potissimum, ac proposita venia, misericorditer adnitantur.

Quisque autem facile novit inter ejusmodi media esse praecipue recensenda spiritualia exercitia, quae tum per se ipsa, tum ex divina gratia magnam ad corrigendos animos, et ad scandala reparanda vim habent. Quamobrem iis in Dioecesibus praesertim, in quibus a Clericis eadem **exercitia** laudabili consuetudine quotannis peraguntur, neque ullam proinde admirationem aut poenae suspicionem excitant, **maxime** optandum, ut praefati Ecclesiastici **simul** cum aliis probis Sacerdotibus ad ipsa **exercitia** paternis hortationibus invitentur, ut ibi ad impetrandam reconciliationem opportune se praeparent. Quam ut facilius assequantur Sacra Poenitentiaria juxta mentem ipsius SS. Dni. Locorum Ordinariis facultates Apostolicas ad annum duraturas communicat, quibus sive per se, sive per alias idoneas personas ab eis deputandas, recensitos Ecclesiasticos, qui praesentibus rebellionibus approbationem, favorem, auxilium, et adhaesionem quoquo modo, directe vel indirecte praestiterint, **aut memoratis** libellis subscripserint, et renunciationem dominii temporalis Summo Pontifici suadere praesumpserint, postquam verae resipiscentiae signa exhibuerint, debitamque emiserint retractationem, a censuris et poenis Ecclesiasticis propterea incursis absolvere, et cum eisdem super irregularitate ex violatione earumdem censurarum contracta dispensare Apostolica auctoritate valeant: injuncta singulis pro modo culparum congrua poenitentia salutari, aliisque injunctis de jure injungendis. Ne autem ullius difficultatis praetextu a facienda praefata retractione detineantur Sacra Poenitentiaria declarat, eam quidem **esse** necessariam ad illatum scandalum reparandum; sed fieri posse juxta discretam formam hisce litteris adnexam, aut aliam prout circumstantiae personarum judicio,

Ordinarii postulaverint, sive scripto, sive voce coram ipso Ordinario, aut persona ab eo deputata, adeo tamen caute evulgandum, ut antequam Poenitentes ad sacra publice accedant fidelibus persuasum sit eos fuisse cum Ecclesia reconciliatos. Non dubitat profecto Sacra Poenitentiaria, quin haec summa SSi. Dni. benignitas praefatos Sacerdotes ad resipiscientiam adducat; atsi qui inventi fuerint adeo mente superba, ac duro corde ut hasce Apostolicae clementiae voces audire recusaverint, nihil aliud restat, quam ut illis cum Apostolo Paulo edicatur: quid vultis? in virga veniam ad vos. Primo quidem hujusmodi pertinaces removendi omnino sunt ab officio audiendi Sacramentales confessiones, ac praedicandi verbum Dei, ob periculum ne venenatis Doctrinis Christifideles inficiant, aut jam infectos in eis confirment. Deinde si his omnibus spretis, ac Pastorum suorum monitionibus non auditis in suis erroribus pertinaciter insordescant, sedulo ab Ordinariis Locorum certior S. Poenitentiaria de illorum agendi ratione est facienda, ut, per ipsam re ad SSmum. Dnum. relata, efficacioribus juris remediis, meritisque poenis contra illos procedi possit.

Datum Romae in S. Poenit. die 10 Martii 1865.

CARDINALIS CAGIANO, M.P.
S. PEIRANUS, S. P. SEGRTJ.

FORMOLA DI RITRATTAZIONE.

Io N. N. confesso ed affermo essere errore e temerità contradire alle dotirine manifestate dalla Chiesa, e non potersi senza grave peccato ricusare ossequio, e sincera sottomessione all' autorità della S. Sede, e perciò rispetto e mi uniformo a tutte le dichiarazioni della medesima, e specialmente a quelle che riguardano il dominio temporale del Sommo Pontefice, alle quali ha fatto eco l' intero Episcopato Cattolico.

www.ingramcontent.com/pod-product-compliance
Lightning Source LLC
Chambersburg PA
CBHW021353230426
43666CB00006B/515